city baby
dc

Holly Morse Caldwell

Based on the original New York edition by
Kelly Ashton and _Pamela Weinberg_

universe publishing

This edition first published in 2008 by
UNIVERSE PUBLISHING
A division of Rizzoli International Publications Inc.
300 Park Avenue South
New York, NY 10010
www.rizzoliusa.com

© 2008 by Holly Morse Caldwell
Based on City Baby, © 2005, 2003, 2001, 1997
by Kelly Ashton and Pamela Weinberg
Cover Illustration by Sujean Rim
Design by Headcase Design

2008 2009 2010 2011 / 10 9 8 7 6 5 4 3 2 1
First Edition
Printed in the United States of America

ISBN-13: 978-0-7893-1686-8
Library of Congress Control Number: 2007907668

Publisher's Note: Neither Universe Publishing nor the authors have
any interest, financial or personal, in the locations listed in this book.
No fees were paid or services rendered for inclusion in these pages.

contents

acknowledgments

Writing a book of this scope would have been impossible without a lot of help. Many, many thanks to:

My husband, John: My own personal cheering section and the love of my life. Your unconditional love, friendship, humor, intelligence, patience, and acceptance humble me. You are our fearless leader; we would follow you to the ends of the earth.

Connor and Charlie: You are rock stars. I could not have asked for two more interesting, original, and hilarious characters. You inspire me and make me realize how lucky we are for each moment we have together. I love you.

My parents, Jill and Sam: I hope a bit of your work ethic, elegance, and wicked sense of humor have rubbed off on me and that I make you proud.

Molly: You are the best little sis a girl could have asked for, and you've been a lifeline of sanity through thick and thin. Peace out.

The Caldwells: Alice, Jack, Aunt Letty, and Mags. I could not have asked for more wonderful in-laws.

My peeps: Carter Brown, Hayley Pivato, Dan Herlihy, Isabella Johnson, Kelly Stroh, Barret Tilney, Stephanie Hyman, Blair Giannini, and Jill Howson. Simply put, you guys are awesome. I'd be standing out on a ledge without you.

Russell and Randy Katz, who went above and beyond the call of friendship by generously providing me with a place to write and storing the couch.

Caitlin Leffel, my editor, whose anality and subtle use of reverse psychology made the editing process not only painless but thoroughly enjoyable. I look forward to our next endeavor together. I'd also like to thank Jacob Lehman, Kathleen Jayes, Tricia Levi, and Universe Publishing.

Alix Clyburn, whose incredible support made this project happen and whose sense of humor and encouragement cured the occasional (and sometimes often) case of writer's block.

Dedication

To my boys: John, Connor, and Charlie

introduction

*W*hether you've just moved to Washington, DC, or have lived here your whole life, the city changes once you have a baby. Suddenly a neighborhood can be judged on the existence of a good playground, the CVS is only as good as its formula inventory, and that tiny second-floor sushi café you and your husband loved might as well be in Tokyo, since climbing the narrow stairwell with a stroller is out of the question.

When my sons, Connor and Charlie, came into the world (four years and one year ago, respectively) I became familiar with this transformation. In addition to the joy and drama of mommyhood, I realized when they arrived that there was a brand new facet of DC life to learn. And, as I discovered, we did not have the benefit of any road map or guidebook to help us. I had to rely on word of mouth . . . which, thankfully, in most cases was extensive. But what about other new moms? And what about all the information friends and friends of friends didn't know to pass along?

Washington, DC, is the sixth most populous metropolitan area in the United States, and one of the most highly educated. Twenty percent of households have children under the age of five. There are a lot of new parents here, and these are new parents who read, so why wasn't there a book for them? That's what I set out to create. *City Baby DC* is that resource, guiding you through the endless decisions you'll be making about everything from pregnancy to preschool that can stump even the savviest Washingtonian.

I have spent the past year ensuring that *City Baby DC* is, in fact, the ultimate guide. You hold in your hands a book of thoroughly researched information on every topic a city parent needs: how to find an obstetrician or midwife, where to take Mommy and Me classes, who offers great classes for preschoolers, how and where to throw the best first birthday party, which restaurants serve great food and are kid-friendly, where to find the coolest maternity clothes . . . the list goes on (and on).

As you read this book, keep in mind that while the information was accurate at the time of publication, stores go out of business, schedules change, and prices inevitably go up. I always recommend calling ahead to double-check addresses, hours, and prices.

Congratulations! It's an exciting time to be raising a family in DC, and being a parent here has never been more fun. You're about to embark on your greatest adventure, one that will take the rest of your life to complete. Let *City Baby DC* help to make these first few years of parenthood easier—and more fun.

part one

PREPARING FOR YOUR DC BABY:
everything you need to know

from obstetric care to childbirth

Congratulations! You're pregnant, and in just nine short months you will be the proud owner of your very own baby! This incredibly exciting news brings with it many decisions that must be made between now and when your baby arrives. Of course you want to make choices that ensure you and your baby have the best experience possible. But don't worry, this book is here to help. The first things to think about are:

★ Who will provide your prenatal care throughout your pregnancy?

★ Who will deliver your baby?

★ Where will your baby be born?

You have had the good sense (or blind luck) to get pregnant in a city that seems to have an obstetrician on every other block and some of the best hospitals in the world. Finding excellent care won't be a problem. This chapter provides everything you need to know about the birthing business in DC: doctors, midwives, hospitals, birthing centers, childbirth preparation classes, labor coaches, lactation consultants, and more.

During your pregnancy there are two people who can monitor you: a doctor (who may be the obstetrician/gynecologist you saw in your pre-pregnancy days or another doctor you select at this time) or a midwife. Though their approaches differ, both of these professionals will essentially perform the same service: meeting you at different points during your pregnancy to check your progress, and helping deliver your baby on the big day.

Your baby can be born in one of three places: a hospital, a birthing center, or at home. If you deliver your baby at home, hopefully it's because you've planned it that way and not because you didn't make it to the hospital! (Yes, there are some parents who actually want and plan to have their babies at home.) But chances are you will make it to the right place at the right time.

Looking back on my own birthing experiences with my two boys, I know that being comfortable with and confident in my doctor was the most important part of a positive birth experience. All of the hospitals and birthing centers listed have the qualifications to provide an excellent birthing experience, whether you choose to deliver with an obstetrician or a midwife. I will also explain the differences between all of the many choices, so you can decide which option is right for you.

the birth attendant

Whether it's an obstetrician or midwife, you should choose this person as soon as you know you're pregnant.

Obstetricians

Most women in DC deliver their babies in a hospital with an obstetrician, but a growing number are opting for a midwife or even having both in the delivery room. You probably already have an obstetrician/gynecologist whom you see for checkups, and you may have already decided to have him or her deliver your baby. If you're comfortable and happy with your current ob/gyn, stick with that person.

However, you may want to find a new doctor for one of several reasons: Your current ob/gyn is fine for routine checkups, but friends have told you about a wonderful new doctor; your ob/gyn is farther away from your house than you'd like (toward the end you will be seeing the doctor constantly so location is an important consideration); your ob/gyn is affiliated with a hospital that doesn't appeal to you; or you may be over thirty-five years old, considered high risk, and want an ob/gyn who has this focus. If you're laid-back, you also might want an ob/gyn more in keeping with that style; for example, some doctors are adamant that their patients follow a strict prenatal diet and some feel it's perfectly fine to indulge yourself with the occasional glass of wine or double tall latte. The good news: There's no shortage of obstetricians in DC, so you can pick and choose.

If you think you may want to find a new doctor, you should start to look for one immediately. Start with recommendations, ideally based on the personal experiences of people you know. If you don't know of anyone to ask, try to get a referral from your internist or general practitioner. You can also call the hospital where you would like to deliver and ask for recommendations from its obstetrical department.

Check with your insurance company, as well. You can call your provider and ask for a list of doctors within a certain geographical area who take your insurance.

Another good idea is to go online and check out *Washingtonian's* most recent "The Best Doctors in Washington" issue. This is how I found my ob/gyn, whom I love and have since recommended to friends, who have had the same great experience. He took my insurance and delivered at Sibley, two important criteria for me that narrowed my search.

Once you have a candidate or two, call for a consultation. Any doctor should be willing to sit down with you and discuss what you can expect over the next nine months and during the birth. Go to your appointment armed with a list of written questions, a pen and pad, and your husband or partner—two listeners are better than one. Here are some questions to ask:

★ Are you part of a group practice? If so, will I see the other doctors in the practice? What is the likelihood that you rather than one of your colleagues will deliver my baby? (Ask when the doctor typically takes vacation. You will be able to figure out what month you are delivering, so inquire early on. Many doctors take off two weeks in March, when private schools are on break.)

★ How often will I need to come in for appointments?

★ What tests should I expect to have and when?

★ What is the fee for a vaginal birth? Cesarean section? What extra charges should I expect? (Many good doctors now charge the same fee for a vaginal or a cesarean delivery, because they do not want to be accused of performing unnecessary cesareans.)

★ What are your thoughts on natural childbirth, anesthesia, episiotomy, cesarean section, induction of labor? (Ask these and any other questions you have about the doctor's birthing philosophy.)

★ With which hospital are you affiliated? What are the facilities like? Ask about birthing rooms; labor, delivery, and recovery rooms; rooming-in options for baby and partner; neonatal intensive care units and their levels.

★ What do you consider "high risk" birth factors?

★ How do I get answers to my questions between visits? If you are busy, is there another doctor in the office who will take my call?

★ Do you have nurses trained to answer basic prenatal questions? (Obstetricians spend half of the day performing hospital deliveries or patient check-ins, so it is important to know that if your doctor is not there, someone will be available to answer your questions in a timely manner.)

★ Ask whether the doctor works in a collaborative way with patients, making joint decisions, or whether he or she likes to call the shots. Again, the doctor's personality must jibe with yours—this is your pregnancy.

After this initial consultation, you should be able to decide whether this is the doctor for you. He or she should listen to you carefully, answer your questions thoroughly, and inspire your trust. You need to feel confident that this doctor will be there for you any time, day or night, during your pregnancy. I can't stress this enough: feeling confident and comfortable with your ob/gyn is essential.

If your pregnancy is considered low risk and normal the usual schedule for visiting your ob/gyn is every three to four weeks for the first seven months, every two weeks in the eighth month, and every week in the ninth month. Of course, this may vary with different doctors, and if your pregnancy is high risk, you may have to see your doctor more often.

Some common tests to expect over the course of your pregnancy are:

★ **Amniocentesis:** Better known as an amnio, this procedure is performed in the fourth month (sixteen to eighteen weeks) of pregnancy. It is performed in a hospital rather than at your doctor's office. The technician, guided by an ultrasound image of the uterus, inserts a long hollow needle through the woman's abdominal wall and withdraws a small amount of amniotic fluid. From the extracted fluid, the doctor is able to check for chromosomal abnormalities that can cause conditions such as Down's syndrome. Amniocentesis is an optional procedure, and most women with normal low-risk pregnancies choose not to have it done. Amniocentesis is recommended for women over thirty-five (although many women over thirty choose to have it performed as well) and in cases in which genetic disorders or chromosomal abnormalities are suspected.

★ **CVS (Chroionic Villus Sampling):** This is a relatively painless procedure where the doctor extracts chromosomal tissue from the uterus through a small tube guided by an ultrasound. Like the amnio, it is performed in the hospital, but it is done much earlier than the amnio (between ten and twelve weeks). Though this test is optional, many women are choosing to undergo this test because it provides important genetic and chromosomal information about a pregnancy much earlier than an amnio and is also a less invasive procedure than the amnio.

★ **MSAFP (Maternal Serum Alpha-Fetoprotein Screening):** The MSAFP, also called the Triple Marker screening, is performed in the fourth month (sixteen to eighteen weeks). This simple blood test determines the levels of alpha-fetoprotein (blood protein) present in the mother's blood. High or low levels may indicate serious problems in the development of the fetus, but be aware that there are many false positive results. If the MSAFP level comes back either too high or too low, the doctor will probably recommend a second test to confirm the results of the first.

★ **Nuchal Translucency Screening:** This prenatal screening test (also called the nuchal fold scan) uses ultrasound to measure the clear space in the tissue at the back of your developing baby's neck. The measurement can help your doctor assess your baby's risk for Down's syndrome (DS) and other chromosomal abnormalities as well as major congenital heart problems. Babies with abnormalities tend to accumulate more fluid at the back of their necks during the first trimester, causing this clear space to be larger. While the nuchal translu-

cency screening test won't give you the definite diagnosis you'd get from more invasive tests like CVS and amniocentesis, it can help you decide whether you want to undergo more intrusive diagnostic testing. And unlike diagnostic tests, this test is painless and involves no risk to you or your baby.

★ **Ultrasound or Sonogram:** This is a machine that is used to see the baby in utero. Typically, a woman has two or three sonograms during her pregnancy. The first will be done in the second month (at about nine weeks) to date her pregnancy and to locate the fertilized egg and make sure it has attached to the proper place in the uterus; the second, more extensive, sonogram will be done in the fifth month (about twenty weeks), sometimes at the hospital, to check the growth and internal organs of the fetus and, for those inquiring minds, the sex of the baby! Finally, a third may be done in the ninth month (about thirty-six weeks) to gauge the baby's size and position. Trust me, at that point all you'll really want to know is when that baby will be coming out!

These tests and procedures are routine, and the obstetrician you choose will have conducted, ordered, or overseen them on hundreds of pregnant women before you. But remember: this is your pregnancy. You should feel perfectly comfortable asking what you may think are "dumb questions" about the need for tests and what the results mean. You should also make sure your doctor knows your full medical history and give as much family medical history on both sides as you can provide. If you are thirty-five or older, you are considered high risk in DC. Statistics show that women over the age of thirty-five have a slightly greater risk of problems during pregnancy. Other circumstances can also determine a high-risk pregnancy: a previous period of infertility, multiple miscarriages, high blood pressure, diabetes, obesity, and other serious health problems.

Midwives

A growing number of DC women opt for a midwife rather than an obstetrician to guide them through pregnancy and delivery. A midwife may be a good fit for you if you're low risk and are interested in natural childbirth (a delivery without the use of anesthesia or medical interventions). Most midwives believe that a woman's body was intended to give birth, and pain medications, episiotomies, and c-sections are not only unnecessary but make for a longer and more painful recovery for the mother.

Personally, my idea of "natural childbirth" was wearing minimal makeup in the labor and delivery room—I'm a total wimp! However, if this option sounds appealing to you, you will want to find a Certified Nurse Midwife (CNM), a registered nurse who has gone through an accredited nurse-midwifery program. The American College of Nurse Midwives, which provides midwife certification nationally and sets the standards for the practice of nurse-midwifery, happens to be based right here in DC. All certified midwives can prescribe pain medications for women in labor and they can call an anesthesiologist when in a hospital.

Two other categories of midwives are Direct Entry Midwives, often referred to as Lay Midwives, and Physician-Assistant Midwives. Neither of these have the full qualifications of a CNM. Direct Entry Midwives, who are trained through a combination of coursework and apprenticeship, are not permitted to practice in hospitals but do perform or assist at many home births in the DC metro area.

When you choose a CNM, make sure to find out about her hospital affiliation. You may prefer to deliver in a birthing center or at home, but in the event of a medical complication, it is critical that your practitioner have access to a hospital nearby. Many CNMs in DC practice in hospitals and will deliver your baby in the same birthing rooms that the obstetricians use, though fewer hospitals are allowing midwives to practice unless in tandem with an ob/gyn because the liability insurance is too high.

With a CNM you can expect the same schedule you would have with an obstetrician: a visit every three or four weeks at the beginning of your pregnancy, every three weeks in the seventh month, every two weeks in the eighth month, and every week in the ninth month. Like an obstetrician, the midwife will ask how you are feeling and if you have any questions. She will give you an external exam, take your blood pressure and weight, and listen to the baby's heartbeat. You can request to have any of the tests previously mentioned such as an amnio, but they will most likely not be a part of the person's standard practice.

If you would like to learn more about midwifery, call any of the names listed here and set up an appointment for a consultation, just as you would for an obstetrician. Another excellent resource is the ACNM's website, www.acnm.org. When you have settled on a candidate or two, you should interview her and ask the same questions provided on page 12. In addition, you should find out how the midwife will help you through the stages of labor and delivery, the point at which the practices of CNMs and obstetricians usually differ. A certified midwife is usually with you throughout the entire labor. In general, ob/gyns check in periodically and then arrive at the end. Most of the time you are alone in the room with your partner; a nurse will check in on you once an hour. Many CNMs are skilled at relaxing and preparing the perineum (the area between the posterior vulvar junction and the anus) so that anesthesia and episiotomies are rarely necessary.

The following are two independent and popular Certified Nurse Midwife practices in the DC metro area.

★ **LOUDOUN COMMUNITY MIDWIVES**
  (all births take place at Loudoun Hospital
    Center's Birthing Inn)
  44055 Riverside Parkway, Suite 208
  Leesburg, VA 20176
  703-726-1300
  www.lcmidwives.com

★ **THE PHYSICIAN AND MIDWIFE COLLABORATIVE PRACTICE**
  (affiliated with INOVA Alexandria Hospital)
  4660 Kenmore Avenue, Suite 902
  Alexandria, VA 22304
  703-370-4300
  Two other VA office locations
  www.physiciansandmidwives.com

Note: You and your doctor or midwife should decide jointly, based on your wishes and her expertise, on a birthing plan for the big day. Sometime after you begin your visits, but well before your due date, decide what will happen regarding anesthesia, IVs, and episiotomies. Your ideal birthing plan (barring any unexpected complications) should be in writing, *in your doctor's file, and on hand at the hospital when you arrive.*

Labor Doulas

Once you have decided who will deliver your baby, you can decide if you would like the additional support of a labor doula. A doula (pronounced "doo-la") is Greek for "mother the mother." A labor/birth doula doesn't deliver your baby but supports you and your partner emotionally and physically during the labor and birth process. She uses massage and relaxation, attention-focusing, and positioning techniques. Studies have shown that the assistance of a labor doula helps decrease the pain and stress associated with childbirth, enhancing the experience for both mother and partner.

Another option is a postpartum doula, who comes to you after you are home from the hospital, helping to take care of the baby and assisting with breastfeeding. More on this in chapter three.

Because a doula is such an intimate part of the birth experience, you should consider your options carefully. A good way to find one is through a recommendation or through the Doulas of North America website: www.dona.org. Also, many of the childbirth educators listed at the end of this chapter offer doula services.

the birth place

Hospitals

All obstetricians are affiliated with a hospital, or maybe two, so once you have selected your obstetrician you have also found your hospital.

If you are still in the process of choosing an obstetrician, you may want to work backward: figure out the hospital where you want to deliver, and then find an obstetrician who practices there. Knowing as much as you can about the place your baby will be born is very helpful and comforting.

Here are some important things to know about the hospital: the number of birthing rooms, cesarean rate, level of neonatal or NICU care provided (I, II, or III), policies on partners in the delivery room, rooming in (partner and baby staying overnight in your room), and sibling and family visitors. The DC metro area has many hospitals, but some are newer and more comfortable than others; for example, Sibley and George Washington hospitals were recently renovated, and therefore are able to offer a larger number of private rooms and amenities like DVD players and Wi-Fi in each room.

I toured all of the hospitals listed on the following pages and found them to be similar in many ways. They all provide birthing beds, showers, or squatting bars to help your labor and delivery. If you don't know what these things are or what you'll need during labor, don't worry. Your doctor or midwife will be able to guide you through all of the decisions concerning your labor.

Other general points to keep in mind:

★ Pre-register at the hospital (all of the hospitals in this book allow you to do this). This is a good idea, because once you are in labor you won't want to fill out forms. Registering in advance keeps paperwork to a minimum upon your arrival. I sent in my registration form to Sibley when I was just four months pregnant, which did seem a little neurotic—until I found myself in the hospital at seven months with preterm labor. I was happy they had all of my information on hand.

★ Contact your insurance company when you become pregnant to find out exactly what they need and when, so there won't be surprises when you submit the forms after delivery. Some insurance companies require notification before you check into the hospital.

★ Know your insurance company's policy on the length of time you can stay in the hospital for childbirth. Most insurance companies cover either a twenty-four- or forty-eight-hour stay for a vaginal delivery and three to four days for a cesarean delivery.

★ Think about storing your baby's cord blood, which is rich in stem cells and can be used if a family member is ill and requires a blood transfusion. To find out more about cord-blood registry, check with your ob/gyn, visit www.cordblood.com, or call 1-800-932-6568. Remember to take the kit when you check in at the hospital, and tell the nurse about your plans; the hospital will take care of this once your baby is born. You will be responsible for getting it to the storage bank, though, so make one person responsible for reading the instructions regarding when and where it is to be sent.

★ Private rooms are available at each of the hospitals listed here. But keep in mind that the cost of a private room is not covered by insurance unless there are no other rooms available at the time of your stay. Your out-of-pocket expenses will range from $150–$400 per night. Some hospitals will let you pre-register for a private room, but in reality they are only available on a first-come, first-served basis. If you really want a private postpartum room, tell your nurse when you get into the labor/delivery room. Your nurse will quickly become your new best friend, and he or she will have an inside track to setting that up for you if it's available. Rooming-in for partners and newborns is permitted in all hospitals in a private room. (In some hospitals it is also permitted in a semi-private room as long as your roommate doesn't object.) Personally, I thought springing for the private room was worth every penny.

★ All the hospitals have twenty-four-hour parking lots nearby and can provide you with a list of them. Be sure to find out which hospital entrance to use in case you arrive in the middle of the night. If you do find yourself "hee-hee-heeing" in the wee hours of the morning, you will in most cases enter the hospital through the twenty-four-hour emergency entrance.

★ All hospitals offer weekly classes for new mothers, on topics such as bathing the baby, breastfeeding, and basic childcare. If you cannot make it to a class, ask the nurses in the maternity ward for a crash course. The postpartum nurses are trained to help with the baby, and in my experience were more than happy to do so. Take advantage of the twenty-four-hour on-call help you'll have during your hospital stay. This is what the nurses are there for—and remember, they won't be going home with you.

★ Many hospitals have generous visiting hours. However, be selfish about seeing visitors for your own health and well-being and for that of the baby. Don't feel guilty about using your hospital stay to get some rest and to bond with your baby. There will be plenty of time for visitors when you're home.

★ Take a couple of pillows from home for your postpartum room. You will be a lot more comfortable with your own pillows, considering most hospital pillows more closely resemble sixteenth-century torture devices. To avoid having your six-hundred-thread-count linens mixed in with the hospital's laundry, make sure your pillowcases are any color but white.

★ You should also consider taking towels from home. Actually, disregard that; go ahead and pack your towels now. The first thing I did after each of my deliveries was take a shower. Having a real towel from home—as opposed to the washcloth-sized piece of sandpaper that the hospital offered—felt extremely luxurious. At that point, little comforts make a big difference.

The following section provides information to consider while evaluating the hospital where you will deliver your baby. It includes:

★ **Hospital:** The name, address, key phone numbers, website, and visiting hours.

★ **Rooms:** The number and types of delivery rooms you'll visit depend on the hospital and what type of delivery you'll be having. All of the hospitals listed here have what are known as LDR rooms (for labor, delivery, and recovery), and only on the off chance that everyone in DC decided to deliver at the same time would they have to use separate labor and delivery rooms. In an LDR room, you will do just that before you are transferred to your own room (also called a postpartum room). An operating room is where cesareans and complicated vaginal births take place. From delivery you go to a recovery room for one or two hours before going to your postpartum room, where you will stay until you leave the hospital.

★ **Midwives:** Hospitals with midwives on staff, and those that allow midwives to deliver babies.

★ **Nursery level:** Neonatal intensive care units are classified in Levels I through III, with Level III being the most advanced. Choosing a hospital with a Level III is recommended, especially for high-risk pregnancies.

★ **Childbirth classes:** Prenatal classes for women and their partners, including Lamaze, breastfeeding, and preparation for cesarean birth. These classes are given at the hospital (unless otherwise

noted), and you have to sign up in advance. For second-time moms, many hospitals offer refresher courses and sibling classes.

★ **Other information:** Any unique or notable features about the hospital. Many hospitals have amenities such as Jacuzzi tubs to help ease labor and Web nurseries where out-of-town friends and family can go online and watch the baby in the nursery through a webcam.

District of Columbia

★ **GEORGETOWN UNIVERSITY HOSPITAL**
3800 Reservoir Road, NW
Washington, DC 20007
202-444-2000 (General)
202-342-2400 (Class schedule)
www.georgetownuniversityhospital.org
Visiting Hours: 11 A.M.–9 P.M.
   Fathers have 24-hour privileges.
5 LDR suites/7 LDR rooms/1 operating room
Midwives: No
Cesarean Rate: The hospital declined to release this information.
NICU Level: III
Rated one of America's best hospitals in 2006 by *U.S. News & World Report*, this hospital specializes in high-risk pregnancies and has one of the most highly regarded NICUs in the area. The only procedure not performed here is newborn cardiac surgery. The five larger LDR suites all have Jacuzzi tubs.
   Classes:
      • childbirth methods
      • baby care
      • breastfeeding

★ **GEORGE WASHINGTON UNIVERSITY HOSPITAL**

900 Twenty-third Street, NW

Washington, DC 20037

202-714-4000 (General)

888-449-3627 (Class registration)

www.gwhospital.com

Visiting Hours: 12–8 P.M.

Fathers have 24-hour privileges.

10 LDR/2 operating

Midwives: No

Cesarean Rate: 37.3 percent

NICU Level: III

This hospital specializes in high-risk delivery and neonatal care. It offers couplet care, in which the same nurse takes care of mother and baby in the postpartum room or in the nursery. It also has in-house lactation consultants and a Web nursery.

Classes:

- pregnancy nutrition
- pregnancy massage
- baby care
- breastfeeding
- parents of multiples
- prenatal yoga and tai chi
- preparing for cesarean

★ **SIBLEY MEMORIAL HOSPITAL**

5255 Loughboro Road, NW

Washington, DC 20016

202-537-4000 (General)

202-537-4076 (Education)

www.sibley.org

Visiting Hours: 11 A.M.–8 P.M.

Fathers have 24-hour privileges.

10 LDR/2 operating

Midwives: Yes

Cesarean Rate: 38 percent

NICU Level: II

This hospital is preferred by many NW moms for the nice private rooms and convenient location. Patients and doctors also often prefer the fact that it is not a teaching hospital with interns piling into rooms to watch deliveries. Infants born here with complications are usually transferred to Georgetown's NICU.

Classes:

- baby and me
- breastfeeding
- breathing and relaxation for labor
- prenatal yoga
- grandparenting and siblings

★ **WASHINGTON HOSPITAL CENTER**

110 Irving Street, NW

Washington, DC 20010

202-877-7000 (General)

www.whcenter.org

Visiting Hours: 11 A.M.–9 P.M.

Fathers have 24-hour privileges.

12 LDR/3 operating

Midwives: Yes

Cesarean Rate: 29.68 percent

NICU Level: III

Rated one of America's best hospitals in 2006 by *U.S. News & World Report*, Washington Hospital Center annually delivers the most babies of any hospital in DC.

Classes:

- baby basics
- breastfeeding
- prepared childbirth class
- life as a new mom

- sibling class
- infant & child CPR

Maryland

★ HOLY CROSS HOSPITAL

1500 Forest Glen Road
Silver Spring, MD 20910
301-754-7000 (General)
301-754-8800 (Maternity services)
301-754-7163 (Doula services)
www.holycrosshealth.org

Visiting Hours: 11 A.M–8 P.M.
Fathers have 24-hour privileges.

15 LDR suites/3 operating

Midwives: No

Cesarean Rate: The hospital declined to
release this information.

NICU Level: III

This hospital specializes in high-risk pregnancies.
There are extensive in-patient and out-patient lactation services, as well as a birth and postpartum
doula program and at-home newborn assistance. It
has a Web nursery.

Classes:
- Lamaze
- pre- and postnatal exercise
- prenatal yoga
- infant and child CPR & safety
- baby care
- sibling preparation
- infant massage

★ SHADY GROVE ADVENTIST HOSPITAL

9901 Medical Center Drive
Rockville, MD 20850
301-279-6000 (General)
301-279-6386 (Maternity services)
240-631-8868 (Doula services)
www.adventisthealthcare.com/SGAH

Visiting Hours: Birth suites allow up to three
visitors 24 hours a day. Mother/baby units
allow father and siblings between 9 A.M. and
8 P.M. Other visitors are allowed between 11
A.M. and 8 P.M.

48 LDR/3 operating

Midwives: Yes

Cesarean Rate: 32 percent

NICU Level: III

The hospital went through a complete renovation in
late 2007. Each mother/baby private suite has a sofa
bed for guests, free Internet, movies on demand,
and spa services. Jacuzzis for labor relaxation are in
each birthing suite. Doula services may be arranged
directly through the hospital. It also has couplet care
and in-house lactation consultants.

Classes:
- childbirth/infant care
- breastfeeding
- fatherhood 101
- cesarean childbirth
- pediatric safety and CPR
- prenatal yoga

★ WASHINGTON ADVENTIST HOSPITAL

7600 Carroll Avenue

Takoma Park, MD 20912

301-891-7600 (General)

800-542-5096 (Class scheduling)

301-891-5305 (Maternity and doula services)

www.washingtonadventisthospital.com

Visiting Hours: Labor and delivery unit allows up to two people 24 hours a day. At the mother/baby unit, fathers are allowed between 9 A.M. and 10 P.M. Other visitors are allowed between 1 and 8 P.M.

10 LDR/ 2 operating

Midwives: No

Cesarean Rate: 39 percent

NICU Level: II

Specializing in high-risk pregnancies/deliveries, this hospital also provides a wide range of care for mothers and children in the home after the birth, such as lactation consultants and postpartum doulas. Also available: in-house lactation consultants, breast-pump sales and rentals, and doula services.

Classes:
- childbirth/infant care
- breastfeeding
- fatherhood 101
- cesarean childbirth
- infant care for adoptive parents
- pediatric safety and CPR
- sibling prep

Virginia

★ THE BIRTHING INN

Loudon Hospital Center

44045 Riverside Parkway

Leesburg, VA 20176

703-858-6000 (General)

703-858-6360 (Childbirth education)

Visiting Hours: 11 A.M.–8 P.M. Fathers have 24-hour privileges.

9 LDR/24 private postpartum/2 operating

Midwives: Yes

Cesarean Rate: The hospital declined to release this information.

NICU Level: II

The Birthing Inn is a unique hybrid combining a birthing center and a traditional hospital. It offers a holistic approach to childbirth yet offers all of the most advanced technology available. All rooms are private, with a soaking tub for labor. Both ob/gyns and midwives assist with labor and delivery, and there is a neonatology department available to assist with high-risk births.

Classes:
- preparation for childbirth
- newborn care
- breastfeeding
- pregnancy yoga
- cesarean prep
- unmedicated birth

INOVA ALEXANDRIA HOSPITAL

4320 Seminary Road

Alexandria, VA 22304

703-504-3000 (General)

703-204-3373 (Women's Center)

www.inova.org/inova_alexandria_hospital

Visiting Hours: 10 A.M. to 8 P.M.

Fathers have 24-hour privileges.

11 LDR/3 Operating

Midwives: Yes

Cesarean Rate: The hospital declined to release this information.

NICU Level: III

Description: This 318-bed community hospital has an extensive high-risk perinatal department that offers services from pre-pregnancy genetic testing to postpartum care.

Classes:

- expectant parent
- lamaze
- baby care
- breastfeeding
- parenting

INOVA FAIRFAX HOSPITAL

3300 Gallows Road

Falls Church, VA 22042

703-776-4001 (General)

703-776-6000

www.inova.org

Visiting Hours: 10 A.M.–8 P.M.

Fathers have 24-hour privileges.

22 LDR/3 Operating

Midwives: No midwives on staff.

Cesarean Rate: The hospital declined to release this information.

NICU Level: III

Description: This 833-bed teaching hospital delivers more babies than any other hospital in the DC metro area. With more than 11,000 deliveries in 2006, it is also the sixth busiest obstetrical department in the nation.

Classes:

- expectant parent
- lamaze
- baby care
- breastfeeding
- parenting

★ VIRGINIA HOSPITAL CENTER

1701 North George Mason Drive

Arlington, VA 22205

703-558-5000 (General)

www.virginiahospitalcenter.com

Visiting Hours: 11 A.M.–8 P.M.

Fathers have 24-hour privileges.

16 LDR/3 operating

Midwives: Allowed only through certain approved ob/gyns.

Cesarean Rate: 42 percent

NICU Level: II

Virginia Hospital Center is currently undergoing a renovation of its Women and Infant Health unit; it will be completed in 2008. New amenities will include Wi-Fi, spa services, and a family lounge.

Classes:

- childbirth preparation
- pre- and postnatal yoga
- sibling transition
- infant care
- breastfeeding
- couple massage
- CPR

Birthing Centers

If you choose a midwife, she may deliver at one of the hospitals listed previously or at a birthing center. Many women find the non-hospital-like atmosphere and amenities of a birthing center appealing. But remember that birthing centers are really only an option for those with low-risk normal pregnancies.

The primary ways that birthing centers differ from hospitals are that you will not be hooked up to any monitors or IVs, and you will be allowed to be much more mobile when labor begins. In addition, everyone is welcome to be with you throughout your birth experience, including your partner or coach, your mother, father, best friend, and, if you have them, your other children. During your labor, you can usually walk around, sip tea, relax in a Jacuzzi or tub, or try other activities women often find to be labor-enhancing. At a birthing center you can choose to labor and even deliver your baby in a special tub of soothing warm water. However, keep in mind that if you or your baby experiences complications during delivery, you'll want immediate access to a nearby hospital.

★ **BIRTHCARE & WOMEN'S HEALTH**
1501 King Street
Alexandria, VA 22314
703-549-5070
www.birthcare.org

This freestanding birthing center provides an extremely homey environment in which women with low-risk pregnancies can deliver their babies. There is a labor and birthing area with two private rooms. Both have private bathrooms with access to a larger bathroom with a Jacuzzi tub. BirthCare is not affiliated with any one hospital, but should

hospital intervention become necessary, a transportation procedure is in place.

★ **DC BIRTH CENTER**
801 Seventeenth Street, NE
Washington, DC 20002
202-398-2007
www.developingfamilies.org/dcbc.html

This birthing center specializes in family-focused, low-risk prenatal care, labor, and delivery. It is affiliated with Washington Hospital Center; you may choose to deliver your baby there from the start, or have it as a backup option in case there are complications during delivery at the Birth Center.

childbirth methods

No matter where you'll be delivering, you'll want to know the best, easiest, and most pain-free ways to get your baby out. For me, that was getting the epidural practically in the parking lot of the hospital, but some people want to be more cognizant for their birthing experience. Whether you are one of the brave ones, choosing to deliver naturally, or you're more like me, it's a good idea to take a class to prepare you mentally. Even if you are electively catatonic, the person delivering your baby still expects you to push. (The nerve!) And there's a whole trick to the pushing part that I'm not even going to go into; you'll learn it by taking a class. Trust me, you'll want to be ready.

As you talk with other pregnant women and new mothers, you will hear about the merits of one birthing method over another. It's up to you to decide which one is right for you. Here is a very short primer on the six best known and most popular.

Birth Works

www.birthworks.com

Birth Works was developed by Cathy Daub in 1981 to develop a woman's self-confidence, trust, and faith in her ability to give birth. Birth Works seeks to facilitate a woman's or couple's personal process in childbearing, and not to impart a preconceived method of labor and birth. During the ten-session course, a certified instructor covers topics including positions in labor, nutrition, medical procedures, pros and cons of drugs, and alternative comfort measures.

Birthing From Within

www.birthingfromwithin.com

In 1989 Pam England, a certified nurse midwife and mother, created Birthing From Within, a holistic approach to natural childbirth. Childbirth educators teach the philosophies from Pam's popular book *Birthing From Within: An Extraordinary Guide to Childbirth Preparation*, which include self-hypnosis, discovering personal strength, learning how to cope during unplanned circumstances, and breathing exercises, as well as birth art as a form of creative expression.

The Bradley Method
Husband-Coached Childbirth

www.bradleybirth.com

This method was developed in the 1940s by Dr. Robert A. Bradley, a Toronto-based obstetrician. The Bradley Method is based on a calming pattern of relaxation, deep abdominal breathing, and close teamwork between partner and expectant mother. Bradley's goal is a completely unmedicated pregnancy (not even aspirin or cold remedies), labor, and birth (no epidural block or Pitocin). Classes run for twelve weeks, covering twelve units of instruction.

With Bradley, the pregnant woman learns various positions for first-, second-, and third-stage labor. She is encouraged to approach her entire pregnancy as training for labor and to prepare her muscles for birth and her breasts for nursing.

Many hospitals in the Washington area offer Bradley instruction for childbirth, and there are also many private instructors available as well (I have listed a few below). You can also call The American Academy of Husband-Coached Childbirth at 800-4A-Birth or visit the organization's website.

HypnoBirthing

www.hypnobirthing.com

This technique combines hypnosis with pain management. It was founded by Marie Mongan, who is certified as a hypnotherapist, hypnoanesthesiologist, instructor of hypnotherapy, and the author of *Hypno-Birthing: A Celebration of Life*. HypnoBirthing educators teach women and their partners relaxation techniques and how to overcome fear and pain related to the birth process through the medium of hypnosis. Many educators are practitioners and can attend the labor.

The Lamaze Method

www.lamaze.org

Named after its developer, Dr. Fernand Lamaze, who was head of an obstetrical clinic in Paris in 1950, this method is popularly known as "childbirth without pain." (Wouldn't that be nice.) The method combines learned breathing techniques (the hoo-hoo-hoo, hee-hee-hee) used during contractions, with relaxation exercises designed to help a woman get through labor comfortably.

Most hospitals offer Lamaze classes. Call to sign up. (Also, most of the obstetrical nurses listed are trained in Lamaze and can assist your coach in the labor room if needed.) Couples usually begin Lamaze in the seventh month.

Some large obstetrical practices also offer Lamaze or will make referrals to private instructors, so ask your obstetrician or midwife. You can also sign up for area classes directly through the DC chapter of Lamaze at www.lamaze-dc.com or by calling 301-352-9727.

Water Labor and Water Birth

Water birth, popular in Russia since the 1960s, has attracted a small but enthusiastic number of supporters in the United States. Studies have shown that warm water can reduce the hours and stress of labor, offer support to the laboring woman, and help relax blood flow, making the baby's journey into the world easier.

Some women use this method's water-filled tub only as a comfort during labor. Others deliver while still in the tub, and the baby takes his first breaths while most of his body is submerged in water—a gentle, womblike environment in which to be born.

All three of the birthing centers listed make water labor and water birth available as an option. Should you wish, you can also rent a birthing tub and have a water birth at home with the help of a midwife. I repeat, with the help of a midwife. Please do not attempt this at home alone without the help of a professional!

childbirth educators, classes, and other resources

In addition to the classes offered at the hospitals and birthing centers, the following is a list of independent instructors, many of whom offer more than one type of service. I have tried to include the scope of offerings for each provider, but I suggest calling a few for updated information and to determine the right match. Class length varies, but most are offered as a series, meeting once or twice a week for around eight to ten weeks.

★ **THE BABY DUCK**
   703-217-8733
   www.thebabyduck.com

Owner and primary instructor Melody Kisor has an extensive and varied background that includes a BA in public health and maternal/child health education, and graduate work in clinical research administration and epidemiology. She is certified as an EMT and a CPR instructor, Lamaze and ICEA childbirth instructor, and she is a certified labor doula (CLD). In addition, she is a lactation management specialist. Melody started The Baby Duck in 2003 and offers a wide variety of classes on topics including pain management in labor and childbirth, preconception, infant safety, pets and babies, travel with baby, and parenting.

★ BEAUTIFUL BIRTHS

Rachel Silber

301-412-8847

info@beautiful-births.com

www.beautiful-births.com

Rachel is a doula and childbirth educator who specializes in the Birth Works method. The Birth Works childbirth education classes are offered either in a class setting or in private sessions. Group classes are held over eight weeks at her home in Potomac, Maryland.

★ CHILD BIRTH CARE

2469 Eighteenth Street, NW

Washington, DC

202-276-6474

www.childbirthcare.com

Child Birth Care, run by founder Katja Brandis, offers an array of childbirth education classes, including those based on the Birth Works and HypnoBirthing philosophies. In addition, you'll find classes on breastfeeding, newborn care, and pre- and postnatal yoga (there is even a yoga class to which you can take the new addition). I particularly like the fact that it teaches a prenatal massage class for partners!

★ CONFIDENT BIRTH

Lara Maupin

confidentbirth@verizon.net

www.confidentbirth.com

A certified Lamaze childbirth educator since 2000, Lara teaches weekly classes in Falls Church, Virginia, through the DC chapter of Lamaze. She also teaches other birth-related classes privately which she will tailor to your individual needs. (For example, if you are a second-time parent and would like a refresher course, Lara can create an abridged version for you.) In addition, Lara is a certified DONA birth doula. The doula services she provides include at least two prenatal visits, support during labor and delivery, a written birth story, and one postpartum visit.

★ MOMEASE

300 Montgomery Street, Suite 203

Alexandria, VA

703-739-2832

www.momease.com

Momease started seven years ago and has developed prenatal education products for expectant parents. It has since expanded its offerings to include childbirth and new parenting classes for couples and single moms. (There are also separate classes for new fathers taught by a male instructor.) As your pregnancy proceeds, a variety of classes are available, including baby care, parents of multiples, breastfeeding, and childbirth classes, as well as classes on nutrition and pregnancy massage. Prenatal exercise programs such as tai chi and belly dancing are also offered. Classes are taught at George Washington Hospital or the Alexandria location. Momease also offers complete doula services.

★ SHANTI YOGA CENTER

4209/4217 East-West Highway

Bethesda, MD

301-654-6759

888-384-YOGA (9642)

www.schooloflife.org

Shanti Yoga offers a program emphasizing a balance between body, mind, and spirit through the exploration of Hatha yoga. This program is open to all women, whether or not they practice yoga regularly. Classes take the center's philosophy—based on the five principles of yoga: proper exercise, breathing, diet, relaxation, and positive thinking/meditation—and apply them to mothers and family. In addition to classes on preconception, prenatal yoga, women's water yoga, mother/baby yoga, spiritual motherhood, and family yoga, it also offers a complete childbirth education class based on the HypnoBirthing method.

★ **SUSAN MESSINA BIRTH WORKS**
202-338-3846
http://leep.lis.uiuc.edu/publish/smessina/
    MessinaBirthWorks.htm
Susan has been teaching the Birth Works method of childbirth preparation since 2002. Her very popular classes are taught in her home in NW DC's Palisades neighborhood in a ten-session course format. Each class runs for about two hours twice a week. If you are interested, call early to check current schedules and sign up, as these classes tend to fill up quickly.

★ **WILLOW STREET YOGA**
6930 Carroll Avenue, Suite 100
Takoma Park, MD
301-270-8038
www.willowstreetyoga.com
In addition to a wide range of yoga classes, Willow Street Yoga also offers a class on pregnancy and birth. The instructor, Sara Shelley, specializes in yoga and meditation for the childbearing years and is a certified HypnoBirthing childbirth educator. The workshop is designed to help couples expand their awareness and confidence during pregnancy, labor, and birth. The class emphasizes posture, breath work, massage, and other techniques for relaxing and staying focused during the birthing process.

★ **WISEBIRTHWAYS**
Susan Lucas
301-588-7771
Priscilla McGee
301-740-2578
www.wisebirthways.com
Susan and Priscilla are both certified labor doulas who offer childbirth classes in the Birthing From Within philosophy. Together they have over twenty-five years of experience, and both have trained with Pam England, the founder of Birthing From Within. Class offerings include either a six-week series for first-time parents or a four-week refresher series for second-time parents. They also offer private classes and weekend intensives. Classes are held at the Cameron Medical Building in Silver Spring, Maryland, or you can arrange for private sessions in your home.

taking care of you

After you've assembled your support team, from your doctor or midwife to hypnotherapist, doula, birth instructor, and lactation consultant (why not throw in a makeup artist and Sherpa while we're at it?), it's time to focus on taking care of you. I am a firm believer in doing whatever it takes to feel as fantastic as possible—both physically and mentally—during pregnancy. Happy moms make for happy babies, and, fortunately, being pregnant has become truly chic—babies are the latest "it" accessory. We are incredibly lucky to live in a day and age where a cottage industry has sprung up to cater to the expectant mother. Taking advantage of some of these terrific services to relax and refresh the body, mind, and spirit will make the hardships of pregnancy that much easier to bear. Treating yourself to a manicure or a massage in your ninth month may get you through one of those days when you're ready to reach in and take that baby out yourself! And once your new addition has made its way into the world, you'll probably be desperate to get your pre-pregnancy body back. Yes, ladies, "A Farewell to Arms" might just have a whole new connotation.

This chapter is all about you. It provides information on professionals who offer pre- and postnatal exercise classes, fitness training, yoga, and massage. I have also included a list of nutritionists who can help you eat right. Everything listed here has been tailored for pregnant women, but please always consult with your physician before undertaking any of the activities suggested. If your obstetrician allows it, I recommend getting involved in a physical fitness program early on in your pregnancy. It will help you feel your best through those long, heavy months, prepare you for labor, and can be a great way to meet other moms-to-be.

Unfortunately, some women will be forced to spend some time during their pregnancy on bed rest, as I did. I have some tips and services to help make you more comfortable during those long weeks and months.

exercise

Most experts agree that exercising throughout your pregnancy is safe, healthy, and beneficial to your overall well-being. If your pregnancy is normal and relatively low-risk, you should be able to participate in a moderate exercise program throughout your pregnancy. If you are a serious athlete or have exercised regularly prior to being pregnant, you should be able to maintain that level of activity, with some modifications, throughout pregnancy and postpartum. However, it is extremely important to check with your doctor or midwife before starting or continuing any exercise, whether you are low- or high-risk. Below are some recommendations adapted from the guidelines issued by the American College of Obstetricians and Gynecologists (ACOG):

★ Regular exercise (at least three times per week) is preferable to intermittent activity.

★ Avoid exercise that involves lying flat on your back after the fourth month. Lying on your back is associated with decreased cardiac output in pregnancy. Also avoid prolonged periods of standing.

★ During pregnancy, you have less oxygen available for aerobic exercise. Modify the intensity of your exercise. Stop exercising when fatigued, and never exercise to the point of exhaustion.

★ Weight-bearing exercises, such as jogging, may be continued throughout pregnancy at lower intensities. Non-weight-bearing exercises, such as cycling and swimming, minimize risk of injury.

★ Be sure that your heart rate does not exceed one hundred forty beats per minute.

★ Avoid exercise that could cause you to lose your balance, especially in the third trimester. Avoid any type of exercise with the potential for even minor abdominal trauma.

★ Be sure to eat enough prior to your workout. Pregnancy requires an additional three hundred calories a day just to maintain your weight.

★ Drink water and wear comfortable clothes to augment heat dissipation during exercise.

Many pregnancy-related body changes persist four to six weeks postpartum. After your baby is born, resume your pre-pregnancy routines gradually, according to how you feel.

If you're thinking, *I haven't been to the gym since* Friends *was on the air!* (did I just lose my inner monologue?) but want to keep in shape during your pregnancy, the best advice is to walk every day. Walking is a low-impact activity that is easy to incorporate into your everyday routine. For those of you who would like to add some other activities to your routine in a more structured environment, check out some of the classes offered at gyms around town. There are dozens of health clubs to choose from in the area, ranging from the luxurious Four Seasons Georgetown, where one-time enrollment fees top $4,000, to Bally's Total Fitness, which offers month-to-month memberships for as low as $32 per month (plus enrollment fees).

Unfortunately, most of these clubs are not offering much in the way of specific pre- and postnatal classes as compared to clubs in L.A. and New York. However, most instructors at these gyms are happy to tailor regular activities to suit whichever stage of pregnancy you are in, so be sure to notify them prior to the start of class. Many personal trainers in these health clubs are also certified to work with pre- and postnatal women, so just inquire. Another option: check with the hospital where you are planning to deliver, since some have fitness programs or will refer you to one. The classes offered at area hospitals can be found in chapter one.

The following is a list of classes and professionals specializing in pre- and postnatal exercise programs:

★ BABY BOOT CAMP

Andrea McEvoy
Multiple Maryland locations
301-461-6605
888-990-BABY (2229)
Andrea.mcevoy@babybootcamp.com
www.babybootcamp.com

Baby Boot Camp is a national exercise program that started in 2001 in San Francisco. These seventy-five-minute cardio- and strength-training workouts are done with your baby in a jogging stroller. Andrea McEvoy currently offers a 9:30 A.M. class in a different Maryland location each day. The first class is free; after that classes are $15 each. There is a discount for purchasing a series.

★ CHASE MISHOU

Palisades, DC
202-294-8538
chasemishou@gmail.com

Chase Mishou is the go-to guy to help rid you of the postpartum muffin top, or whatever it is you wish to shed. You will feel like you are on your way to getting your pre-pregnancy (maybe even high school) bod back once he shows up at your house and says "drop and give me twenty!" No in-home gym is necessary, as he comes armed with resistance cords and a medicine ball, and can turn two Pottery Barn kids' chairs into a multifunctional torture device. I swear by him.

Sorry, ladies, the cat's out of the bag. Chase will no longer be the best-kept secret in DC. A sixty-minute session is $80.

★ DAVID KELLER

Fitness for Life
Georgetown, DC
202-338-6765
ffl1417@aol.com

Don't hate him because he's beautiful. Featured every year in *The Washingtonian* as DC's "trainer to the stars," David is the Adonis of trainers with twenty-plus years' experience keeping women (and their partners) fit throughout pregnancy and beyond. And, unlike a lot of trainers, David truly makes you feel like you are the most beautiful woman on the planet—a priceless commodity as your body takes on an alien form. You'll meet with him in his private light-filled Georgetown studio and not want to leave when it's time to go. A fifty-minute session of personally tailored training is $125.

★ NANCY KARABAIC

High Energy Fitness
Silver Spring, MD
301-942-3399
www.nancykarabaic.com

A full-time trainer since 1996, Karabaic specializes in pre- and postnatal personal training. Karabaic started her mom's class in September 1999, the year she gave birth to her son Grant. Her class is personal-training-meets-playgroup, and she encourages you to take your newborn or toddler. Classes are held Monday through Thursday, 10–11 A.M., in her home studio in Kensington, Maryland. The class includes circuit weight training with the use of free weights, thirty minutes of cardio workout, and abdominal work and stretches tailored to each mom's personal level of fitness. For the babies, her gym has a bouncer, activity gym, swing, and

ExerSaucer, and toddlers can jump between the playhouse, rocking horse, small kitchen, and play yard. At $30 a session, it's a bargain that's hard to beat. Nancy will also come to you for one-on-one training sessions; rates start at $80 an hour.

★ SEEMOMMYRUN

www.seeMOMMYrun.com

This non-profit organization is dedicated to improving the health and well-being of mothers and children by providing easy access to family-friendly fitness groups (and, in the near future, training programs). It lets members exercise without having to spend time away from their children because moms in every area or neighborhood can start groups convenient to them. At seeMOMMYrun.com, moms can communicate and make their own arrangements for running or walking together in groups. The website helps members coordinate with other moms based on geographic needs, time constraints, and fitness abilities.

★ STROLLER STRIDES

866-FITT-4MOM

www.strollerstrides.com

DC (AU Park, Capitol Hill, Chevy Chase, U Street, Zoo)

Kathrin Bachrack

888-666-9733

www.strollerstrides.net/washingtondc

kbachrack@strollerstrides.net

Bethesda/Gaithersburg/Germantown/Potomac /Rockville

Corina DuBois

888-232-2496

www.strollerstrides.net/montgomerycounty

corina@strollerstrides.net

Arlington/Alexandria

Jennifer Lungren

888-452-4899

www.strollerstrides.net/alexandria

jlungren@strollerstrides.net

Stroller Strides, which started in San Diego, is a nationwide exercise program that combines power walking, body toning, and stretching using a stroller with your six-week- to five-year-old in it. Each class consists of a warm-up, a power walk and "stations" where you do a variety of body-toning exercises. Exercise tubing (provided for you), your stroller, and the outdoor environment are used to create the "gym." If your baby is fussy, the instructor will show you exercises you can do holding him. The group classes are a great way to meet other moms. Each class is approximately fifty minutes long and indoor locations are provided in inclement weather and during the winter. Classes are $15 each and discounts are offered if you buy a series or a month-long pass. Stroller Strides also offers other great services, such as resources to help moms organize play dates, and a quarterly newsletter. There are more than ten locations in the DC metro area. Check the website for the location nearest you.

★ **YMCA**
Multiple locations
www.ymcadc.org

This gym is the exception to the rule, offering many different pre- and postnatal exercise classes including water aerobics, Pilates, and yoga. True, it's not the sexiest place to be working out as you inch toward "yummy mummy" status, but it is a great bang for the buck and has surprisingly hip offerings for America's original gym, established in 1851. Another perk is the comprehensive website: Once you've established membership, you can check class offerings and schedules and sign up online. I have to say I was pleasantly surprised.

yoga

It has fast become one of the most popular forms of exercise for women, pregnant or not. With its focus on relaxation and breathing techniques, yoga is great for moms-to-be and may help make your pregnancy more comfortable by reducing backaches and other body stresses during your pregnancy.

If you have taken yoga before your pregnancy and want to continue, do so. Don't feel like you need to switch to special prenatal classes entirely. I did advanced yoga with modifications throughout my pregnancy. But it is important to learn these modifications; for example, no lying on your back and no flying crow! If you have never practiced yoga, prenatal classes are a good place to start. The instructors will guide you through safe exercises geared to the various stages of your pregnancy. Prenatal classes usually allow more time than traditional yoga for resting and relaxation. You will also learn breathing and postures that are helpful during birth and labor. It's also a great way to meet other expectant moms in your neighborhood.

In the past five years the number of yoga studios in DC has increased exponentially, but not all studios offer prenatal classes. Below are some private yoga instructors and studios, and classes offered for pregnant women or women who have just given birth. Many of these studios also offer Mommy and Me yoga, Itsy Bitsy yoga, and other yoga classes for kids. Please see chapter twelve for those listings.

★ **CAPITOL HILL YOGA**
221 Fifth Street, NE
Capitol Hill, DC
202-544-0011
www.capitolhillyoga.com

This studio offers yoga for the entire family, including parents-to-be. From prenatal to Itsy Bitsy and Tots Itsy Bitsy yoga, the whole family can enjoy the benefits of the more than thirty classes with excellent instructors. Individual classes are $18; ten classes are $150. Mommy and Me classes are $10 each.

★ **CIRCLE YOGA**
3838 Northampton Street, NW
Chevy Chase, DC
202-686-1104
www.circleyoga.com

Pre- and postnatal yoga classes are offered in this newly renovated studio in Chevy Chase. It offers classes for the entire family from Itsy Bitsy yoga to family yoga. A single class is $18, or you can buy a fourteen-week-session package that allows you to drop in on any class for $210.

★ FLOW YOGA CENTER

1450 P Street, NW

Dupont Circle, DC

202-462-FLOW

www.flowyogacenter.com

Prenatal and Mommy and Me yoga classes are taught in the Hatha style in these two light-filled studios, designed according to the princicples of feng shui. The space is immediately relaxing and the instructors all have the highest levels of certification. Each class is $16; a ten-class pass is $135; and a one-month unlimited pass is $120.

★ GEORGETOWN YOGA

1053 Thirty-first Street, NW

Georgetown, DC

202-342-7779

www.georgetownyoga.com

Moms-to-be love the laid-back yet encouraging approach at Georgetown Yoga, founded by fellow mom Margaret Burns Vap. In the bright and airy studio overlooking the canal, Ashtanga-trained instructors apply this approach to prenatal yoga. This is a great place to go if you find yourself wanting to try yoga for the first time while pregnant. Each class is $17; an unlimited monthly pass is $145.

★ INSPIRED YOGA

1115 U Street, NW

U Street Corridor, DC

202-462-1800

www.inspiredyoga.com

While many great yoga studios around DC offer prenatal classes, few make it a focus of their overall practice as Inspired Yoga does. It offers a popular prenatal class on Sunday mornings where soon-to-be moms are encouraged to attend with their partners. Regular prenatal and mom and baby classes are offered as well. Classes are $17 each; an unlimited-class pass that is good for three months is $300.

★ JOY OF MOTION

7315 Wisconsin Avenue, Suite 180E

Bethesda, MD

301-986-0016

1643 Connecticut Avenue, NW

Dupont Circle, DC

202-387-0911

5207 Wisconsin Avenue, NW

Friendship Heights, DC

202-362-3042

www.joyofmotion.com

Joy of Motion offers a wide range of dance and exercise classes including pre- and postnatal yoga. The instructors are very knowledgeable about different stages of pregnancy and how to adjust the intensity of a class accordingly; however, I found the facilities a bit grungy. Classes cost $17 each; an eight-week unlimited session pass is $120.

★ MELISSA FELDMAN

240-678-3617

www.melissafeldman.com

Melissa teaches private and group pre- and postnatal yoga instruction with an emphasis on the Vinyasa flow method. Having been pregnant herself, she has a true understanding of what women are going through during this time. She charges $100 an hour for a private session, which can include up to five people. Melissa also teaches at various locations around the city. A friend who recently had twins took private in-home sessions with Melissa throughout her pregnancy and swears by her. She carried the twins all the way up to forty-one weeks—almost unheard of with twins—and each baby weighed eight pounds at birth. Yikes!

★ **MOORE THAN YOGA**
  4347 Arlington Boulevard
  Arlington, VA
  703-671-2435
  www.moorethanyoga.com
Founded by Jennifer Moore, Moore than Yoga offers Hatha yoga for the entire family. There are pre- and postnatal classes for the beginner, as well as Mommy and Me and Little Tots yoga. Jennifer even offers Pajama Yoga, where families can spend some relaxing, playful time together in their pajamas. Classes start at $9 each; an eight-class pass is $112.

★ **PURE PRANA YOGA**
  100 South Patrick Street
  Alexandria, VA
  703-836-PURE (7873)
  www.pureprana.com
Prenatal, postnatal, Mommy and Me, and traditional yoga classes are offered in Pure Prana's second-floor studio in the heart of Old Town. Class participants are encouraged to stay after each class to chat, relax, and enjoy tea and cookies. All classes are $15.

★ **SPIRAL FLIGHT**
  1826 Wisconsin Avenue, NW
  Georgetown, DC
  202-965-1645
  www.spiralflightyoga.com
Pre- and postnatal yoga are offered at this two-story studio located in upper Georgetown. Each class is $18; a ten-class pass is $150.

★ **TRANQUIL SPACE YOGA**
  2024 P Street, NW
  Dupont Circle, DC
  202-223-YOGA (9642)

  7475 Wisconsin Avenue
  Bethesda, MD
  301-654-YOGA
  www.tranquilspace.com
Pre- and postnatal yoga classes are taught by Anne Thiel, a certified prenatal yoga instructor and certified midwife. Gentle Vinyasa yoga is coupled with breath work and meditation designed to help expectant mothers adjust to the changes of pregnancy. Instruction also helps to physically, mentally, and emotionally prepare women for childbirth and labor, and for their lives as new parents. Each class is $17; three classes are $33.

massage

Frankly, who needs to be talked into getting a massage when she is pregnant, and what better excuse could you have to get one? Many women suffer from lower-back pain, especially during those last few months. Your body produces a hormone called Relaxin which, much like it sounds, relaxes the muscles and ligaments in your body, allowing it to compensate for your growing bundle of joy. However, this often causes strain in the back and hips. Getting a massage can help to keep everything in alignment and relieve some of the discomfort. (Though you should not schedule a massage until you are through your first trimester.)

A massage therapist should be licensed, and I don't mean via correspondence course. Let's leave that to motorcycle repair, shall we? Certain pressure points can actually induce labor, so ideally, a massage therapist should be certified in prenatal massage, or at least have extensive experience working with pregnant women. When I was in my seventh month with Charlie, I went to a well-known and upscale spa in West Virginia with friends and we all got massages. My so-called massage therapist's first words to me were, "You're here for a prenatal massage, right? I haven't done one of these in a long time so just holler, okay?" That scary theme song from Deliverance started going through my head. I still shudder at the thought. Every massage therapist listed here is licensed in prenatal massage.

Communication with your therapist is vital. If you feel lightheaded, short of breath, or uncomfortable, let him or her know. Women are advised not to lie on their backs after the fourth month of pregnancy, therefore prenatal massages are often given to a woman as she lies on her side with pillows under her head and between her arms and legs. There is actually a special pregnancy massage table—which is basically a table with a hole for your stomach—but I have never used one and find the pillows to be incredibly comfortable.

Some of the therapists listed here will come to your home for an additional fee. Personally, the idea of having a massage at home just didn't sound relaxing to me. With phones ringing, dogs barking, and, during my second pregnancy, a toddler calling, I preferred to go to a spa, where the sounds of babbling brooks and whale song, and subtle aromas wafting through the air soothed the savage beast I had become. However, if you're pregnant for the first time or are lucky enough to have a well-insulated massage room (or a padded cell) in your home, the convenience of home is nice.

The downside to calling a spa and asking for a prenatal massage therapist blindly is you don't know who you are going to get the first time. I had a great prenatal massage at The Four Seasons Georgetown when pregnant with Connor. When I called to schedule a massage with the same person while pregnant with Charlie, the therapist was no longer working there and the new therapist wasn't as good.

In addition to the therapists listed in this chapter, two additional resources that provide online referrals are the American Massage Therapy Association at www.amtamassage.org and The Potomac Massage Training Institute at www.pmti.org. All therapists work by appointment only, so call ahead.

★ CLAUDETTE PLATER

Ashburn, VA

703-724-4210

www.tranquilmoment.com

Before becoming a certified prenatal massage therapist, Claudette was a labor and delivery RN as well as a doula and birth assistant. She runs her practice out of her Ashburn home. She charges $70 for an hour-long prenatal massage (and does not do home visits).

★ ELIZABETH ARDEN RED DOOR SALON AND SPA

5225 Wisconsin Avenue, NW

Chevy Chase, DC

202-362-9890

1101 South Joyce Street, Suite B-36

Arlington, VA

703-373-5888

11838 Spectrum Center Drive

Reston, VA

703-467-8488

4210 Fairfax Corner West Avenue

Fairfax, VA

703-968-2922

10213 Old Georgetown Road

Bethesda, MD

240-644-1319

www.reddoorspas.com

The Red Door Salon and Spa offers prenatal massages and many other services for the expectant mother in need of some pampering. Treatments are relaxing and help to relieve stress on weight-bearing joints, in addition to reducing neck and back

pain, and edema. Packages include Great Expectations (a prenatal massage, skin-illuminating facial, warm cream manicure and pedicure, and spa lunch) and Bundle of Joy (a Red Door facial or prenatal massage, shampoo and style, warm cream manicure, and spa lunch). Treatments start at $120.

★ FOUR SEASONS GEORGETOWN

2800 Pennsylvania Avenue, NW

Georgetown, DC

202-342-0444

www.fourseasons.com/washington/spa.html

An oasis in Georgetown, the spa has eight treatment rooms and at least two certified prenatal massage therapists on staff at all times. Upon check-in, you are offered your choice of refreshing flavored spring waters or herbal tea, and you have full use of the gym, steam room, and sauna. (Unfortunately, your doctor will prohibit the use of steam or sauna until postpartum.) The changing and waiting rooms are always quiet and the treatment rooms are wonderfully womblike: dimly lit, warm, and quiet. The prenatal massage costs $90 for fifty-five minutes.

★ THE MANDARIN ORIENTAL HOTEL

1330 Maryland Avenue, SW

Downtown, DC

202-554-8588

www.mandarinoriental.com

They went all out when designing the spa at this downtown DC location of the premier hotel chain. You will feel truly indulgent when whisked away into one of the gorgeous treatment rooms. Even though partaking while pregnant is a no-no, take a peek at the awesome steam room. An eighty-minute prenatal massage is $225. Here you are paying for the "Mandarin" name and the multimillion-dollar spa. It's definitely a splurge.

★ **THE MASSAGE STUDIO**

James Montgomery

2602 Connecticut Avenue, NW

Woodley Park, DC

202-288-4911

www.massagedc.net

James runs his Woodley Park practice out of the fourth floor of Salon Roi, in the famous "Marilyn Monroe" building. If you are longing to be able to lie on your stomach again, this is the place to go. James's prenatal massage table has an ovoid opening for the belly, and breast recesses, which enable the shoulder blades to retract slightly, and allows superior access (and much-needed relief) to the musculature in the center of the back. Fathers are encouraged to tag along and learn a thing or two about massage, both for the mother and newborn (personally, I'd rather John stay at home and have James do his thing). He charges $85 for an hour massage in the salon; in-home visits are $130 an hour.

★ **MELISSA FELDMAN**

240-678-3617

www.melissafeldman.com

Melissa is trained in the Swedish and shiatsu methods of massage. She also incorporates acupressure and vocal meditation and relaxation techniques during the home session. She charges $100 for an hour-long massage.

★ **NUSTA SPA**

1129 Twentieth Street, NW

Penn Quarter, DC

202-530-5700

www.nustaspa.com

The Nusta Spa strives to treat the tired expectant mom or new mom like royalty. Its therapists will focus on the lower back, neck, hips, and legs for relief from muscle cramps, spasms, and myofascial pain. Fifty- and eighty-minute massages are offered; for a full spa experience, you can add other treatments such as facials, manicures, and pedicures. A fifty-minute massage is $105.

★ **ROBBIN PHELPS**

Takoma Park, DC

202-288-9017

robbin_mp@hotmail.com

Not only is Robbin certified in prenatal massage therapy, she's also a mother. She thoroughly enjoys the process of "nurturing the mother and baby" throughout the nine months of pregnancy and believes that prenatal massage can make for an easier delivery and higher APGAR score for baby. She practices both out of her office in Takoma, DC, and at Boundless Yoga Studio in the U Street corridor. Rates start at $70 per hour.

★ **SHERYL STURGES**

Adams Morgan, DC

202-232-4138

www.sdswellness.com

With two children of her own, Sheryl knows firsthand the pangs of pregnancy. She has been practicing prenatal massage since 2000. During her own labor and delivery, she found the use of acupressure so helpful as a way to manage pain that she has incorporated instruction of accupressure points with the pregnancy massages she gives. She charges $75 for an hour massage at her Adams Morgan studio and $110 for home visits.

nutrition and food delivery

Now that you're eating for two, it's important to make sure you are eating more of the right foods—not just eating more. In fact, "eating for two" is a bit of a misconception; according to The American College of Obstetricians and Gynecologists, on average women really only need to add about three hundred calories a day to their diets during pregnancy. So put down the tub of ice cream and read on.

Your doctor or midwife should address dietary issues with you, but for a more comprehensive plan to follow over the next nine months, consult a nutritionist. Moreover, to avoid some of the lovely side effects of pregnancy—constipation, nausea, and heartburn (one of my personal favorites)—a dietitian can help to steer you from certain foods. If you are underweight, overweight, a diabetic, or want to maintain a vegetarian diet during pregnancy, he or she can address those needs as well.

Some women have to spend time during their pregnancy on bed rest. (I did.) I have included home-delivery services that will help make it a bit easier to stay healthy during this time.

★ **AMERICAN DIETETIC ASSOCIATION**
800-366-1655
www.eatright.org
The American Dietetic Association will provide a list of certified dieticians in your area that specialize in prenatal nutrition.

★ **DOOR TO DOOR ORGANICS**
888-283-4443
www.doortodoororganics.com
Door to Door Organics is based out of Bucks County, Pennsylvania, and has been family owned and operated since 1996. The service ships farm-fresh organic fruit and vegetables directly to your door overnight each Wednesday by UPS. Prices are somewhat high but are competitive with other high-end organic-produce providers. The site is easy to navigate and once you set up an account, you can easily repeat previous saved orders.

★ **F².U.E.L**
202-351-6818
www.fueledup.com
If finding the time to shop for groceries and cook a nutritious meal just isn't happening, then you'll need to call F2.U.E.L and have its chefs do it for you. After an initial consultation with one of the company's registered dieticians, a meal plan will be completely customized for you. Professional chefs will then prepare for you up to four healthy gourmet meals a day that are delivered to your doorstep by 5 a.m each morning. Meal plans range between $18 and $24 a day.

★ PEAPOD

800-5-PEAPOD (573-2763)

www.peapod.com

Peapod is the online-delivery arm of Giant Grocery, and it serves the entire DC metro area. When shopping online, the website allows you to browse by food category, by aisle, or by specific product or brand name. You then schedule a convenient time for the groceries to be delivered to your home. Delivery fees are between $7 and $10 with a required minimum order of $50. This service is great if you are on bed rest, too tired to shop for groceries with a newborn, or are back at work and want to save time.

★ SAFEWAY.COM

877-505-4040

www.safeway.com

Safeway.com is the online-delivery arm of Safeway grocery store. The service is very similar to Peapod and the website has comparable search functions to enable easy ordering. When scheduling a delivery time, you are given the choice of either a two- or four-hour window, and delivery fees range from $6 to $10. It is recommended to schedule your delivery at least two days ahead, as schedules get booked up.

★ WASHINGTON'S GREEN GROCER

301-333-3696

www.washingtonsgreengrocer.com

In 1994, tired of buying "tired" produce, John and Lisa Zechiel decided they probably weren't alone. The husband-and-wife team decided to leave careers in the restaurant business and embark on their dream of delivering fresh organic produce directly to consumers. Each week a selection of twelve to fourteen different types of fruits and vegetables is delivered to your doorstep. You have a choice of a combination of organic and conventional or 100 percent certified organic produce. You can also add fresh organic milk, cheese, eggs, and pasta to your order. Prices range from $27.50 for a small box to $39.50 for a large box.

★ WHOLESOME BODY

1622 Fourteenth Street, NW

U Street Corridor, DC

202-745-0003

www.wholesomebodydc.com

clorenze@wholesomebodydc.com

Certified nutritionists make up Wholesome Body. They work with clients on everything from stabilizing blood sugar to creating healthy diets for pregnancy, breastfeeding, and post-pregnancy weight loss. Their goal is to create nutrition plans that achieve their clients' goals and match their lifestyles; for example, some people enjoy cooking while others eat out almost exclusively. In both cases, women can enjoy a healthy and varied diet. Rates start at $135 for an initial consultation.

from health care to day care

Though it may be hard to envision now, that belly impeding the view of your toes will soon be an actual, living person in your home—a little baby with inscrutable demands and health needs. It's a good idea to get your postpartum support system—perhaps a nurse or a doula, as well as day care, nanny, and baby-sitter—in place before the swaddled bundle is in your arms, because those first few months can be harrowing!

Baby needs a pediatrician, and it's best to line one up in your third trimester. Get recommendations from your ob/gyn (that's how I found mine) or from friends or relatives. In case you don't know a slew of people with families already underway, I've included some resources to help you find one, as well as a list of the DC area's most popular practices.

If you think you might want some extra help, I've also recommended a few nurses and doulas, and I show you how to find more in your area. We had a night nurse for several weeks when we came home with each of our boys. My husband John and I were both so glad we made that decision as she left us feeling well rested in addition to confident in our new roles as parents. In the first month, a nurse or doula will visit you in the home, overnight if you like, and help you get your baby on feeding and sleeping schedules. This can be very luxurious, as she can even give baby those midnight feedings so you can sleep.

You won't believe it in those first few weeks, but one day you will want to get back to work, go out to dinner with friends, or just spend a couple of hours without your beloved babe. Start lining up childcare while you're still pregnant, especially day care or nannies. This chapter will make it easy, and by the end you'll be able to find a baby-sitting teen in your neighborhood and learn how to line up the right care for your Harvard-bound daughter.

selecting a pediatrician

Start looking for a pediatrician in your third trimester. When my doctor took me off bed rest at thirty-six weeks, I practically stood up and had Connor. I was glad to have had the blind luck of settling on a good doctor ahead of time. Upon delivery, the hospital will also contact your pediatrician so that he or she can come to the hospital and examine the baby before you are both released.

Here are some good starting points to help you find a pediatrician:

★ Ask your ob/gyn for a recommendation. This is how I found our pediatrician. My ob/gyn had actually taught her at Georgetown University and had referred other patients who were happy. I love our doctor but, more importantly, both of my boys love her. I have yet to experience those legendary meltdowns some kids have at the mere mention of the word doctor. Much like the criteria for finding a good ob/gyn, you want to find a pediatrician that you feel comfortable with and who shares the same basic philosophies as you. Some doctors will have you see a specialist at every sneeze or if your child doesn't crawl at exactly five months. Other doctors are more relaxed and feel that each baby develops in his or her own good time and that worrying too much is unnecessary. Find a doctor that fits your family's personality. This relationship is one that will span at least the next eighteen years, if not longer.

★ Ask friends whose judgment you trust for a recommendation.

★ Call the hospital where you plan to deliver and ask for a referral from its pediatric department.

★ Location, location, location. You will be at the pediatrician constantly, especially in the beginning, and being able to get to the doctor's office easily and quickly is just plain practical. Also, if you will be driving, check out the parking situation and how convenient it is or how accessible the office is to public transportation.

★ Check with your insurance company to find out which area doctors are covered in your plan.

Once you have the names of two or three pediatricians, set up a meeting. Most practices will set aside a time each week to meet with parents of prospective patients.

Some questions to ask the doctor when you meet are:

★ Do sick and healthy children wait in the same waiting room?

★ Is there an on-site lab for quick blood and urine tests, ear wave sonograms, etc.?

★ How many doctors are in the practice?

★ How does the doctor answer non-emergency calls throughout the day? Is there a call-in hour or does the doctor return calls intermittently between patients? Is there a nurse practitioner who can answer questions?

★ What is the doctor's philosophy on breastfeeding versus formula? Does he or she have a lactation consultant on staff?

★ What is the schedule for newborn visits?

★ If your doctor is a solo practitioner, who handles phone calls when he or she is on vacation?

baby nurses and doulas

I remember the surreal feeling of driving back from the hospital with John after giving birth with an actual baby in the back seat—two days earlier it had just been the two of us. Only an hour prior there were what felt like hundreds of doctors and nurses working around the clock caring for this baby's every need. All of a sudden a nurse just wheels you to the curb and hands you your baby. I remember thinking, "You're going to let this baby go home with us? Do you have any idea what you're doing? I can't even keep a goldfish alive!" Reality sets in quickly, and we were very grateful when the baby nurse arrived at our doorstep a few (very long) hours later.

Most people arrange to have the baby nurse come the day they bring their baby home from the hospital. The term "baby nurse" can be a bit misleading, though, as it does not necessarily mean she is a trained RN. The word "nurse" is used loosely and is an antiquated term for someone who has many years of experience taking care of infants. A baby nurse stays with you in your house twenty-four hours a day and does everything for the baby. She gets up with the baby at night to change diapers and do feedings. If you are breastfeeding, she will bring your baby to you to nurse, but then burp him, change him, and put him back down so you can go back to sleep. (Believe me, that extra bit of sleep can make a big difference.) Each baby nurse works differently but usually she will take a few hours off during the day, and if she is with you for two weeks or more, she will take a full day off at some mutually agreeable time. This luxury does not come cheap—baby nurses cost between $200 and $300 a day—

but trust me when I say it is money well spent.

Another option is a postpartum doula. The easy way to remember the difference between the two is that a nurse does everything for the baby and a doula does everything for the mother. Doulas usually come for a few hours a day and will go grocery shopping, do laundry, and prepare meals. She will also help troubleshoot if you're having a hard time breastfeeding (almost everyone I know does in the beginning). A doula may also assist in taking care of the baby by giving her a bath or changing her. But really a doula's job is to give mothers more time with the baby.

The charge for postpartum doula services ranges from $25–$35 per hour depending on location and how many hours of support you need a day. You can usually book blocks of time or longer-term contracts, which are more cost-efficient.

The best way to find a baby nurse or doula is through a friend who has used the person herself. Though you'll have moments when you'd accept anyone with a pulse (my friend Carter and I jest that we've been to the point of desperation where we've even considered pulling into the Duron parking lot to solicit a babysitting job instead of painting from the day laborers there), for some it's hard to imagine a complete stranger coming into your house every day, or even living with you for several weeks during such an important time. You should make sure you feel comfortable with the person. I found my nurse through my friend Melissa. Melissa had said great things about her baby nurse, Agnes, and I was also able to go to her house while Agnes was taking care of Melissa's daughter and meet her in person. I booked her eight months before my due date, and you'll want to do the same, if possible. The good ones are busy and are booked far in advance.

If you use an agency, it will send three or four candidates for you to meet with and interview while you are pregnant. If you like one, you can reserve that nurse or doula based on your estimated due date. The agency will factor in a two-week cushion on either end if you are early or late.

The following is a list of baby nurse and doula agencies and resources in the DC metro area:

★ **CAPITAL CITY NURSES**

4600 North Park Avenue

Chevy Chase, MD

301-986-9129

866-687-7307

www.capitalcitynurses.com

Since 1976 Capital City Nurses has been providing in-home care for newborns and children through the placement of highly qualified and experienced care providers. Most care providers have at least one year's experience working in a hospital and are certified RNs who have gone through extensive background checks. Employees of Capital City Nurses pride themselves on being very attentive yet respectful of families' privacy while living in their homes. Baby nurses work with new parents to help them learn to care for the newborn themselves, as well as assist them with running their households during the transition from hospital to home. Nurses will also help with meal preparation, housekeeping, and looking after other children.

★ **CHILD BIRTH CARE**

2469 Eighteenth Street, NW

Washington, DC

202-491-4151

www.childbirthcare.com

email: info@childbirthcare.com

Child Birth Care provides doulas, and also holds monthly "Meet the Doula" events for parents, where they can meet local doulas and find out about their services and fees.

★ **DOULAS OF NORTH AMERICA, INTERNATIONAL (DONA)**

P.O. Box 626

Jasper, IN

888-788-DONA (3662)

www.dona.org

email: info@dona.org

DONA provides certification for both birth and postpartum doulas. The organization's website is a great source for information on anything related to doulas, and it has a user-friendly search engine to help find a certified doula who fits your needs.

★ **MOMEASE**

300 Montgomery Street, Suite 203

Alexandria, VA

703-739-2831

www.momease.com

email: carolyn@momease.com

Momease provides both doula and baby-nurse services depending on the need and preference of the mother. Its doulas are experienced practitioners who will assist with a birth and support the mother during delivery. When mother and baby head home, Momease can provide a nurse to stay day and night to help with feedings, bathing, and breastfeeding support.

★ **MOTHER & BABY MATTERS, INC.**
12001 Market Street, Suite 301
Reston, VA
703-787-4007
www.motherandbabymatters.com
email: motherbaby_office@juno.com
Mother & Baby Matters, Inc. provides a variety of services, from consultation visits to day and overnight plans. Travel doulas are also available for international or national destinations.

★ **NANNIES + MORE . . .**
3 Bethesda Metro Center, Suite 700
Bethesda, MD
888-466-4525
www.nanniesandmore.com
email: clients@nanniesandmore.com
Based out of Atlanta, Nannies + more . . . places nannies around the world (see page 47). It also provides baby-nurse placements for a minimum two-week stay. There is a $250 application fee. Should you hire a candidate through the company, the one-time placement fee is based upon a percentage of the estimated gross salary package of the candidate. All fees are non-refundable.

★ **WHITE HOUSE NANNIES, INC.**
7200 Wisconsin Avenue, Suite 409
Bethesda, MD
301-652-8088
800-266-9024
www.whitehousenannies.com

Founded in 1985 by Barbara Kline, White House Nannies is considered the premier nanny agency in DC (see page 48). Strictly local, it also places night nurses and will provide short-term and emergency placements for families visiting the area. The agency charges a $275 application fee and takes a percentage of the gross salary.

nannies

It's hard to imagine, but someday you'll have to leave your baby in someone else's arms. The time will come when you will either return to work, need to run errands, or just want some "mommy time." Hiring someone to take care of your baby while you are away can put a pit in your stomach. You want a good, kind, smart, honest, reliable, sober, kid-loving, CPR-knowing, cookie-baking caretaker who thinks your child is the most adorable genius she has ever met. Basically, you want another you.

Obviously, cloning yourself isn't a possibility at this point. However, with determination and time, you will find someone who will meet most of these requirements—someone with whom you will feel confident leaving your baby.

A nanny is usually responsible for all child-related duties, including the child's laundry and meal preparation. Some nannies will also perform light or heavy housecleaning, errands, and cooking for the parents. It is important to decide what you need to make your and your family's lives easier, and to have a clear definition of those responsibilities before you begin looking for someone to fill that role. Decide if you want a live-in or live-out nanny. Decide what hours you will need someone to work on a weekly basis and what your overtime and vacation policies will be. Decide what her scope of responsibilities will be.

Full-time live-out nannies with little experience usually start at around $500 a week. For an experienced, educated caregiver who speaks fluent English and drives, you can pay over $1,000 a week. Live-in nannies for whom you provide room and board start at $400 per week. Prices vary depending on the number of children they will be caring for, and their experience, education, and legal status.

You can find nannies many different ways. Most of my friends have found someone through word-of-mouth or through an agency. There are pros and cons to both.

Agencies

The advantage to using an agency is they will do most of the preliminary legwork for you. Most agencies will provide a candidate's agency application, work history, DMV background check, and letters of reference. They will also run their own background checks. Based on the criteria you provide, agencies will then send you several candidates to interview. It is very important to follow up on the references provided and to make sure you interview candidates thoroughly.

If you hire a nanny through an agency, you will pay an agency fee. Keep in mind that this can sometimes create a conflict of interest, since high turnover is actually good for the agency's business. But you want a reliable caregiver who will stay with you and your family for a long time. Typically fees range between 12 and 15 percent of the nanny's annual salary. Agencies should provide a one- to two-week trial period. Moreover, some agencies will offer what is a called a "replacement guarantee," for anywhere from three months to one year. During this time, if a nanny leaves or is fired a new search will be undertaken without an additional fee to you. Be sure to find out what the agency's policy is in the beginning.

The following is a list of top nanny agencies that make placements in the DC metro area:

★ **ALL-AMERICAN NANNY, LTD.**
2120 Staples Mill Road, Suite 107
Richmond, VA
800-3-NANNYS
www.allamericannanny.com
email: ananny@mindspring.com
All-American Nanny was established in 1990 and has placed over six thousand nannies with families all over the United States. The agency performs complete background, DMV, and health checks on all candidates. It charges a one-time fee of $2,500 for all nannies placed with a family.

★ **A CHOICE NANNY**
2429 Twenty-sixth Road South
Arlington, VA
703-685-BABY (2229)
www.achoicenanny.com
Serving the Washington Metro area since 1989, A Choice Nanny places both full-time and part-time childcare. The agency charges a one-time $2,000 fee for permanent full-time placements and $1,400 for permanent part-time placements.

★ **METROPOLITAN NANNIES**
12801 Worldgate Drive, Suite 500
Herndon, VA
703-481-3181
www.metropolitannannies.com

Owned and operated by local resident Jaclyn Gob-uluk, Metropolitan Nannies places childcare solely within the DC metro area. It places full-time, part-time, emergency, and temporary caregivers. The fee is $3,000 for permanent full-time placements. It also has a Temporary Service program that allows you to schedule a nanny for last-minute emergencies, vacations, or evening baby-sitting. The membership for this program is $175.

★ NANNIES + MORE . . .

3 Bethesda Metro Center, Suite 700
Bethesda, MD
888-466-4525
www.nanniesandmore.com
email: clients@nanniesandmore.com

Based out of Atlanta, Nannies + More . . . places domestic help all over the world. It has an application fee of $250. Should you hire a candidate through this service, the one-time placement fee is based upon a percentage of the gross estimated salary package of the candidate. All fees are non-refundable.

★ NANNIES, INC.

Vienna, VA
703-255-5312
www.nanniesinc.net

As a single dad, John Joyce was experienced hiring nannies through local agencies, but he felt there was room for improvement. In 1989 he started Nannies, Inc., out of Vienna, Virginia, which places childcare givers with local families who meet specific criteria. All the nannies at this agency are over the age of thirty, are long-time local residents, have years of local references, and in most cases have raised their own children. The agency boasts the lowest turnover placement rate in the area, and it was voted "best nanny agency in the DC metro area" by Family magazine. There's a $200 application fee to begin a search, and $2,500 is charged upon placement.

★ POTOMAC NANNIES

7910 Woodmont Avenue, Suite 1120
Bethesda, MD
301-986-0048

Potomac Nannies has been around since 1985. It provides full-service placements for both live-in and live-out nannies and conducts prescreening, and reference and background checks.

★ SPECIAL CARE NANNIES

6842 Elm Street, Suite 101
McLean, VA
703-356-3118
www.specialcarenannies.com

Based in McLean, Special Care Nannies provides placements for local families who have children with special needs. Agency caregivers have specialized training in caring for children with autism, AD/HD, Down's syndrome, and other disabilities. Placements are available on a full- or part-time basis and are available to either live in the home or out. In addition, Special Care Nannies has an on-call division for short-term or emergency placements and it will provide training for a family's existing nanny where needed. For permanent placements, there is a $350 application fee; upon placement, the agency charges 15 percent of the caregiver's first annual salary.

★ **TEACHER CARE**

3 Bethesda Metro Center

Bethesda, MD

888-TEACH-07

703-204-0511

www.teachercare.com

Teacher Care places individuals who have specific training and background in early childhood development, Montessori, education, and/or child psychology. It will also find placements for children with special needs, or who are gifted and talented. It is a small national chain with six national offices including DC. The agency charges a fee of 12 percent of the caregiver's first annual salary. There is no application fee.

★ **WHITE HOUSE NANNIES, INC.**

7200 Wisconsin Avenue, Suite 409

Bethesda, MD

301-652-8088

www.whitehousenannies.com

Founded in 1985 by Barbara Kline, White House Nannies is considered the premier nanny agency in DC. This agency places nannies with families in the DC metro area only. It will also provide short-term and emergency placements for families visiting the area. The agency charges a $275 application fee and takes a percentage of the first year's salary.

Referrals

As with many services, finding a nanny through word of mouth is a great way to go, and also saves you from having to pay the high agency fees. Start with friends who have childcare; their nannies often will know someone who is looking for work. You can also go to a local park and ask nannies there. Don't be shy! In Georgetown, for instance, Rose Park at 3 P.M. is the daily nanny meeting place. I have found fantastic nannies for multiple friends while out in the park with Connor and Charlie. But remember, if you find a nanny through a referral, it is up to you to do a complete background check.

Newspaper and List Serve Ads

If you find you're not having much luck finding someone through word of mouth, placing an ad can be another good way to find someone. When you place an ad, be as specific as possible. Check the classified sections to see examples of other help-wanted ads, or refer to the example I have provided here:

In Search of Playful, Loving Nanny

Live-out nanny needed for three-year-old and eight-month-old boys and five-year-old dog. Light housekeeping and shopping. Must have experience with infants and toddlers. Excellent references required. Nonsmoker. English speaking. Must swim, drive, and know CPR. Legal working papers a must. Hours are Monday–Friday 8 A.M.–7 P.M., Saturday evenings. Call 555-5555.

Interview candidates over the phone before you meet them in person. Screen them carefully; it will save you time later. When you call newspapers, check their deadlines. Most will let you fax your ad and pay by credit card.

★ **CRAIGSLIST**

www.washingtondc.craigslist.org/kid/

Free online listserv where both nannies and employers post their job searches.

★ **THE CURRENT**

202-244-7223

Fax: 202-363-9850

www.currentnewspapers.com

The Current runs four weekly papers, *The Georgetown Current*, *The Northwest Current*, *The Dupont Current*, and *The Foggy Bottom Current*. An ad submission will run in all four periodicals. Deadline for classified line ads is 5 P.M. the Monday prior to publication.

★ **DC CHILDCARE LISTSERV**

http://groups.yahoo.com/group/dcchildcare

This is a free listserv whose nine hundred members are parents and childcare providers in the DC metro area. Again, with any online listserv, the responsibility of screening, interviewing, and performing background checks is up to the parent.

★ **DCNANNY.COM**

www.dcnanny.com

DCNanny.com is an online job board where both nannies and parents post their want ads. There is no fee to register, post, or to search through listings. However, nannies who post here are not prescreened in any way. It is the responsibility of the parent to perform a background check and screening, and to interview all candidates sourced through DCNanny.com.

★ **DC URBAN MOMS AND DADS**

www.dcurbanmom.com

DCUM is a free online listserv for DC moms (and dads). There is a nanny and baby-sitter exchange where both families and nannies post their want ads. It is also a great way to connect with other parents and get answers to anything child- or parent-related.

★ **GEORGETOWN MOMS LISTSERV**

georgetownmoms-subscribe@yahoogroups.com

Georgetown Moms is a free online listserv for parents living in Georgetown. The listserv was started in 2004 and currently has about one hundred thirty members. There is no advertising allowed but members are encouraged to post recommendations for their favorite shops and services.

★ **THE GEORGETOWNER**

202-338-4833

www.georgetowner.com

A weekly publication serving Georgetown and other NW areas. Ads can be emailed to classifieds@georgetowner.com

★ **THE WASHINGTON POST**

703-469-2585

www.washingtonpost.com

While it is the largest daily newspaper, serving all areas of the DC metro area, ads can cost in excess of $300, and I have yet to meet someone who has had success finding a nanny through it.

The Interview

To determine whether a candidate is the right person to take care of your baby, nothing is as important as the interview. Are you looking for someone to join the family, or will this person be more of an employee with formal working arrangements? It may be a good idea to have your child nearby to see how the candidate interacts with her or him. Most importantly, trust your instincts. Here is a suggested list of interview questions:

★ Why are you looking for a job now? Why did you leave your previous job?

★ What is your previous childcare experience?

★ What other jobs outside of childcare have you held in the past?

★ What was a typical day like in your previous job as a nanny? What were your responsibilities? Did you drive, prepare meals, host play dates, bathe the children, and perform light housekeeping?

★ How many children did you take care of in your previous jobs? What were their ages? How old were they when you began? How long did you work for those families? Did your responsibilities change as they got older?

★ Do you have family here? Do you have children of your own? How old are they? Who cares for them while you are at work?

★ What did you like best and least about your previous jobs?

★ Did your previous employers work? (If you are not working full time or work from home, be sure to ask how she feels about having you around the house.)

★ Do you smoke?

★ Do you have CPR or first-aid training?

★ If the candidate has a history of high turnover, ask why.

★ Can you stay late during the week or work on weekends, if necessary?

★ Describe an emergency situation and how you handled it.

★ What are your child-rearing philosophies and how do you feel about discipline? Do you believe in spanking or time-outs?

★ What are you looking for in a family?

★ Do you know your way around the city? Do you drive? Do you own a car?

★ Can you travel with the family, if necessary? Are you able to travel outside of the United States?

★ Do you have any health or dietary restrictions?

★ Do you like to swim? Do you like to be outside? (Think of other activities that are important to you.)

★ Do you like to read?

★ When can you start? What are your salary requirements?

Checking References and Background Checks

Checking references with previous employers can be one of the more challenging aspects of the nanny search. Who are you calling? How can you be sure the person you are contacting isn't just the candidate's friend or relative? Be wary of handwritten letters of reference. When calling to verify references, my experience has been that people are generally pretty nice and willing to talk to you about their previous employee. I think this is especially true if they had a good relationship with her and want to help her find a good job. However, some people aren't that talkative on the phone. Don't worry about it, but be diligent, as this is an important opportunity to find out what the candidate is really like.

Use your common sense and intuition. Be open and friendly and identify yourself in detail. Tell the person about your family, as this will sometimes help to break the ice and allow you to ask questions about her or his family. You need to know the kind of household your potential nanny has worked in, as it may be very different from yours. If she was part of a large staff, she may not be used to housekeeping and cooking. If she worked for a family where both parents were away at work most of the time and your situation is different, she may not be used to having an employer around during the day and would prefer to run the show.

There are many national agencies that verify references and perform background checks on domestic help. A complete background check will cost around $100 and take between three and five busi-

ness days. The agency will conduct checks on everything from references to DMV records, and criminal records, and perform social-security-number traces. You will need the candidate's signed consent to order a pre-employment background check.

Beware of online "instant" credit or background checks. Most are a scam and provide little information. Many instant searches are not FCRA- (Fair Credit Reporting Act) compliant and cannot legally be used for pre-employment screening. More importantly, the instant searches do not search source records. They rely on incomplete and outdated databases and are not comprehensive. The firm conducting the background check should provide a document available for your use.

★ **CHOICEPOINT**
877-547-2518
www.choicepoint.com

★ **SCREENTHEM (a division of Beltrante & Associates)**
703-360-5000
www.screenthem.com

★ **STERLING**
800-899-2272
www.sterlingtesting.com

★ **VERIFICATIONS, INC.**
800-247-0717
www.verificationsinc.com

When the Nanny Starts

Once you have found the right person, it is important to watch how she interacts with your baby and/or children to make sure everyone is comfortable. If you are going back to work, have the person start at least a couple of weeks prior to help ease the transition. This will provide an opportunity for you to observe her with the children and to show her around your neighborhood. Take her to the grocery store, parks, playgroup, pediatrician, and anywhere else she'll need to get used to going when you aren't there. Spell things out, literally. I like to have a typewritten list of the children's schedules, emergency numbers, and a list of things to be done around the house.

Some people will give a nanny a "trial" period. This is especially useful if you're hiring a live-in nanny. Try her out for a week or so before she actually moves in, and see if it's a match to hire her full time. Remember, you don't have to settle. There are plenty of people out there so if the person isn't a fit for whatever reason, keep looking.

You may also want the person to get a physical examination. Definitely find out about her health and vaccinations. Depending on where your nanny is from and how long she's been in the United States, she may not be vaccinated against measles, mumps, rubella, and chicken pox. If not, arrange with your doctor for her to get these shots before she starts.

Taxes and Insurance

Once you have hired a nanny, you have become an employer. The Internal Revenue Service publishes a helpful guide called "Household Employer's Tax Guide" detailing your responsibilities as a household employer. The publication helps you determine if you are responsible for paying employment taxes, and provides a checklist of documents and obligations as an employer. You can download a copy of the guide at www.irs.gov or call 1-800-829-3676.

The IRS requires payroll tax filings by a domestic employer who pays a household employee more than $1,400 cash wages in a calendar year. Payroll withholdings and taxes that may need to be factored in include Social Security, Medicare, federal unemployment taxes, state unemployment taxes, and disability insurance. If you employ a childcare provider for more than forty hours a week, you should buy workers' compensation and disability policies.

The following companies offer tax- and insurance-related services for household employers:

★ **BREEDLOVE & ASSOCIATES**
888-273-3356
www.breedlove-online.com
Breedlove provides payroll and tax services as well as insurance plans for domestic employees. The website has a paycheck calculator if you want to determine how much tax must be withheld for different salary levels.

★ **ESSENTIA SOFTWARE CORPORATION**
888-999-1722
www.essentia-soft.com
Essentia Software offers a Windows-based payroll program for household employers called Nanny-Pay. This service will calculate all federal and state withholding taxes and also helps guide employers to tax compliance. Compared to other services, this program is reasonably priced and is upgradeable every tax year.

★ 4NANNIES.COM

2 Pidgeon Hill Drive #550
Potomac Falls, VA
800-810-2611
www.4nannies.com

This online recruiting site offers a variety of services, including a nanny search, background checks (through Verifications, Inc.), and payroll services (including tax remittance), as well as a ton of information on employing a nanny. The company offers a service called NaniPay, which features payroll and tax remittance through electronic funds transferred from your bank account or credit card. NaniTax prepares quarterly and annual payroll taxes.

au pairs

Many parents find the au pair program, a government-regulated educational and cultural exchange, to be practical and economical. Au pairs come to the United States from different countries, mostly in Europe. They can legally remain in this country for two years and can work a forty-five-hour week. In most cases, an au pair has a weeklong orientation after she or he arrives in the United States and takes one academic course during her stay. In addition, she is provided with support counselors and a health plan under the umbrella organization.

An au pair lives with you and is paid a weekly stipend (roughly $140) determined by the government, based upon the minimum wage, less an allowance for room and board. In addition, there is an application and program fee. Most agencies provide background information on several candidates. Always interview a prospective au pair over the phone or in person when possible.

Things to consider: Most au pairs tend to be inexperienced childcare providers. They most often work in homes with stay-at-home mothers. They are not allowed to remain alone with the children overnight, so an au pair is not a great option for parents who travel without their children. Au pairs are usually on a two-year visa, which means you will be replacing them every two years. Good friends of mine had great success with the first two au pairs they hired, but they "exchanged" their third after she crashed two cars in the first month. One of the drawbacks with an au pair is that they are young and usually want to have an active social life, which is not always compatible with childcare. However, I have friends who swear by au pairs, vowing that the influence of a young, educated person on their children is invaluable. There are six sponsoring organizations that place au pairs in the United States.

★ AUPAIRCARE

800-4-AUPAIR
www.aupaircare.com

★ AU PAIR IN AMERICA ONLINE, INC.

800-928-7247
www.aupairinamerica.com

★ AU PAIR USA/INTEREXCHANGE

800-AU-PAIRS
www.aupairUSA.org

★ CHI AU PAIR USA

703-528-5152
www.chiaupairusa.org

* **CULTURAL CARE AU PAIR**
  800-333-6056
  www.culturalcare.com

* **GREATAUPAIR**
  925-478-4100
  www.greataupair.com

day-care centers

The DC metro area has more than one thousand licensed day-care centers and large family childcare homes, which are private homes that legally offer day care for up to fourteen children. Licensing for DC, Virginia, and Maryland is overseen by the Department of Social Services in each state. The highest accreditation a day-care center can receive is by the National Association for the Education of Young Children (NAEYC). There are an estimated four hundred eighty centers in the DC metro area with this accreditation. For a list of these day-care centers, check the organization's website at www.naeyc.org. The site also lists guidelines and what to look for when selecting a day-care center.

In addition, your employer may provide day-care options. Many large companies offer on-site day care or are willing to contribute to day-care costs. Make sure you begin your investigating and research as early as possible as there are often long wait-lists.

Additional resources for researching and finding day-care centers are listed below:

* **DAYCAREVIRGINIA.COM**
  www.daycarevirginia.com

* **FAIRFAX COUNTY OFFICE FOR CHILDREN, CHILD CARE REFERRALS**
  703-324-8000
  www.fairfaxcounty.gov/childcare

* **MONTGOMERY COUNTY CHILD CARE REFERRALS**
  301-279-1773
  www.montgomerycountymd.gov/earlychild-hoodservices

* **NATIONAL ASSOCIATION FOR THE EDUCATION OF YOUNG CHILDREN (NAEYC)**
  www.naeyc.org

* **WASHINGTON CHILD DEVELOPMENT COUNCIL**
  202-387-0002
  www.wcdconline.org

baby-sitting

If you are a stay-at-home mom who needs a little childcare on a Saturday or a few afternoons a week, a baby-sitter is key. Even if you have a nanny, there may be times when she is not available or could use a break herself, especially on the weekends. It's good to have the number of a baby-sitter you like as a backup. You can find a sitter the same way you would find a nanny: through word of mouth or agencies. College job boards are a great place to find students who have extra time in the evenings and on the weekends. The following is a list of services and resources for finding a baby-sitter:

★ AMERICAN UNIVERSITY JOB CORPS

www.jobcorps.ausg.org

The site is free for both students and parents and is a great way to find college student baby-sitters if you live in Tenley, Glover Park, Georgetown, or other nearby areas.

★ ARLINGTON, VA AREA BABY-SITTING CO-OP

www.geocities.com/Heartland/Meadows/6989

This is an established baby-sitting co-op for families in Arlington and the surrounding areas. Its network of parents trades baby-sitting services on the barter system: families baby-sit for other families on a rotating schedule.

★ BABY-SITTERS.COM

www.babysitters.com

This national web-based referral service provides listings for sitters in the DC metro area. Sitters pay an annual fee of $25, and parents join for free.

★ CHEVY CHASE BABY-SITTING CO-OP

Nedra Weinstein

301-654-2419

Families in the Chevy Chase neighborhood have been exchanging childcare with one another through this co-op since the '60s. Schedules are coordinated each month by volunteers on a rotating basis. You must apply for membership.

★ HILLZOO

www.hillzoo.com

A free service that connects parents with Hill staffers looking for supplemental income.

★ MARYMOUNT UNIVERSITY JOB BOARD

www.marymountjobs.com

Great for families in the Arlington area. The job posting site is open to the public.

★ MONA

www.monamoms.org

Moms of North Arlington (MONA) is an organization for mothers in the area. Members trade baby-sitting on the barter system.

★ MONSTERTRAK

www.monstertrak.com

This website is the easiest way to reach a large number of job-seeking college students. After you select the schools you want to access ($25 per school), MonsterTrak posts your job listing and students contact you.

★ SITTERCITY

888-211-9749

www.sittercity.com

This is a national web-based baby-sitter network that allows you to narrow your search by zip code. Sitters register for free; parents pay an annual fee of $40.

★ STUDENT SITTERS

www.student-sitters.com

A $25 membership fee allows you to sort through résumés of baby-sitting college students for up to three months. Renewals are $20 for three months. Sitters are paid an average of $10 an hour.

★ **WEE SIT**

703-764-1542

www.weesit.net

weesit@aol.com

Wee Sit is a family-owned and -operated baby-sitting service for families in DC and Northern Virginia; it was founded in 1984. All sitters are over the age of twenty-one and have been with the agency an average of five years. All sitters are prescreened and CPR certified. Rates range from $15–$18 an hour with a four-hour minimum.

adjusting to new motherhood

At some point during the first days of motherhood, you will glance at the tiny stranger in your house, and it will hit you that life as you've known it is, well . . . over. You are a mom now. It is as wonderful as every Hallmark card would have you believe, but it's also probably the biggest change you will undergo as a woman. If you think getting to know your new baby is overwhelming, wait until you get to know yourself in your new role as a mother.

Forgive yourself if the first few weeks and months at home are bumpy. You will be exhausted, and postpartum hormones can wreak havoc on your normally cool, calm, collected self. Life will seem to become a relentless cycle of feedings, diaper changes, and laundry. Just fifteen minutes to check TMZ.com seems impossible to find, let alone time to read a book, exercise, even take a shower. It can make a girl justifiably panicky. But remember, this is normal and it will get better. I promise.

If you have been able to line up help ahead of time, you are in good shape. Get as much help as you can afford, and if paying for it is not an option, say yes whenever friends or family members volunteer. I think a lot of new moms feel guilty about hiring help or accepting help from friends. I did. With Connor, I was determined to not accept help from anyone (except the night nurse my mother paid for).

By the time Charlie came, I just started answering the phone with a "yes, please!" Let friends drop off dinner and let your mother-in-law come over and change a diaper or two. Sleep when the baby sleeps and try to get outside at least once a day for a stroll around the block. I cannot stress enough how important it is to have a network of other new and veteran moms. If you don't have friends with kids, join (or form) a playgroup with moms who have babies the same age as yours. Your three-month-olds will barely notice one another, but you moms will be so relieved to have one another. In fact, it shouldn't even be called a "playgroup." At this stage, it's more like group therapy.

Childcare and parenting classes are one of the best ways to meet new moms and get the know-how you need, and there are plenty of great ones listed in this chapter. Join a breastfeeding support group, join a new-parent class, or just get out to a park. In no time, you and your baby will have a set of new friends. And you'll be wearing your new identity of "mom" like it's your favorite cashmere sweater.

new parent classes and support groups

Hospitals are a great resource for a wide variety of new-parent and infant classes. Refer back to chapter one for the complete offerings at each hospital or birth center. They vary, so if your hospital doesn't offer something you are interested in, ask for other resources or referrals while you are there. And remember, you aren't limited to the classes offered where you are delivering. Another good place to get referrals is at your ob/gyn's or pediatrician's office.

The following are non-hospital-based support and discussion resources throughout the DC metro area. Unless otherwise noted, classes are given throughout the DC metro area. Contact the organization to find out about specific offerings in your area. Always check schedules and fees for the most up-to-date information, as they are subject to change.

⋆ AMERICAN RED CROSS OF THE NATIONAL CAPITAL AREA
703-584-8400

www.redcrossnca.org

The Red Cross offers infant and child CPR training, as well as first-aid basics and baby-sitting training for young adults. Classes are given throughout the DC Metro area.

⋆ ATTACHMENT PARENTING INTERNATIONAL
615-298-4334

www.attachmentparentingdc.org

Attachment Parenting International is a nonprofit organization that promotes parenting practices that create strong, healthy emotional bonds between children and their parents. There are play-groups, support groups, and speaker series throughout the DC Metro area.

⋆ THE BABY DUCK
Alexandria, VA

www.thebabyduck.com

Run by Melody Kisor, The Baby Duck offers courses on everything from general baby care to special-interest offerings, like a class on pets and babies. The Baby Boot Camp class covers baby-care basics, and Melissa's infant safety class is a fantastic crash course for the nervous new parent.

⋆ DC METRO DADS
www.dcmetrodads.com

Started by a group of stay-at-home dads in DC, this group provides a network for fathers who are the primary caregivers. Originally a listserv, DC metro Dads has grown to host playgroups and dads' nights out for both couples and single fathers.

⋆ DC WORKING MOMS
www.dcworkingmoms.com

This group also evolved from a listserv into a highly organized group of—you guessed it—working moms. It provides a great support network of local part-time and full-time professional mothers through lunches, playgroups, and happy hours held throughout the DC metro area.

★ MAGIC OF MOTHERHOOD

202-230-4126

www.magicofmotherhood.com

Jill Chasse, a childbirth educator and perinatal development consultant, teaches a class called Welcome Baby. Parents and caregivers learn infant safety, wellness and development, infant mental health, and cognitive, psychosocial, and emotional exercises. Classes start at $75, and are offered in several locations throughout DC metro area.

★ MARIA COHN, PH.D. & ASSOCIATES

1230 Thirty-first Street, NW, 2nd floor

Georgetown, DC

202-333-6251

www.mariacohnassociates.com

In addition to being a highly-sought-after family therapist, Dr. Kohn offers a popular lecture series for parents. Topics covered in the series are sleeping, confidence building, toilet training, and behavioral strategies for young children. In addition, she offers a reading group for preschoolers and a support group for new moms. Rates begin at $75 an hour.

★ MOMEASE

2210 Mount Vernon Avenue, Suite 203

Alexandria, VA 22301

703-739-2832

www.momease.com

Momease is one of the few resources out there that offers parenting classes for both moms and dads. The two-hour monthly "Dadease" course is led by a veteran dad and not only covers basics such as diaper changing and feeding but also gives advice on navigating postpartum with mom. Also offered are CPR classes for new moms and their babies as well

as breastfeeding. The "Positive Parenting" class focuses on how to raise confident children through positive reinforcement. Classes start at $40.

★ MOMS CLUB OF WASHINGTON, DC

Chapters in DC, Maryland and Virginia.

www.momsclub.org

momsdcnw@yahoo.com

Moms Offering Moms Support (MOMS) is a national organization that provides support to mothers who choose to stay home either full or part time. With chapters throughout the DC metro area, the group organizes playgroups, moms' nights out, family activities, and community service opportunities that benefit children.

★ MONA

Arlington, VA

www.monamoms.org

Mothers of North Arlington (MONA) is a support group for stay-at-home mothers, including moms who work part time from home. The group organizes playgroups and family activities, and it also has an online support group.

★ PARENTING PLAYGROUPS, INC.

6161 Fuller Court

Alexandria, VA

Rachel Eppard

703-922-0044

www.parentingplaygroups.com

Rachel has a master's degree in psychology, and she offers an eight-week parenting course for expectant couples and those with newborns that goes beyond the basics of infant care. Temperament, attachment, the role of fathers, and early milestones are all covered. Visiting professionals discuss newborn health issues, infant massage, marriage issues, infant sign language, and baby-proofing and safety. The course meets once a week for an hour and costs $160 per family.

breastfeeding & pumping resources

★ BABIES 'N BUSINESS

Bethesda, MD

301-656-2526

www.worksitelactation.com

Located in Bethesda, Babies 'n Business is a lactation consulting firm specializing in corporate lactation programs. It helps companies support mothers returning to the workplace who are planning to pump, and works one-on-one with the mothers themselves. No need to be a working mom to benefit from its services, though. The staff of knowledgeable lactation consultants will help you with everything from proper breastfeeding techniques to choosing the right pump. The company sells and rents hospital-grade pumps.

★ THE BREASTFEEDING CENTER FOR GREATER WASHINGTON

2141 K Street, NW

Washington, DC

703-978-2000

www.breastfeedingcenter.org

The nonprofit organization offers a variety of free classes for new moms, such as Breast Pump Basics, Breastfeeding Basics, and a class for mothers

returning to work. Lactation consultants are also available for private sessions in-home or on the phone, which start at $85 per hour.

★ INTERNATIONAL LACTATION CONSULTANT ASSOCIATION (ILCA)

919-861-5577

www.ilca.org

ILCA is the professional association for International Board Certified Lactation Consultants (IBCLCs) and other health-care professionals who help breastfeeding families. The site has an easy-to-use tool to find hundreds of board-certified consultants in the DC metro area.

★ LA LECHE LEAGUE INTERNATIONAL

800-LA-LECHE

202-269-444 (DC)

www.lalecheleague.org

Started in the 1950s, La Leche League has become the mainstay for helping mothers all over the world with everything related to breastfeeding. Local chapters organize support groups led by veteran mothers who breastfed. Annual membership is $40.

★ MOTHER & BABY MATTERS

12001 Market Street, Suite 301

Reston, VA

703-787-4007

www.motherandbabymatters.com

In addition to labor and postpartum doula services, Mother and baby Matters also has lactation specialists and consultants on staff. Depending on the amount of support you need, a specialist or consultant can meet with you during pregnancy and while in the hospital, and then make home visits after birth as the baby's needs develop. Mother and baby Matters also sells and rents both Medela and Supplemental Nursing System pumps and accessories.

★ **NORTHERN VIRGINIA LACTATION CONSULTANTS**

10721 Main Street, Suite 2300, Bldg #2
Fairfax, VA
703-425-2229
www.northernvirginialactation.com

This group of board-certified lactation consultants provides breastfeeding support and instruction for clients who rent or purchase Medela and Ameda pumps and accessories through the organization. It also offers free weekly weigh-ins for babies, so moms can easily track their success.

★ **PUMPING MOMS**

www.pumpingmoms.org

Pumping Moms is a network of women dedicated to providing breast milk for their babies but who are unable to breastfeed. Moms include those who have babies who cannot latch properly, those whose babies have health issues that prevent them from breastfeeding, and moms who are returning to work and want to provide breast milk through the use of a pump. The website contains updates on the latest research and health benefits as well as a listserv where pumping moms looking for support and guidance can post questions for other pumping moms.

sleep consultants

Twelve weeks or twelve pounds, whichever comes first: This is the general target for when both you and baby should be sleeping through the night. A favorite reference widely regarded as the sleep bible is Dr. Marc Weissbluth's book *Healthy Sleep Habits, Happy Child*. If you weren't already given six copies at your baby shower, stop what you're doing and pick up a copy and a highlighter right now. As one of the nation's leading researchers on sleep, as well as a top pediatrician and father of four, Weissbluth provides an invaluable how-to that will guide you through getting baby on a sleep schedule and getting you a good night's sleep. If you need some extra hand-holding, I have listed some professionals who will make this sometimes overwhelming task go a bit more smoothly.

★ **ANNIKA BRINDLEY**

Annika's Little Sleepers
301-915-0731
www.littlesleepers.com

Armed with research from top sleep specialists and a master's degree in clinical psychology, Annika Brindley has helped hundreds of families nationwide establish sound day and night sleep schedules for their babies. Based in DC, she works one-on-one with parents to tailor a program that addresses a baby's sleep issues, and then is on-call 24/7 through the "training" period, which is usually around three days. Rates start at $400 for an in-home consultation and forty-eight-hour on-call availability.

★ **KIM WEST**
The Sleep Lady
410-647-6005
www.thesleeplady.com

Kim West is a mother of two and a Licensed Certified Social Worker-Clinical (LCSW-C) who has practiced as a child and family therapist for more than thirteen years. Over the past ten years, she has helped more than a thousand tired parents learn to listen to their intuition, recognize their children's important cues and behaviors, and gently create changes that promote and preserve their children's healthy sleep habits. A comprehensive consultation begins with a one-and-a-half-hour evaluation either in her Annapolis office or over the phone, and an individualized plan. She also offers group phone classes, a DVD lecture, and has recently published *Good Night, Sleep Tight*. Packages start at $300.

★ **SUZY GIORDANO**
A Baby Coach
703-675-7801
www.babycoach.net
suzygiordano@babycoach.net

Suzy Giordano has been helping parents in the DC metro area for the past thirteen years. Her business, A Baby Coach, trains new parents to get their babies to sleep twelve hours by twelve weeks with different packages that include overnight help, training sessions, and assessments. She has five team members who are trained in her magical methods, including her mother, sister, and daughter. If having her on-call through cell phone and email isn't enough for you, you can hire her or a team member to come and do it for you! She has

experience with twins, triplets, and even quadruplets. She has also put her method in book form, *Twelve Hours by Twelve Weeks*. Prices start at $250 for a phone consultation.

diaper services

★ **MODERN DIAPER DUTY**
703-823-3993
www.moderndiaperservice.com

Located in Alexandria, Modern Diaper Duty provides an old-school service that has recently been making a comeback among eco-conscious parents. The service supplies cloth diapers that they will deliver (clean) and pick up (dirty) on a weekly basis. It also offers several different packages, all of which include a diaper pail and deodorizer. Prices start at $15 a week.

part two

SHOPPING FOR YOUR DC BABY:
everything you
need to buy

maternity clothes

Being pregnant is no longer an excuse to drop off the style radar. In fact, top-notch designers have established winning lines specifically for expectant moms. These days you can walk into any cafe wearing the same outfit as the size-two honey in the corner—you just happen to be hiding a baby under that baby-doll top. But before you run off and buy a maternity trousseau, read this. Your body is changing like a creature in a B-movie sci-fi flick. And the worst part is at the beginning. There's an awkward time in the first trimester where your normal clothes don't quite fit and the maternity clothes are still too big. You don't have that lovely mythic belly that just screams fertility goddess. You just look bloated and plump. During this time, elastic and Lycra will be your allies.

Early on in my first pregnancy, convinced I couldn't possibly grow any bigger, I ran out and invested in an entire wardrobe of maternity clothes. Before I knew it, I was so large that I never wore half of it. Learn from my mistake: Hold off for as long as you can with just a few transitional pieces, then buy in stages. I have friends that went all-out shopping, creating a completely new wardrobe entirely of maternity clothes. I also have friends that were able to get by with just a few pieces. You can go either way. Remember the sci-fi-flick element: you have no idea how your body might change. I knew a gal who made it through her entire pregnancy with a larger-sized pair of great-looking non-maternity jeans that just happened to have a low waist.

Maternity clothes are also the first place you'll experience the sisterhood of motherhood. As soon as we hear that a friend is expecting, all of us with maternity duds hanging in our closets are eager to free up the space. It's a never-ending cycle; one day, you will do the same. Once when I was at a cocktail party, I recognized an old maternity dress of mine being worn by a woman I didn't even know!

Another trick is to have your clothes "maternitized" by taking your good-quality clothes to a tailor and having him or her sew elastic fabric or stretch panels to waistbands and hip seams. I did this with a few pieces that I loved and felt that it was worth the investment as I was able to have them refitted post-pregnancy.

This chapter provides a list of stores in DC that either specialize in maternity clothes or have maternity sections. DC doesn't have the wealth of options you'll find in New York and L.A., so I have also included some great online stores in the website directory.

the stores

★ **APPLE SEED BOUTIQUE**
115 South Columbus Street
Old Town, VA
703-535-5446

414 Main Street
Gaithersburg, MD
240-683-5446
www.appleseedboutique.com
Return Policy: Returns may be made up to 10
    days after purchase for store credit or
    exchange. Special occasion, intimates,
    swimwear, and sale items are final sale.

Apple Seed Boutique specializes in fashionable,
fun, and practical clothes for the expectant mom. It
carries a range of inventory from fun casual wear to
hip evening dresses. Salespeople are very person-
able, and they'll even pull together an entire
wardrobe to get you through the next nine months
(this service is by appointment). The boutique carries such lines as Liz Lange, Childish, Japanese
Weekend, and Citizens of Humanity.

★ **CRADLE & CRAYON**
Reston Town Center
11913 Freedom Drive
Reston, VA
703-437-0900
www.cradleandcrayon.com
Return Policy: Returns and exchanges may be
    made up to 14 days after purchase. Special
    occasion, intimates, swimwear, babygear, and
    sale items are final sale.

When owner Stella Guillen was shopping while
pregnant with her first child, she thought that it
would be easy to find an array of choices and
knowledgeable and caring people who could help
her prepare for something she'd never done
before. But her choices seemed the same everywhere, and the shopping experience made Stella's
partner feel like a glorified porter. So after their
baby was born, she set to work and started Cradle
& Crayon, which carries furniture, toys, and baby
gear and clothes, as well as apparel for expectant
moms. She carries Olian, Japanese Weekend, Ripe,
and Noppies, among other labels.

★ **H&M**
1025 F Street, NW
202-347-3306
Downtown, DC

Dulles Town Center
21100 Dulles Town Circle
703-430-5520
Sterling, VA
www.hm.com
Return Policy: Exchange or refund with receipt
    within 30 days of original purchase. Store credit
    for returns after 30 days of original purchase.

H&M is known for offering trendy clothes at
extremely inexpensive prices, and the chain's Mama
maternity line is no exception. You'll find everything
from basic T-shirts to cool wrap dresses. It's a great
place to stock up on edgy everyday clothes as well
as hip duds for the office. Sale items might as well
be free. Customer service seems to be limited to
restocking racks and opening changing-room doors,
though, so don't expect personalized service.

★ GAPMATERNITY

622 King Street
Old Town Alexandria, VA
703-683-0181

Fair Oaks Mall
11750 Fair Oaks
Fair Oaks, VA
703-352-2162
www.gap.com

Return Policy: You can return any item that has
not been washed or worn for a full refund
with receipt and for store credit without.
Items washed and worn must be returned
within 14 days.

The Gap's maternity line has vastly improved in the past couple of years and continues to get better. These stores have a good selection of form-fitting, stylish, and classic basics. You can choose from their four different styles of pants, from Full Panel to No Panel and Roll Panel styles, among others. Unfortunately, both DC locations are just small sections within a Gap store, so I found that inventory wasn't great. But it was worth the trip—I walked out each time with some pieces I ended up living in. Once you figure out what size and styles work best for you, you can order items online, and return them, if necessary, at the stores.

★ MIMI MATERNITY

Mazza Gallery
5300 Wisconsin Avenue, NW
Chevy Chase, DC
202-362-1400

Montgomery Mall
7107 Democracy Boulevard
Rockville, MD
301-469-0308

White Flint Mall
11301 Rockville Pike
Rockville, MD
240-221-0472

11943 Grand Commons Avenue
Fairfax, VA
703-266-9469
www.mimimaternity.com

Return Policy: Store credit or exchange within
10 days of purchase. Sale items are final sale.

Mimi Maternity, owned by the same parent company as A Pea in the Pod, is essentially a downscale version of that store chain in both style and pricing. The chain carries a large selection of reasonably priced casual and evening wear, and work clothes. Its Mimi Essentials line offers inexpensive active wear such as tanks, T-shirts, shorts, and jeans. The stores also carry a good selection of lingerie, sleepwear, and nursing wear. Salespeople are very friendly and helpful.

★ MOTHERHOOD MATERNITY

Montgomery Mall
7101 Democracy Boulevard
Rockville, MD
301-365-4770

Landmark Mall
5839 Duke Street
Alexandria, VA
703-354-8175

Fashion Centre at Pentagon City
1100 Hayes Street
Pentagon City, VA
703-412-0184

Dulles Town Center
211000 Dulles Town Center
Sterling, VA
703-404-6810

Fair Oaks Mall
11750 Fair Oaks
Fair Oaks, VA
703-385-2755

Macy's at Tyson Galleria
1651 International Drive
McLean, VA
703-556-0000
www.motherhood.com

Return Policy: Store credit or exchange within 10 days of purchase. Sale items are final sale.

Motherhood Maternity is owned by the same parent company as A Pea in the Pod and Mimi Maternity, but in my opinion is like the ugly stepsister to those stores. It carries inexpensive, OK-looking maternity clothes as well as nursing bras, breast pumps, diaper bags, and books. I found the stores to be messy and disorganized, and the few basic T-shirts I did buy were such an unflattering cut that I ended up not wearing them at all. For the same price point I was much happier with my finds at Old Navy and Gap.

★ **9 MATERNITY**
12246 Rockville Pike
Rockville, MD
301-468-2022
www.9maternity.com

Return Policy: Exchange and store credit within 14 days. Sale items are final sale.

9 maternity is a great DC-mom-owned boutique that carries a fabulous selection of designer maternity labels such as Naissance (NOM), Michael Stars, Japanese Weekend, 7 for All Mankind, and Citizens of Humanity. In addition, it has cool diaper bags and a small section of baby clothes. The salespeople are very attentive and can suggest which labels work best with your body type and stage of pregnancy.

★ **OLD NAVY**
3621 Jefferson Davis Highway
Alexandria, VA
703-739-6240

Dulles Town Center
21100 Dulles Town Circle
Sterling, VA
703-404-0270

5800 Crossroads Center Way
Falls Church, VA
703-845-8155
www.oldnavy.com

Return Policy: Within 90 days of purchase, full refund with receipt; without receipt, store credit.

Old Navy has really cute maternity clothes that are unbelievably cheap, but inventory is not always consistent, so plan on hitting the store more than once. It's definitely not the place to go if you are looking for clothes to wear to the office, as everything is very casual. The generally college-age salespeople are not particularly knowledgeable about sizing.

★ **A PEA IN THE POD**

Fashion Centre Pentagon City
1100 South Hayes Street
Pentagon City, VA
703-418-2900

Tysons Galleria
1760 International Drive
McLean, VA
703-917-8959
www.apeainthepod.com

Return Policy: Exchange and store credit within 10 days only. Special occasion, intimates, swimwear, and sale items are final sale.

A Pea in the Pod carries a wide range of trendy high-end maternity clothes great for work and play. Designers such as Three Dot, Diane von Fursten-berg, Lilly Pulitzer, and Chaiken are some of the harder-to-find-in-DC lines this chain carries. These stores carry clothes to wear to work, out on the town, and for special occasions. They also carry exercise clothes, nursing bras, and underwear as well as a large selection of bathing suits. I find the service to be very attentive but not pushy. They always have plenty of items on sale.

★ **TARGET**

3101 Jefferson Davis Highway
Alexandria, VA
703-706-3840

10301 New Guinea Road
Fairfax, VA
703-764-5100

13047 Fair Lakes Shopping Center
Fairfax, VA
703-449-7100

6100 Arlington Boulevard
Falls Church, VA
703-392-5630

12197 Sunset Hills Road
Reston, VA
703-478-0770

46201 Potomac Run Plaza
Sterling, VA
703-444-8440
www.target.com

Return Policy: Refund or exchange with receipt within 90 days of purchase.

Target has two lines of maternity clothes. In Due Time offers fairly basic pieces that in my experience run big. Target made a vast improvement five years ago when the company brought on Liz Lange to design a second line specifically for the store. The Liz Lange line is a cheaper version of what you'll find in her flagship Madison Avenue store, but all items are stylish. All of the maternity wear at Target is very affordable, with most pieces averaging under $20.

Chapter Six

baby furniture, strollers, and accessories

Shopping for your baby starts long before he or she graces you with his or her presence in the world, and the shopping most likely will begin with feathering the little one's nest. But let's face it: the nursery is really a room decorated to the parents' liking (usually, to Mom's taste). Your newborn comes into this world without the ability to see colors, acting only on basic instincts, and will not critique your decorating skills. So now that you're focused on who you are really decorating for, let's get down to business.

Walk into any baby furniture store and you'll be faced with a sea of cribs, changing tables, strollers, bouncy seats, high chairs . . . and the list goes on. A year from now you will be an expert, blogging on the merits of one brand of crib over another. In the meantime, here's some advice. This chapter provides a rundown of what you need and why you need it.

While cost and style will influence your choices, DC mothers-to-be must also consider space and logistics. Do you live in a two-bedroom apartment in Dupont or a McMansion in Potomac? Will you need a stroller that's easy to throw in the back of the SUV ten times a day or will you need something that easily navigates the bumpy bricks of Georgetown?

Try not to run out and buy everything all at once. You will need a crib and a car seat immediately, but pace yourself on the rest. If you are having a baby shower and have registered somewhere, wait and see what you get.

Order your furniture at least ten to twelve weeks in advance: the bigger pieces take longer to ship and some items may be back-ordered. Also, factor in assembly time. John and I ordered a darling bassinet from Jacadi that arrived in plenty of time, but it also arrived in about ten thousand pieces—not including the screws, bolts, and tools required to put it together. Not only were the directions in French, but they were wrong and in French. We're still convinced they sent us the assembly instructions for a Peugeot.

I recommend picking up the latest copy of the *Consumer Reports Guide to Baby Products*. This comprehensive guide covers the pros and cons of basic products. Also, it is important to double-check recent product recalls, especially if you are a second-time parent or are considering using a hand-me-down from a friend; For example, certain car seats have been recalled in the last few years. My mother-in-law was given a hand-me-down car seat from a friend as a sort of "welcome to the grandmother club" offering. I swear it was the first car seat ever made. When I mentioned this, her response was, "We never even had car seats, I would just throw the kids in a playpen that I set up in the back of the station wagon and take the turns a little slower." It's a miracle that we all survived. The Juvenile Products Manufacturers Association (JPMA) has a website (www.jpma.org) that is updated daily, with recall information supplied by the Consumer Product Safety Commission (CPSC) on everything from strollers to playpens. You can also call the CPSC at 800-638-2772.

the necessities

Baby Carriers

More commonly referred to as a "Bjorn," this product was a much-needed improvement upon the versions of baby carriers our parents used. They're great for keeping the baby close and your hands free; Dr. Evil made good use of one while carrying around Mini Me in the second Austin Powers movie. Newborns love to be close to your body and can sleep soundly in it. The Baby Bjorn retails for about $75. Many experts don't recommend using carriers until a baby is old enough to hold his head up on his own, though. Once your baby is older, he will love to face out in the carrier.

The baby carrier is another item that you will only use for a short time. If you can, borrow one from a friend and take it around the block for a test drive. I didn't use ours all that often, as I found it hot and the boys felt too heavy. Nojo and Maya make popular slings, which cost around $40. People who like the sling say that because the baby rests more horizontally, he or she is more comfortable inside it.

Baby Monitors

A good baby monitor will allow you to hear every little noise your baby makes wherever you are in your house. Most are either A/C or battery operated, and are easy to move throughout your home. You can also purchase video monitors that allow you to both hear and see your baby, which is nice if you don't want to be running to the nursery every time you hear a gurgle. Hold on to your receipt, though; sometimes you'll pick up static from other household electronics and will want to exchange it. A friend of mine was even picking up the neighbor's baby, since they had coincidentally bought the same monitor. If you have two children to monitor, buy two different brands that will operate on different frequencies. Monitors range in price from $40 for a basic 900-megahertz model that you can find at your local drugstore to $200 for a wireless video monitor found at buy buy BABY.

Baby Swings

A swing may or may not be your lifesaver during your baby's first few months. Connor wanted absolutely nothing to do with it, and screamed if I even walked toward it, while Charlie would swing happily for a good length of time. The most popular swings are made by Graco and Fisher-Price, and each comes with a variety of features, including different speeds, reclining seats, and musical tunes and timers. Prices range from $40–$120.

Bassinets/Co-Sleepers

A bassinet is basically a smaller version of a crib that can be easily transported from room to room. It's used for approximately three months, sometimes longer depending on its size and the size of your baby. Since babies sleep so much during those first few months, these can be very handy if you live in a house with several floors and do not want to be running up and down the stairs every time the baby naps. You can keep a bassinet close to whereever you'll be most of the day. You can also keep one in your bedroom if you want to have the baby sleeping near you at night. Styles range from bassinets with wheels to bassinets that rock and those that lift off from the stand. Some come with full bedding ensembles. Prices generally range from $50–$150, though you can pay up to $750 for a top-of-the-line bassinet at some of the more expensive boutiques around town.

Co-sleepers enable babies to sleep next to parents, but in their own bassinet-sized bed that has an opening on one side and attaches to your bed. The Arm's Reach Co-Sleeper and Baby Style's Baby Delight Snuggle Nest also make the padding separate from the bassinet for parents who want their infant to sleep in their bed but in their own cocoon-like padding. Arm's Reach has patented its Original Co-Sleeper plus Bassinet, which actually attaches to the side of your bed, allowing your baby to sleep at "arm's reach" but not in your bed with you; it also converts into a freestanding bassinet. Prices start at $50 for the padding alone, and $179 for the Original Co-Sleeper with Bassinet. There is also a Mini Co-Sleeper from Arm's Reach that doesn't take up as much room and is perfect for smaller bedrooms and apartments. It also converts into a freestanding bassinet and a changing table. Prices start at $139.

These are the most popular bassinet and co-sleeper brands:
- Arm's Reach
- Badger Basket Company
- Century
- J. Mason
- Kids Line

Bathtubs

Before your baby's umbilical cord falls off, you will most likely be giving your baby a sponge bath in the kitchen or bathroom sink. After this, however, it is safest to use a baby tub. It can be dangerous to bathe your baby in the sink, as the baby is slippery and can easily hit his or her head on the faucet.

Most baby tubs are similar in size. They come either with or without a sponge insert. The Cuddle Tub by Graco ($25) is a great one. It has an adjustable foam cushion and mesh hammocklike attachment for newborns to rest on that can be removed later once your baby can sit up on his own. Once your baby can sit up, try the Safety 1st Tubside Bath Seat ($25), which attaches to the tub with suction cups.

Bouncy Seats

The bouncy seat was probably invented by some poor mother in desperate need of a shower who needed a safe spot to put her baby for five minutes. Bouncy seats are portable and can be moved from room to room, usually carried with one hand while the baby is in the other. It allows babies to be angled enough so they can see around the room until they are old enough to sit in a high chair, Bumbo, or ExerSaucer. Most bouncy seats have a vibrating feature that can help calm even the fussiest babies. The most popular bouncy seats are Baby Bjorn, Combi, Kids II, and Oeuf. They retail from $35–$120.

Car Seats

An infant car seat is one of the most important things to buy before your baby arrives. State and district laws require that all babies be in a car seat when in an automobile. Hospitals will not let you leave without seeing you put your newborn into one.

Safety is the number one consideration when purchasing an infant car seat. The first step in choosing a car seat is to check the latest recalls. Besides the JPMA website, you can also find information on recalls at the Consumer Product Safety Commission's website (www.cpsc.gov) or by calling the Department of Transportation Automobile Safety Hotline (888-327-4236). Next, remember that all infant car seats must be rear-facing until your child is both a year old and twenty pounds. Last, it is safest to install the car seat in the rear center seat.

I strongly recommend having your car seat professionally installed. This can be done at either your local police or fire station or at car dealers that have experts who know how to install car seats correctly in just about any type of car. A great resource in finding the closest car-seat safety-inspection location is Safe Kids Worldwide. Safe Kids is a national non-profit organization located right here in DC that focuses solely on children's safety education. The easiest way to find an inspection station is to go to its website (www.safekids.org) or by calling at 202-662-0600. It also organizes monthly free inspections at various locations throughout the Metro area.

Since September 1, 2002, all car seats have been equipped with the LATCH (Lower Anchors and Tethers for Children) system, which makes using car seats easier and safer. The LATCH system allows you to secure your car seat with tethers located in all cars manufactured after September 1, 1999. Most cars can be retrofitted as well. The LATCH is not required by law, but if you are buying a new car and/or car seat, be sure it is equipped with LATCH.

Three designs of restraining straps or harnesses are available in car seats: the five-point harness, the T-shield, and the bar shield. While all designs are considered safe, most experts agree that the five-point harness is the best. The best overall sellers are Britax, Century, and Evenflo. They retail for $70–$300 and are available at just about every superstore including buy buy BABY, Babies "R" Us, and Target.

Booster seats and high-back boosters are designed for kids over forty pounds (when a child is too big for a convertible seat), but the law requires them to be in a booster until they are six years old or sixty pounds. Boosters have a raised, rigid base that allows children to use an adult seat belt. Britax and Graco are the most popular models. Prices range from $25–$150. Another option is to buy a car with a built-in booster seat. Most Volvos and Chrysler/Dodge minivans offer a factory option. Be sure to check with the car manufacturer to find out about weight, age, and height limitations.

Changing Tables

A conventional changing table is a completely separate piece of furniture that has a guardrail that goes all the way around the top and is fitted with a small cushioned pad. It usually has shelving space below to store diapers, wipes, and diaper cream, and the cost is typically $100 and up. When the baby grows out of diapers or is too big to be lifted up and changed on the table, the piece of furniture becomes obsolete in the nursery, as it really has no other use to transition into.

A better option is a changing table of the flip-top/dresser variety. The top of the dresser becomes a changing area when you place the padded flip top on top of a dresser. Once you are beyond the diaper stage, just remove the flip top and you will have a standard chest of drawers perfect for a toddler's room. Most of the major baby furniture companies manufacture flip tops coordinated with the cribs they sell. Costs run about $120 and up. Another option is to have a flip top made for your own dresser. Or you can simply buy a contoured changing pad and attach it to any dresser you already have, which is what I did. I found a cute dresser that I liked at Crate & Barrel and attached a pad to the top of it. There are attachments that allow you to snap it securely to the dresser and then easily remove it when you no longer need it. These are available at most baby stores and cost about $25.

Cribs

You can find cribs to meet any style and budget requirements. All cribs sold today should be certified by the JPMA. Its safety specifications require the following: the space between the crib bars be no more than two and three-eighths inches apart; the mattress should fit snugly in the crib; and all cribs should have a locking drop-side with a childproof lock-release mechanism.

Here are the questions you should ask when shopping for a crib:

★ Do both sides of the crib drop or just one side?

★ Can you raise or lower the crib's side with one hand while holding the baby, or do you need both hands?

★ Is the crib stable when you shake it?

★ Does the crib include stabilizer bars (metal rods fastening the end boards and located underneath the crib)?

★ If it has wheels, do they have locks to prevent the crib from rolling?

★ Can the crib be converted into a youth bed?

When you are choosing the bedding for the crib, make sure the bumpers can be securely tied on with at least six ties or snaps. Keep the crib clear of any items like mobiles, clothes, and toys that have strings longer than seven inches. Don't set up the crib near any potential hazards in the room, such as a heater, window, or cords from blinds.

Below are the crib manufacturers whose products are widely available in DC. You should know that because of the strict JPMA regulations, many boutique furniture stores do not actually manufacture their own cribs; instead, they buy them from JPMA-approved manufacturers and paint them to match their own furniture lines. Most of these manufacturers are well-known and established in the baby market, and some lines, like Legacy and Renaissance, are exclusive divisions of established lines (Child Craft and Simmons, respectively). The choice comes down to what you like and how much you are willing to spend. Prices range from less than $200 for a Cosco crib to more than $3,000 for a crib from an exclusive boutique. Cribs from companies like Nurseryworks (www.nurseryworks.net, available at Daisy Baby & Mommies Too) and Netto Collection (www.nettocollection.com) have become popular with parents who are looking for something more modern and sleek. Be sure to ask whether the store charges for delivery and assembly. While you can assemble the furniture yourself (think Peugeot), the stores generally send delivery people who know what they are doing.

These are the most popular crib brands sold in DC:

- Bassett
- Bellini
- Child Craft
- Cosco
- Legacy
- Million Dollar Baby
- Morigeau-Lépine
- Ragazzi
- Simmons

ExerSaucer

I can't even begin to describe to you what this ingenious invention is, but trust me when I say you need one. Babies can go in it at four months and are basically safely surrounded by complete sensory overload, which will keep them happily occupied for hours at a time. (Not that I'm suggesting you really leave them in there for that long.) The newest model, jam-packed with the most bells and whistles, costs around $120.

Gliders

A glider or a rocking chair is optional but if you have the space, you'll love having one when you're feeding the baby or trying to get him or her to sleep at two in the morning. A glider is better if you want to avoid little toes or a dog's tail getting pinched under a rocking chair leg. Dutailier gliders are the most readily available and, in my opinion, the best made. They retail for about $250–$450, depending on the finish and fabric you choose.

High Chairs

When you are buying a high chair, it's advisable to:

1. Buy a chair with a wide base to limit chances of the chair tipping over.

2. Make sure the chair comes with a built-in safety belt.

3. Find a chair with a one-hand tray-release mechanism, which makes it easy to take your baby out.

4. Find a high chair that has removable chair cushions for easy cleanup. Babies and food are a messy combination.

Most high chair accidents occur with children under a year old, usually because the child has not been properly strapped in and falls out. Don't just use the tray to keep your baby in the seat; use the safety belt. Also, do not place the chair too close to a surface that the baby could push off of, tipping the chair over.

The most popular high chair on the market is the Peg Perego Prima Pappa, which has a one-handed tray-release and adjustable reclining and height features. The newest version has a removable chair cushion that is machine washable. It also has a dinner tray with a cup holder that sits on top of the tray attached to the high chair. I like it because it folds easily for storage. It retails for around $170. While most old-fashioned wooden, hand-painted high chairs are pretty, they generally tip over easily and are hard to keep sterile. If you want a modern non-plastic version try the Svan infant high chair, which costs $225 (available at www.babystyle.com). This Scandinavian-designed wooden high chair is both aesthetically pleasing and easy to keep clean. It also converts to a toddler seat once your child has outgrown the high chair.

Playpens/Portable Cribs

Playpens are a great place to park your baby when you need a few minutes to yourself to shower, check email, or pour yourself a glass of wine. Some babies can amuse themselves in a playpen for up to thirty minutes at a time, while others stand at the side and cry as if they were in jail. As great as they can be, playpens are big and difficult to store. The portable crib is a more versatile alternative. Portable cribs have thin mattresses and sheets, so they can be used as a crib when traveling. The most popular brand is the Graco Pack 'n' Play, which offers several different models; some have a bassinet that attaches to the top for newborns, a built-in musical mobile, and a vibrating mattress. My advice is to buy the most basic model in the least offensive color or pattern you can find. I bought the one with every add-on and never used any of them. They retail from $80–$189.

Strollers

When choosing a stroller, keep in mind your lifestyle and the neighborhood you live in. DC babies spend many hours in the stroller going to the park, the supermarket, or window-shopping on M Street. Moms and babies are also hopping in and out of cars daily to scoot around the Metro area. Versatility is a must when it comes to living in a city that has it all.

There are five basic types of strollers: light-weight, umbrella, full-size, jogger, and, more recently, the "hybrid." The popularity of the hybrid stroller started with the introduction of the Bugaboo Frog. It is a combination of full-size and jogger strollers. The baby can relax in a bassinet while the larger wheels and shocks absorb the bumps of uneven paving or brick sidewalks. The Bugaboo Frog is the most well-known, but there are many others on the market these days.

All strollers sold today must be JPMA compli-ant, so finding a safe stroller shouldn't be a concern. However, not every type may be right for you. Con-sider what time of year your baby will be born. For winter babies, a stroller with a boot (an enclosed end) might be the best bet to keep your newborn warm. For summer babies, look for one that has good ventilation and a sufficient sunshade. Several strollers on the market come with both, like the Maclaren XT. Also, the weight of a stroller is impor-tant. If you will need to carry a stroller up and down front steps to get into your house, or will need to throw it into the back of your car, look for one that's light and portable. Practice folding it with one hand to make sure that it's user-friendly.

Other desirable features include a stroller seat that reclines (a must for newborn to three-month-olds), plenty of storage space underneath, brakes on all four wheels, and a handle that reverses to allow the baby to face you or face out. Most brands now come with a conversion kit of some kind that allows you to fit an infant car seat into the stroller. If not, you can buy a Snap 'N Go, a lightweight stroller frame that the infant car seat snaps into, and which ranges in price from $50–$120.

the stores

★ **BABIES "R" US**
800-869-7787

12012 Cherry Hill Road
Silver Spring, MD
301-586-8630

2969 Festival Way
Waldorf, MD
301-396-8037

5700 Leesburg Pike
Falls Church, VA
703-575-9542

14173 Crossing Place
Woodbridge, MD
703-492-0209

13954 Metro Tech Drive
Chantilly, VA
703-502-9200

21300 Signal Hill Plaza
Sterling, VA
571-434-8850
www.babiesrus.com

Return Policy: Returns may be made within 90 days from the date of purchase with the receipt for store credit.

Babies "R" Us carries everything from strollers to breast pumps, nursery furniture, and toys. The chain generally has the best prices but I don't recommend going there if you haven't decided on a particular item and are looking for a recommendation. The store is not known for service, and the salespeople aren't particularly knowledgeable. These stores carry just about every mass-market brand, though, and will assemble items for a fee.

★ **BABY DEPOT**
3524 South Jefferson Street
Bailey's Crossroads, VA
703-379-7878

11284 James Swart Circle
Fairfax, VA
703-267-6939

47100 Community Place Drive
Sterling, VA
703-404-0497

600 North Frederick Avenue
Gaithersburg, MD
301-527-1461
www.babydepot.com

Return Policy: A refund, credit, or exchange will be made for merchandise returned within 30 days of purchase with tags attached, in original packaging and accompanied by the original sales receipt.

The Baby Depot is a division of The Burlington Coat Factory and carries everything you'll want, including cribs, high chairs, strollers, clothes, and accessories. Prices are very good. These stores carry a large selection of Kolcraft and Child Craft cribs. Stroller selection includes Peg Perego, Aprica, Graco, Combi, Kolcraft, and Maclaren. It's best to know what you are looking for when you are shopping at Baby Depot, as the service can be hit or miss.

★ **BELLINI**

12113 Rockville Pike

Rockville, MD

301-770-3944

www.bellini.com

Return Policies: Varies by item; contact store directly for policies on specific items.

Before there were so many boutique baby stores, Bellini was the place to go for upscale baby furniture. You can still find quality furniture and accessories here. The staff is very helpful and will work within your budget to come up with a complete design scheme for your nursery. The store has a good selection of cribs on display and has endless catalogs of both cribs and bedding that can be custom ordered.

★ **BUY BUY BABY**

11683 Rockville Pike

Rockville, MD

301-984-1123

6398 Springfield Plaza

Springfield, VA

703-932-9797

www.buybuybaby.com

Return Policy: Full refund within 30 days of purchase. Store credit anytime thereafter.

Buy buy BABY is a baby superstore. But while it has the same look and feel as a Babies "R" Us or Great Beginnings, the service is far superior and the salespeople are very knowledgeable. These stores carry a range of brands, including full lines of some of those at the higher end of the spectrum such as Bugaboo, Baby Bjorn, Medela, and Maclaren. Each store has a large section dedicated to nursery furniture and bedding with a large number of items on display.

★ **COSTCO**

1200 South Fern Street

Pentagon City, VA

4725 West Ox Road

Fairfax, VA

880 Russell Avenue

Gaithersburg, MD

21398 Price/Cascades Plaza

Sterling, VA

800-607-6861

www.costco.com

Return Policy: Satisfaction is guaranteed on every product with a full refund.

Costco carries nursery furniture, bedding, strollers, car seats, and toys from makers such as Child Craft, Zooper, Combi, and Graco. Costco is a great place for bargain-basement prices, but it's best if you go knowing what you want. These stores also carry their own Kirkland brand of diapers, wipes, and formula for much less than other brands.

★ CRADLE & CRAYON

Reston Town Center

11913 Freedom Drive

Reston, VA

703-437-0900

www.cradleandcrayon.com

Return Policy: Full refund on items returned within 14 days of purchase. Anytime thereafter, items can be exchanged or returned for store credit only.

While shopping for her first child, Stella Guillen thought that it would be easy to find an array of choices and knowledgeable and caring people who could help her prepare for something she'd never done before. But her choices seemed the same everywhere, and the shopping experience made Stella's partner feel like a glorified porter. So after their baby was born, she set to work and started Cradle & Crayon, which carries furniture, toys, baby gear, and clothes, as well as apparel for expectant moms. Some of the furniture and gear lines are: Morigeau-Lépine, Best Chairs, Phil & Teds, Britax, Bumbleride, Mountain Buggy, BOB, and Britax.

★ DAWN PRICE BABY

325 Seventh Street, SE

Capitol Hill, DC

202-543-2920

3112 M Street, NW

Georgetown, DC

202-333-3939

www.dawnpricebaby.com

Return Policy: Standard purchases may be returned within the first 14 days for a refund, exchange, or store credit.

Dawn Price Baby now has two locations and both have a great selection of very cool nursery bedding and furnishings among other items. These stores are good for one-stop shopping; if needed, you could accomplish everything from furnishing the entire nursery to dressing baby in the hippest threads. They specialize in carrying the cooler, harder-to-find lines of linens, cribs, and strollers, including Serena & Lily, ducduc, Oeuf, and Phil & Ted's. The stores are owned by a local mom and the service is very friendly.

★ JACADI

1732M International Drive

Tysons Corner Center

McLean, VA

703-356-2844

www.jacadiusa.com

Return Policy: Store credit only for returns made within 30 days.

Jacadi is based in Paris and opened its first US store twenty years ago on Madison Avenue and Rodeo Drive. In addition to darling clothes for infants and toddlers from different brands, Jacadi carries original bedding, furniture, and accessories of its own design. The DC branch has everything you could possibly need to decorate a nursery—from floor coverings, bedding, furniture, and wallpaper—in a theme of your choice.

★ LULLABY BABY

9130 Red Branch Road

Columbia, MD

410-997-8090

www.lullaby-baby.com

Return Policy: No returns on custom ordered items.

Lullaby Baby carries quality nursery decor and furnishings in styles ranging from traditional to contemporary. Custom cribs and furniture can be painted to suit any design scheme that they help you to put together. The store carries lines such as Morigeau-Lépine, Dutailier, and Paintbox Designs. Very few furniture items are kept in stock as most are custom ordered, so make sure to leave at least ten to twelve weeks for delivery.

★ PETITE DEKOR AND SO MUCH MORE

22 West Market Street, NW
Leesburg, VA
703-777-7030
www.petitedekor.com
Return Policy: No returns may be made on custom orders.

Petite Dekor is a one-stop shop for infant and children's furniture, bedding, room decor, toys, stationery, and linens. Some of the brands it carries are Maine Cottage, Bratt Décor, and Little Castle Furniture.

★ POTTERY BARN KIDS

11301 Rockville Pike
Rockville, MD
301-231-5831

8084 Tysons Corner Center
McLean, VA
703-934-4795
www.potterybarnkids.com
Return Policy: Items may be returned for up to 30 days after purchase for full refund.

If you haven't already received the catalog, shamelessly delivered on a daily basis, I don't know where you've been hiding. Pottery Barn Kids sells complete nursery furniture sets of its own design at reasonable prices. It offers everything from monogrammed bedding to light fixtures and baby clothes. Everything is available online and usually ships within a couple of weeks.

★ RIGHT START

11658 Plaza America Drive
Reston, VA
703-464-8320
www.rightstart.com
Return Policy: Returns may be made within 30 days for refund or store credit. No returns on special orders.

Right Start is good for one-stop shopping for just about every stage of your baby's development. The store has a large stroller and car seat section; products include Bugaboo, Peg Perego, and Maclaren. The "feeding" section carries everything from pumps to nipples, forks, and spoons. It does not carry cribs, but it has a small selection of co-sleepers and bassinets. The service is good and salespeople are fairly knowledgeable.

★ TARGET

3101 Jefferson Davis Highway
Alexandria, VA
703-706-3840

10301 New Guinea Road
Fairfax, VA
703-764-5100

13047 Fair Lakes Shopping Center
Fairfax, VA
703-449-7100

6100 Arlington Boulevard
Falls Church, VA
703-392-5630

12197 Sunset Hills Road
Reston, VA
703-478-0770

46201 Potomac Run Plaza
Sterling, VA
703-444-8440
www.target.com

Return Policy: Refund or exchange with receipt within 90 days.

Target carries a small but decent selection of cribs, high chairs, swings, and portable cribs. Brands carried include Graco, Evenflo, and Cosco, but what the stores have in stock can be hit-or-miss. The drawback with this inexpensive chain is that finding someone who actually works there can be a task in and of itself, let alone someone who knows about baby equipment.

★ **WREN & DIVINE**
6645 Old Dominion Drive
McLean, VA
703-356-WREN
www.wrenanddivine.com

Return Policy: No returns may be made on special-order items. All other returns may be made within 10 days of original purchase.

Wren & Divine carries beautiful high-end furniture and accessories for babies and toddlers. It specializes in custom furnishings and bedding for the most posh nurseries. The store also carries strollers, prams, diaper bags, specialty stuffed toys, and layette sets. You could go absolutely crazy in this store.

birth announcements and stationery

Your husband may have sent the exciting news from his BlackBerry in the middle of the delivery room, but like most of us you will still probably want to send out a more traditional birth announcement via snail mail. After all, you've just spent the past nine months growing an entire human being. You want the world to know (on pretty paper, that is) that baby has arrived!

Options abound. You can purchase ready-made cards at a stationery or party store and fill in your baby's name, weight, size, and birth date. These can either be filled in by hand or, depending on how computer savvy you are, fed through your home printer.

Or you can order traditional printed cards, with or without a picture of your new addition. I personally thought I would never include a picture on my children's birth announcements after getting ones from friends who had included snapshots. Picture after picture bore a striking resemblance to Ellen Ripley's offspring in Alien. But when my own little aliens came into the world, I wanted everyone to see how adorable they were. However, if you do decide to include a photograph, factor in the extra time that it takes trying to get your newborn to turn and smile for the camera. It may add unnecessary stress if you don't plan ahead.

Keep your budget in mind. It's easy to go crazy with all of the adorable options out there, and just as easy to find yourself dipping into the Third's college savings account. Announcements can quickly become pricey depending on how customized you want them to be. It can be just as special to create hand-written or computerized announcements as it is to get original letterpress on handmade paper.

I recommend choosing your announcements a month or so in advance, to allow time to print and address your envelopes before the baby arrives. Once your baby is born, you can call the store and provide all of the pertinent stats (name, sex, weight, length, and date and time of birth) to print your final order. Consider ordering matching thank-you cards at this time. Be sure to order enough, as you have no idea how many people will send you gifts—and you can always use extras. Most printing companies charge less if you order larger quantities at one time, so it actually saves money to order more than you think you will need the first time around.

Photo-printing websites are hugely popular. The ability to design an announcement from your home with a few clicks of a mouse is very appealing. We have received tons of birth announcements, holiday cards, and party invitations that were printed this way, and they actually looked cute.

Shutterfly.com and Kodakgallery.com are popular websites that will even address and send them out for you. Many of the websites' cards are the same price as store-bought cards, with the bonus of at-home convenience.

I have listed the most popular stationery stores in the area; each stocks books that the stationery companies provide with product samples. If you already have something in mind, tell the salespeople; they will usually be able to pull books from stationers that are suited to your style.

the stores

★ **CREATIVE PARTIES LTD.**
8011 Woodmont Avenue
Bethesda, MD
301-654-9292
www.cparties.com

Moms-to-be have been ordering from this Bethesda institution forever. Creative Parties stocks a variety of announcements from Sweet Pea, Prentiss Douthit, Wren Press, and many others. It has hundreds of samples from each supplier along the walls of the store, which makes it easy to find what you want. The staff is extremely knowledgeable and will do everything from helping to select do-it-yourself cards to designing fully customized announcements.

★ **FINGERS IN INK**
2642 North Pershing Drive
Arlington, VA
703-465-9100
www.fingersinink.com

Owned and operated by Arlington local Nicole Fingers Woodward, Fingers In Ink offers a high-end selection of the top stationers in the business. The experience here is very hands-on and you are encouraged to call ahead and make an appointment for a ninety-minute consultation when designing your announcements, invites, or stationery. Though custom announcements are this store's specialty, there is also a nice selection of boxed cards that you can hand write or print at home.

★ **JUST PAPER AND TEA**
3232 P Street, NW
Georgetown, DC
202-333-9141
www.justpaperandtea.com

Owned and operated by a husband-and-wife team, Just Paper and Tea carries every major line of stationery including William Arthur, Crane's, Stacy Claire Boyd, and Boatman Geller, among many others. The mom and pop of this "mom and pop shop" are very knowledgeable, and they will help you to quickly narrow your search based on what you have in mind. Service is excellent, with attention to every detail and quick turnaround. The store also carries printer-ready announcements and invitations that can either be printed at home or printed for you for a nominal fee.

★ PAPER SOURCE

118 King Street
Alexandria, VA
703-299-9950

3019 M Street, NW
Georgetown, DC
202-298-5545
www.paper-source.com

In addition to custom-printed letterpress, Paper Source is a great place for the creative mom-to-be who wants to customize her own announcements. With literally thousands of paper options, your imagination is the limit. For those of us who get overwhelmed by the endless possibilities, the Paper Source has an equally numerous selection of hip announcement "kits" that can be printed at home and easily assembled. Service is good and its artsy employees are full of creative ideas. It also offers workshops from designing and making your own announcements to pulling together a cool scrapbook for baby.

★ THE PAPERY

4852 Bethesda Avenue
Bethesda, MD
240-497-1420

2871 Clarendon Boulevard
Arlington, VA
703-875-0390
www.thepapery.com

The Papery stocks a variety of announcements from Crane's, William Arthur, The Wren Press, and many others. The walls are covered with cute boxed cards that you can fill in yourself either by hand or on the computer, but the store can also print them for you.

★ PAPYRUS

40 Massachusetts Avenue, NE
Union Station, DC
202-551-0757

1300 Wisconsin Avenue
Georgetown, DC
202-337-0720

7101 Democracy Boulevard
Bethesda, MD
301-365-5511

5457 Wisconsin Avenue
Chevy Chase, MD
301-913-0360

721 King Street
Alexandria, VA
571-721-0070

1100 South Hayes Street
Arlington, VA
703-415-4319

11912 Fair Oaks Mall
Fairfax, VA
703-359-6810

7934 Tysons Corner Center
McLean, VA
703-893-5640
www.papyrusonline.com

Papyrus is an upscale national retailer of stationery and cards. The stores carry over twenty-five lines of popular brand-name stationers such as Checkerbox, William Arthur, and Stacy Claire Boyd that can be customized and ordered in one of the many locations around town or online. Boxed invitations, thank-you cards, and announcements that can be customized on your printer at home or by the store (for an extra fee) are also available. Papyrus has a very quick turnaround time so it's great for moms in a hurry.

★ **TIFFANY & CO.**
5481 Wisconsin Avenue
Chevy Chase, MD
301-657-8777
www.tiffany.com

Tiffany & Co. has a large stationery department offering both its own line and some Crane's. True to form, Tiffany offers a wide selection of classic, understated engraved announcements and cards. It also continues to add fresh, more playful designs to the collection each year.

★ **WRITE FOR YOU**
3807 McKinley Street, NW
Chevy Chase, DC
202-686-7060

Write For You has a large selection of announcements and cards. The store carries popular brands such as Stacy Claire Boyd, Blue Mug, Sweet Pea, Prentiss Douthit, Crane's, and William Arthur. There is also a large selection of letterpress invitations and stationery, as well as boxed announcements.

★ **THE WRITTEN WORD**
1427 P Street, NW
Dupont Circle, DC
888-755-4640
202-223-1400
www.writtenwordstudio.com

The Written Word has been designing and printing high-end stationery, announcements, and invitations for more than twenty-five years. Using a one-hundred-fifty-year-old letterpress, it produces wonderful handcrafted birth announcements on paper that is imported from around the world. This is the place to go for the highly individualized, original announcement that you're sure no one will have seen before.

Chapter Eight

baby and toddler clothes

Fashion for little ones really comes down to one fundamental question: What is your position on appliqués? If you choose to eschew them, it won't be easy, but you will sleep soundly knowing you haven't let your child be branded daily with a dump truck on his T-shirt, or some cheesy rabbit playing tennis on her skirt. And do not get me started on the shameless marketing opportunities. These poor kids look like miniature billboards, covered from head to toe with ads for Winnie the Pooh, Nemo, Elmo, Dora, and the like. It's enough to make you want to go really old school and dress them in white for the first five years.

I am a big believer that style starts young. Regardless of your budget or your taste, you should instill it in your child while he or she is still in diapers. With all that DC has to offer, your City Baby can be decked out in any look imaginable, from prep to punk. In this chapter, I'll help you navigate the stores—from the reliable retail chains to obscure little boutiques off the beaten track. Get psyched, because this is about to be some of the most fun you've had with your credit card in a long time.

shopping tips

★ Wait until after the baby shower to see where you may need to fill in the gaps. If your shower gifts include too many outfits in three- and six-month sizes, return most of them for credit or exchange them for twelve- and eighteen-month sizes. Don't wait too long to exchange or return items, though. If you put it off for too long, you'll find some stores won't take them back or they will have marked them down when you finally do.

★ Pay attention to a store's return policy. In general, the big retail chains have much more liberal return policies; smaller boutiques are a bit more strict.

★ Don't go crazy buying dresses or pants for babies under six months. They sleep most of the time, and those cotton, terrycloth, and velvet onesies are much more comfortable for them, and easier to change often.

★ Infants grow incredibly fast. Try not to buy too much at any one time. If you do your laundry as often as we do, your baby can get by with two or three pairs of pajamas.

★ If you plan to shop with your little one in tow, use the Baby Bjorn or small stroller. Some of these stores are small and get crowded, and you may have to walk up a flight of steps.

layette

The following is a list of things to have before baby's arrival that will carry you at least through the first three months. Some stores will offer you a much more lengthy list; however, they have their own sales in mind, and store lists usually have many unnecessary items.

★ 6 onesies (the little cotton short-sleeve shirts with snaps in the crotch)

★ 2 side-snap or side-tie shirts (the hospital will give you some and you only use them until the umbilical cord falls off)

★ 5 sleeper onesies with feet (the velvety full body suits with snaps)

★ 1 sun or snow hat (depending on when baby is born)

★ 6 pairs of socks

★ 1 snowsuit (for winter babies)

★ 4 receiving blankets (to lay baby down on or swaddle him in)

★ 2 SwaddleMes (great for those of us who can't figure out the swaddle fold with a normal blanket)

★ 1 heavier blanket

★ 1 Bundle Me (this is basically a thick fleece and wool blanket that zips into your stroller)

★ 2 hooded towel/washcloth sets (a normal towel works just as well but these are cuter)

★ 12 burp cloths (because babies do more than just burp)

★ 4 bibs

★ 1 kit containing nail scissors, thermometer, aspirator, and hairbrush

the stores

★ **APPLE SEED BOUTIQUE**
115 South Columbus Street
Alexandria, VA
703-535-5446

4141 Main Street
Gaithersburg, MD
240-683-5446
www.appleseedboutique.com
Return Policy: Exchange or store credit within 10 days of purchase with original tags.

Apple Seed Boutique specializes in outfitting the youngest set of DC fashionistas with the latest in hip children's clothing from around the world. In addition, you'll find everything from stylish shower gifts to the latest designer diaper bags. These stores carry such lines as Petit Bateau, Malina, Noa Lily, Pediped, Larucci, and Patachou.

★ BABYGAP

Locations throughout the DC metro area
800-GAP-STYLE
www.babygap.com

Return Policy: Full refund with receipt. Store
credit for amount paid with gift receipt.
Returns without receipt receive store credit.

If you aren't already familiar with babyGap then I don't know where you've been hiding. These stores are everywhere, and they have fashionable, decent-quality clothes at good prices. They are great for all the staples, especially for boys. Not all babyGaps carry the same inventory, so check online for full offerings.

★ BENETTON

1666 Connecticut Avenue, NW
Dupont, DC
202-232-1770

785 Seventh Street, NW
Downtown, DC
202-393-8209

1200 Wisconsin Avenue, NW
Georgetown, DC
202-625-0443

7101 Democracy Boulevard
Bethesda, MD
301-365-2997

1100 South Hayes Street
Arlington, VA
703-412-0950

11750 Fair Oaks
Fair Oaks, VA
703-218-3980

1961 Chain Bridge Road
McLean, VA
703-749-9064
www.benetton.com

Return Policy: Unworn full-price merchandise
may be returned within 14 days of purchase
with receipt. No cash refunds.

The United Colors of Benetton's children's collection is a miniaturized take on the preppy European looks that this chain is known for. For clothes, there are brightly colored coordinating ensembles and comfortable knits as well as a wide range of accessories, pajamas, winter coats, and much more. Sizes range from infant to age twelve, and prices are moderate.

★ BUY BUY BABY

1683 Rockville Pike
Rockville, MD
301-984-1123

6398 Springfield Plaza,
Springfield, VA
703-932-9797
www.buybuybaby.com

Return Policy: Full refund within 30 days of
purchase. Store credit anytime thereafter.

Buy buy BABY has a large clothing section that stocks everything from packs of Carter's onesies to cute outfits from Ralph Lauren and Tommy Hilfiger. If you really want to be efficient, you could also get everything from formula to diapers, a stroller, and a car seat as well. It truly is the baby-supply superstore. The service is excellent and anything you can't find can be ordered and shipped directly to you.

★ THE CHILDREN'S PLACE

1100 South Hayes Street
Arlington, VA
703-413-7875

1663 Rockville Pike
Rockville, MD
301-255-0439

7101 Democracy Boulevard
Bethesda, MD
301-767-1863

11930 Lee Jackson Highway
Fairfax, VA
703-691-1020

21100 Dulles Town Circle
Dulles, VA
703-421-3430

8034 Tysons Corner Center
McLean, VA
703-448-0233
www.thechildrensplace.com

Return Policy: No sale is ever final.

The Children's Place is a growing chain with locations throughout the Metro area. Offering clothes for boys and girls from newborns to age fourteen, the store is good for basics, on par with Target and Old Navy in terms of quality and price. The clothes are fairly well made and very affordable.

★ CRADLE & CRAYON

Reston Town Center
11913 Freedom Drive
Reston, VA
703-437-0900
www.cradleandcrayon.com

Return Policy: Full refund on items returned within 14 days of purchase. Anytime thereafter, items can be exchanged or returned for store credit only.

Cradle & Crayon is one of those great locally owned boutiques that has made shopping for both babies and mothers a lot of fun. All of the clothes are hand-picked by store owner and fellow mom Stella Guillen. The service is extremely attentive and the staff is full of helpful suggestions for building a layette or wardrobe. Baby lines carried are Tea Collection, Cakewalk, Zutano, and Petit Bateau, among others.

★ DAISY BABY & MOMMIES TOO

4924 Del Ray Avenue
Bethesda, MD
301-654-7477

Return Policy: Purchases with tags intact may be returned for up to 2 weeks for exchange or store credit.

Daisy Baby is a darling boutique that carries very chic moderate- to high-priced lines of baby clothes, as well as maternity clothes, nursery furniture, and bedding. Daisy Baby & Mommies Too offers lines such as Margery Ellen, Splendid, and Monsters with Sideburns baby clothes. This is perfect boutique-style shopping for both expectant and new mothers, and the store is great for shower gifts, too.

★ DAWN PRICE BABY

325 Seventh Street, SE
Capitol Hill, DC
202-543-2920

3112 M Street, NW
Georgetown, DC
202-333-3939
www.dawnpricebaby.com

Return Policy: Standard purchases may be
   returned within the first 14 days for a refund,
   exchange, or store credit.

Dawn Price Baby is a store where you will want to
spend some time, since it is packed with the
coolest baby clothes and gear. It has such a strong
local following that it added a second location in
Georgetown, which was enthusiastically welcomed.
These are boutique superstores, offering much
more than you would think by their size; they sell
furniture, strollers, clothes, and decor. Baby clothing lines you'll find are Tea Collection, Ralph Lauren,
Barefoot Dreams, and Under the Nile.

★ DOODLEHOPPER 4 KIDS

228 West Broad Street
Falls Church, VA
703-241-2262

7521 Huntsman Boulevard
Springfield, VA
703-912-7200
www.huntsmandoodlehopper.com

Return Policy: Items with tags may be returned
   for a full refund within 30 days of purchase.

Doodlehopper 4 Kids carries clothes for newborns
up to age ten for girls and up to age seven for boys.
It has a large selection of fashions, ranging from

traditional to playful and unique, from Hartstrings,
Kitestrings, Absorba, E.Land, Sweet Potatoes, Le
Top, Plum Pudding, Mulberribush, Wes & Willy,
Deux par Deux, Biscotti, and many more. It also car-
ries everything you'll need to outfit your child for
her or his first ballet class.

★ EMISSARY

5300 Wisconsin Avenue, NW
Mazza Galleria
Chevy Chase, MD
202-363-1760

2001 International Drive
Tysons Galleria, VA
703-827-7700

Return Policy: Full refund on items returned
   within the first 7 days, and store credit
   thereafter.

Emissary carries beautiful layette and children's
clothes up through size 2T. I love the Absorba line
of cozy little onesies the stores carry, as well as the
beautiful hand-smocked dresses and other special-
occasion clothes. Each store has a good selection
of silver spoons, cups, and brush sets, which can be
monogrammed and make easy shower gifts. It is a
wonderful little boutique filled with specialty items.

★ FILENE'S BASEMENT

1133 Connecticut Avenue, NW
Downtown, DC
202-872-8430

529 Fourteenth Street, NW
Downtown, DC
202-638-4110

5300 Wisconsin Avenue, NW

Mazza Galleria

Chevy Chase, DC

202-966-0208

11840 Rockville Pike

Rockville, MD

301-816-7805

www.filenesbasement.com

Return Policy: Full refund within 30 days of purchase with tags and receipt.

Filene's Basement is the original go-to store for deeply discounted designer clothes. The infant and toddler sections can be hit-or-miss, but can be worth the trip to find great deals on clothes from Ralph Lauren, Anavini, Tommy Hilfiger, and Absorba. Service is virtually nonexistent so be ready to work for your bargain-basement togs.

★ **FULL OF BEANS**

5502 Connecticut Avenue, NW

Chevy Chase, DC

202-362-8566

10144 River Road

Potomac, MD

301-983-6569

Return Policy: Full refund if items are returned within 2 weeks; after 2 weeks, store credit only.

Full of Beans is where to go if you're looking for cool clothes for your little hipster from newborn to age twelve. These boutiques carry a wide selection of designer clothes including Flapdoodles, Cakewalk, Baby Lulu, Biscotti, and Cherry Tree outerwear. The store also carries a good selection of classic toys and books. Staffpeople are very helpful.

★ **GRANDMOTHER'S BACK ROOM**

756 East Walker Road

Great Falls, VA

703-759-2680

www.grandmothersbackroom.com

Return Policy: Sale items may be returned for store credit only. All other items may be returned up to 1 week after purchase for refund.

Locals warmly welcomed the opening of this store back in 1996 as a place to buy tasteful children's gifts and quality children's clothes. The clothes range from sizes newborn up to sixteen for girls and twelve for boys. You can find discounted children's apparel from top brands on the permanent well-stocked sales rack, including seasonal items. Hartstrings, Sweet Potatoes, E.Land, Anavini, and Zutano are just a few of the long list of designers the store stocks.

★ **GYMBOREE**

1100 South Hayes Street

Arlington, VA

703-413-5009

7970-L Tysons Corner Center

McLean, VA

703-790-8858

www.gymboree.com

Return Policy: Full refund on returns made with receipt within 30 days of original purchase.

Gymboree carries very affordable clothes for infants through age twelve. Some of the clothes may not be the most stylish but occasionally you can find basic coordinating pieces that are good for play. Customer service is very good, and if you can't find a certain size salespeople will happily locate it in another store and have it shipped to you.

★ H&M

1025 F Street, NW

Downtown, DC

202-347-3306

Dulles Town Center

21100 Dulles Town Circle

Sterling, VA

703-430-5520

www.hm.com

Return Policy: Exchange or refund with receipt within 30 days of original purchase. Store credit for returns after 30 days of original purchase.

H&M is known for offering hip clothes at inexpensive prices, and its kids' line is no exception. You'll find everything from the basics to cool coordinates for the mini-hipster. Sale items might as well be free. Salespeople seem to focus on restocking racks and opening changing-room doors, so don't expect personalized service.

★ J. CREW

Montgomery Mall

7101 Democracy Boulevard

Bethesda, MD

301-365-2000

Tysons Galleria

17426 G International Drive

McLean, VA

703-734-9555

www.jcrew.com

Return Policy: All items with receipt can be returned for full refund or exchange within 60 days.

J. Crew took the preppy, clean styles it's well-known for and miniaturized them for its kids' line called Crewcuts. The clothing sizes are for children age two through ten years and are moderately priced. Not all locations carry the children's line yet, so keep checking as stores expand their stock.

★ JACADI

1732 M International Drive

McLean, VA

703-356-2844

www.jacadiusa.com

Return Policy: Store credit only for returns made within 30 days.

Jacadi is based in Paris and opened its first U.S. stores twenty years ago on Madison Avenue and Rodeo Drive. At that time the clothes were more traditional, with a Parisian flair; my mother used to buy beautiful smocked dresses there for my sister and me. The clothes are still very well made and full of style, but with a sort of Euro-mod look. It carries clothes for infants through age twelve as well as shoes and accessories. All clothes are the company's own design and brand.

★ JANIE AND JACK

1961 Chain Bridge Road

McLean, VA

703-356-7526

11750 Lee Jackson Memorial Highway

Fairfax, VA

703-352-6738

21100 Dulles Town Circle

Sterling, VA

703-444-6970

www.janieandjack.com

Return Policy: There is no time limit on returns with tags still intact.

Janie and Jack is a division of Gymboree, and was created as a more upscale alternative to the clothes found in the Gymboree retail stores. Janie and Jack locations have a more boutique-y feel, carrying sizes ranging from preemie to 5T for both boys and girls. It's great for everyday play clothes, with classic designs that are a bit more playful than you might find at GapKids. Clothes are inexpensive to moderately priced. The stores have deeply discounted seasonal sales that are worth checking out.

★ KIDS CLOSET

1226 Connecticut Avenue, NW

South Dupont, DC

202-429-9247

Return Policy: Items with receipt may be returned within 2 weeks for full refund. After 2 weeks, returns may be made for store credit or exchange.

Located in a relatively small storefront right off of Dupont Circle, Kids Closet carries a surprisingly large selection of children's clothing, toys, and gifts. Clothes from brands such as Absorba, Carter's and OshKosh run from newborn to age twelve for both boys and girls.

★ KINDER HAUS TOYS & CLOTHES

1220 North Fillmore Street

Arlington, VA

703-527-5929

www.kinderhaus.com

Return Policy: Returns for full refund may be made up to thirty days after purchase.

This independently owned toy and clothing store —packed from floor to ceiling with merchandise— will send you into sensory overload. From play clothes to dress clothes, there are countless choices for both boys and girls in sizes newborn to twelve. A large play area where children are encouraged to test drive toys while their parents shop is a bonus, but also ensures you won't be leaving without some new toys.

★ LACOSTE

3146 M Street, NW

Georgetown, DC

202-965-1893

5445 Wisconsin Avenue

Chevy Chase, MD

301-654-3367

Tysons Galleria

1757 M International Drive

McLean, VA

571-633-0241

www.lacoste.com

Return Policy: Returns may be made within 14 days of purchase for a full refund.

After declining from its height of popularity during the 1980s prep craze, Lacoste has finally made a comeback. (I'm proud to say I've been loyal throughout.) It offers brightly colored preppy staples, including its signature alligator polo shirts. The store stocks children's clothes in sizes four and up for boys and girls, as well as tennis shoes in sizes ten and up.

★ LEMONDROP

8530 Connecticut Avenue

Chevy Chase, MD

301-656-1357

Return Policy: Exchanges and returns may be made for up to 2 weeks for store credit.

The longtime mainstay for traditional party dresses and boys' first blazers, Lemondrop is where one can still find classic, traditional clothes for boys and girls newborn through age 16. In addition to special-occasion outfits, Lemondrop carries a wide array of casual and play clothes. The store is all about customer service, and manager Toni Roddy will even look for specialty items for longtime repeat customers while on buying trips. Lemondrop carries moderate to high-end lines from Lilly Pulitzer, Vineyard Vines, Anavini, Sarah Louise, Hartstrings, and Flap Happy.

★ LORD & TAYLOR

5255 Western Avenue, NW

Chevy Chase, DC

202-362-9600

11311 Rockville Pike

Kensington, MD

301-770-9000

Tysons Corner Center

701 Russell Avenue

Gaithersburg, MD

301-947-0502

10300 Little Patuxent Parkway

Columbia, MD

410-997-7518

www.lordandtaylor.com

Return Policy: Returns may be made for up to 30 days from original purchase date for full refund. Returns made with no receipt will be issued a refund at the lowest in-store selling price in the last 30 days as a merchandise certificate.

Opened in 1826 on Manhattan's Fifth Avenue, Lord & Taylor has been helping to fashionably clothe American families since the beginning and continues to do so today. The store maintains a reliable stock of big-name designers such as Ralph Lauren and Guess for boys and girls sizes newborn through age sixteen. A constant sale seems to be taking place, offering large discounts on everything from clothing to accessories such as socks and underwear.

★ MACY'S

1201 G Street, NW

Downtown, DC

202-628-6661

701 North Glebe Road

Arlington, VA

703-524-5100

1000 South Hayes Street

Arlington, VA

703-418-4488

5701 Duke Street

Alexandria, VA

703-354-1900

8000 Tysons Corner Center

McLean, VA

703-893-4900

7125 Democracy Boulevard

Bethesda, MD

301-469-6800

www.macys.com

Return Policy: Full refund with receipt.

Calling itself "the world's largest store," Macy's offers shopping's self-proclaimed antithesis to the boutique experience. However, a parent looking to dress every child in the family from head to toe will never be disappointed here (and may find something for the adults in the family, too). With a huge children's department filled with clothing priced to fly off the shelves, and from familiar brands such as Carter's and Polo Ralph Lauren, the convenience of this big-box retailer is hard to deny.

★ **THE MAGIC WARDROBE**

108 West Washington Street

Middleburg, VA

540-687-3363

www.themagicwardrobe.com

Return Policy: Items with receipt may be returned for up to 30 days for a full refund. Items without original receipt may be returned within 30 days for store credit.

The Magic Wardrobe is a wonderful place for beautiful, traditional imported clothing for infants and children through age twelve. Located in Middleburg, it is a pretty good trek for most people in the DC area, but it has seasonal trunk shows in the District, which you can find out about by calling and asking to be put on its mailing list. Magic Wardrobe carries lines such as Papo d'Anjo, Bella Bliss, and Vineyard Vines, and it is a great store to find special-occasion outfits, complete with accessories and shoes. Also, if you are looking for a particular item, Bridget, the store owner, will send you clothes on consignment (you are only charged for the things you decide to keep . . . or forget to send back.).

★ **MONDAY'S CHILD**

218 North Lee Street

Alexandria, VA

703-548-3505

http://mondayschildofalexandria.com

Return Policy: Store credit and exchanges on regular-priced merchandise.

Monday's Child offers traditional clothing for boys and girls, from layette and christening gowns to special-occasion and everyday outfits. Florence Eisman, Feltman Brothers, Kissy Kissy, and Katie & Co. are just a few of the lines carried at this boutique.

★ **NEIMAN MARCUS**

Mazza Galleria

5300 Wisconsin Avenue, NW

Friendship Heights, DC

202-966-9700

Tysons Galleria

2255 International Drive

McLean, VA

703-761-1600

www.neimanmarcus.com

Return Policy: All unworn items may be returned for full credit.

Neiman Marcus has a large department of trendy and traditional clothes for newborns to sixteen-year-olds. The trendier set can trick out their tots in duds from designers such as Juicy Couture, True Religion, and Dolce & Gabbana. More traditional designers carried are Burberry, Lilly Pulitzer, and Neiman Marcus's own line of beautiful christening gowns and accessories. The store also carries baby bags, silver sets, and blanket and towel sets.

★ NORDSTROM

1400 South Hayes Street
Arlington, VA
703-415-1121

8075 Tysons Corner Center
McLean, VA
703-761-1121

7111 Democracy Boulevard
Bethesda, MD
301-365-4111
www.nordstrom.com

Return Policy: Full refund with receipt.

Nordstrom has just about everything you could need for your child, newborn and up. The stores carry their own well-priced layette line (Nordstrom Baby) and toddler line (Pine Peak Blues) both priced from $10 to $28, as well as Tommy Hilfiger, Ralph Lauren, Little Me, Carter's, Skechers, Aster, Nike, and Adidas. They also boast the largest shoe section of any department store in the area; see entry on page 103.

★ OILILY

1866 G International Drive
McLean, VA
703-556-0697
www.oilily-world.com

Return Policy: Full refund on all returns with receipts within 30 days of purchase.

This Dutch design house has been creating bold clothing in bright prints and colors since 1964. The moderate- to high-priced clothes for newborns through age ten include cotton coordinating pieces in an array of rainbow-colored floral prints. Oilily also carries a line of children's shoes, socks, and accessories.

★ OLD NAVY

3621 Jefferson Davis Highway
Alexandria, VA
703-739-6240

5800 Crossroads Center Way
Falls Church, VA
703-845-8155
www.oldnavy.com

Return Policy: Purchases with receipt may be returned within 90 days for full refund. Anytime thereafter, refund will be granted in the form of a gift card. Any items returned without receipt will be refunded on a gift card.

Old Navy is filled with adorable well-made basics great for everyday wear. The clothes are very well priced, so sale items are a virtual giveaway. Sizes run from preemie to 5T for both boys and girls. Customer service can be hit-or-miss.

★ POTTERY BARN KIDS

11301 Rockville Pike
North Bethesda, MD
301-231-5831

Fair Oaks Mall
11750 Fair Oaks
Fair Oaks, VA
703-934-4795

8084-L Tysons Corner Center
McLean, VA
703-356-2172
www.potterybarnkids.com

Return Policy: Items may be returned for up to 30 days after purchase for full refund.

In the past year Pottery Barn has expanded into yet another growing market by adding a line of baby and toddler clothing to its offerings. The cotton pastel-colored clothes are available for newborns up to age twenty-four months. For an extra $5, many of the items can be personalized, making great shower gifts. I found all of the clothes to be reasonably priced and the customer service was attentive and helpful.

★ PROPER TOPPER

1350 Connecticut Avenue, NW
Dupont Circle, DC
202-842-3055

3213 P Street, NW
Georgetown, DC
202-333-6200
www.propertopper.com

Return Policy: Returns may be made for store credit within 14 days of purchase.

The Proper Topper carries a very nice selection of baby clothes at both the Georgetown and Dupont locations. It carries Tea Collection, Sckoon, Zutano, Pluie Pluie, and Bobux for newborns to age twenty-four months. It is also a great place to find a cute gift for a shower or first birthday, as it has fun novelty baby gifts such as the Kidorable line of animal umbrellas and rain boots, animal finger puppets, and icky baby's line of burp cloths and lunch bags. Prices are moderate to high; customer service is excellent.

★ RALPH LAUREN

1245 Wisconsin Avenue, NW
Georgetown, DC
202-965-0905

5471A Wisconsin Avenue
Chevy Chase, MD
301-718-4223
www.polo.com

Return Policy: Returns with receipt must be made within 30 days for full refund.

Exchanges may be made for up to 60 days.

You could go crazy in the layette and baby section of this Chevy Chase flagship store. From heirloom-worthy christening gowns to gorgeous cashmere sweaters and monogrammed polos, my suppressed inner prepster comes out like a Tasmanian devil here. Prices are moderate to high for clothes for newborns through age sixteen, and I always find the customer service to be excellent. (I've received thank-you notes from salespeople . . . which I quickly hide from my husband.) One quick jaunt and your babe will be ready for cocktail hour at the Chevy Chase Club.

★ ROBCYNS

3660 King Street
Alexandria, VA
703-379-7800

Return Policy: Returns for store credit or exchange.

Robcyns carries a wide range of high-quality kids' clothing for boys and girls. Among the brands you'll find are Absorba, Le Top, Hartstrings, Zutano, Flap Happy, Healthtex, and Robeez.

★ TALBOTS KIDS

7101 Democracy Boulevard
Bethesda, MD
301-469-9761

7914 Tysons Corner Center
McLean, VA
703-442-4931

11741-L Fair Oaks Mall
Fair Oaks, VA
703-934-8360
www.talbots.com

Return Policy: No time limit on any exchanges
   or refunds.

Talbots Kids stores carry clothing of their own label
and design for newborns to seven-year-olds. The
sixty-year-old company offers a large selection of
well-made, reasonably priced coordinates for both
everyday play and special occasions. They have
some convincing Florence Eisman knockoffs for
about a third of the price. They are also a reliable
source for classic khakis and navy blazers for boys
as well as dress shirts, belts, ties, and loafers.

★ **TARGET**
   3101 Jefferson Davis Highway
   Alexandria, VA
   703-706-3840

   10301 New Guinea Road
   Fairfax, VA
   703-764-5100

   13047 Fair Lakes Shopping Center
   Fairfax, VA
   703-449-7100

   6100 Arlington Boulevard
   Falls Church, VA
   703-392-5630

12197 Sunset Hills Road
Reston, VA
703-478-0770

46201 Potomac Run Plaza
Sterling, VA
703-444-8440
www.target.com

Return Policy: Refund or exchange with receipt
   within 90 days.

Target has great prices on clothing and shoes for
toddlers. Brands include Graco, Carter's, and
Cosco. The drawback to this inexpensive chain is
that salespeople are few and far between.

★ **TICKLED PINK**
   103 South Saint Asaph Street
   Alexandria, VA
   703-518-5459

   7259 Woodmont Avenue
   Bethesda, MD
   301-913-9191
   www.tickledpinkapparel.com

   Return Policy: Items may be returned within 7
      days of receipt of merchandise. After the sev-
      enth day, merchandise can be exchanged for
      store credit. No returns after 14 days.

Tickled Pink offers the full line of Lilly Pulitzer
apparel, shoes, and accessories for men, women,
and children, as well as her home collection. In
addition, the store also carries kids' wear from
other lines, such as Tibi, Juicy Couture, Lacoste,
Shoshanna, Susana Monaco, Alice and Trixie, Laundry, CK Bradley, Nicole Miller, Julie Haus, Hanky
Panky, Kenneth Jay Lane and Sarah Briggs Jewelry,

Vineyard Vines, Eliza B, and Jack Rogers Shoes. Children's clothing starts at size twelve months.

★ **T.J. MAXX**
4350 Jenifer Street, NW
Friendship Heights, DC
202-237-7616

3504 South Jefferson Street
Falls Church, VA
703-578-3335

3451 Jefferson Davis Highway
Alexandria, VA
703-519-9420

8389 Leesburg Pike
Vienna, VA
703-893-2420

1776 East Jefferson Street
Rockville, MD
301-881-3857

7730 Richmond Highway
Alexandria, VA
703-781-3051

10300 Main Street
Fairfax, VA
703-352-0197

12170 Fairfax Towne Center
Fairfax County, VA
703-691-9030
www.tjmaxx.com
Return Policy: Items with tags still intact may be returned for full refund for up to 30 days after original purchase date.

Deeply discounted designer brands is what this large national retailer offers. For kids, there is clothing for newborns to preteen boys and girls from brands such as Ralph Lauren, Absorba, Tommy Hilfiger, and the like. Stores receive weekly shipments of new inventory so it's best to check back often—stock is constantly changing. In most of these stores, be prepared to roll up your sleeves and work for your savings as customer service and organizational skills seem to be a foreign concept.

★ **TREE TOP KIDS**
7505 Leesburg Pike
Falls Church, VA
703-356-0088

11895 Grand Commons Avenue
Fairfax, VA
703-815-2121

10219 Old Georgetown Road
Bethesda, VA
301-897-4940

11325 Seven Locks Road
Potomac, MD
301-299-8300

3301 New Mexico Avenue, NW
Wesley Heights, DC
202-244-3500

1382 Chain Bridge Road
McLean, VA
703-356-1400
www.treetopkids.com
Return Policy: Returns with receipt may be made within 2 weeks for full refund. Returns without receipt receive store credit.

Tree Top Kids stores carry clothes for newborns to twelve-year-olds. Everything from pajamas to play ensembles and party clothes can be found at this local boutique chain. What these stores lack in square footage they certainly make up for in the amount and variety of children's clothing offered. Kissy Kissy, Robeez, Bella Bella, Journey, Kate Mack, Lilly Pulitzer, Vive la Fête, and Urban Smalls are just a few of the lines from the extensive selection you'll find here. Prices are moderate to high.

★ WHY NOT?

200 King Street

Alexandria, VA

703-548-4420

Return Policy: Returns may be made within 7 days for full refund.

Since 1962 this store has been the trusted source among local families for unique imported and domestic infant and children's clothes. Sweet Potatoes, Spuds, and E.Land are just a few lines that may be found in the store's extensive clothing section. It also stocks a wide selection of books, board games, model trucks and trains, and other toys. The customer service could not be more helpful and friendly.

★ YIRO

3236 P Street, NW

Georgetown, DC

202-338-9476

www.yirostores.com

Return Policy: Items may be returned within 7 days of original purchase for full refund.

Yiro is the first organic children's clothing store to hit the retail scene in DC. Located in Georgetown,

the store carries fun and funky play and dress clothes from around the world. All items in the store—clothes, shoes, and toys—are chemical-free, and made with all-natural dyes and according to fair-trade practices. Sizes range from newborn to eight years for both boys and girls. Prices are moderate to high and customer service is attentive, especially when owner Grace is in the store.

Consignment Stores

★ ONCE UPON A CHILD

7692 Stream Walk Lane

Manassas, VA

703-257-5055

www.ouac.com

This national chain carries both new and gently used children's clothing, furniture, baby gear, books, and toys. If you are looking to sell things, Once Upon a Child is a great place to do it because it pays on the spot rather than requiring consigners to go through a waiting period of several months.

★ RED BEANS & RICE

4710 Fourteenth Street, NW

Downtown, DC

202-291-0337

www.redbeanchildren.com

Red Beans & Rice offers quality new and used children's clothes, toys, and books at affordable prices. Most of the clothes are either new with tags or very slightly used. The store carries new pieces from Mulberribush, Zutano, Flap Happy, eeBoo, Mudpuppy Press, Fun Bath, and Robeez, to name a few. On the consignment side, it has brand-name items from all the popular children's lines such as Ralph Lauren, Janie and Jack, DKNY, Hanna Andersson, and Lilly Pulitzer.

shoes

Buying your child's first walking shoes is an exciting and important task. First, it is important to take your child to a store where true "first walkers" are sold, and where you can get your child's foot properly measured. Because your one- or two-year-old can't tell you whether the shoes are comfortable, watch carefully as he or she is being fitted. If it seems difficult to get the shoes on and off, they are probably too small. Shoes should generally last at least two months; if they seem small three weeks after you bought them, go back and have them checked.

The salesperson at the shoe store should measure your child's foot while he is standing with his toes uncurled. Ask about the width of your child's foot and don't buy a shoe that narrows greatly at the toes. Also, look for a soft, flexible sole. A soft sole is necessary for the first year. After that, when your child is really walking and running, you can buy any shoe your heart desires. Although many of the children's clothing stores listed in this chapter also carry shoes, the following is a list of shoe stores that I recommend when buying baby's first pair of "walkers."

★ **BRADSHAW'S CHILDREN'S SHOES**
4532 Lee Highway
Arlington, VA
703-527-1546
Return Policy: Returns with receipt may be made for up to 14 days from original purchase. Items must be unworn and in original packaging.

Bradshaw's Children's Shoes has a wide selection of American and European shoes for first walkers, including ones from popular brand names such as Stride Rite, Ecco, Umi, Merrell, and Teva. It also carries girls' dress shoes up to size five and boys' dress shoes up to size seven.

★ **GUCCI**
5481 Wisconsin Avenue
Chevy Chase, MD
301-986-8902
www.gucci.com
Return Policy: Returns within 10 days of original purchase may be made for full refund. Anytime thereafter items may be returned for exchange or store credit.

Gucci Gucci Goo! It doesn't get any cuter than this. A bit of a splurge, I'll admit, but my friend Blaire cited a pair of Gucci loafers as one of the best baby presents she received and is having them nickel plated. (Bronzing them would be far too pedestrian.) From Mary Janes with Gucci's signature red and green accents to driving moccasins complete with horse bit, styles change seasonally, and prices usually start at around $195 a pair for sizes eight to twelve months. Although I wouldn't necessarily recommend Gucci specifically for first walkers, I couldn't resist adding the store to this section.

★ JEANNE'S SHOES

5110 Ridgefield Road

Bethesda, MD

301-654-3877

Return Policy: Returns may be made within 10 days of original purchase for full refund. Anytime thereafter unworn items in original packaging may be returned for store credit.

Jeanne's Shoes of Bethesda carries children's shoes for sizes infants and up. Brands stocked include Stride Rite, Nike, Adidas, Primigi, and Ecco among others.

★ NORDSTROM CHILDREN'S SHOE DEPARTMENT

7111 Democracy Boulevard

Bethesda, MD

301-365-4111

21090 Dulles Town Circle

Dulles, VA

571-434-4000

8075 Tysons Corner Center

McLean, VA

703-761-1121

1400 South Hayes Street

Arlington, VA

703-415-1121

www.nordstrom.com

Return Policy: Returns may be made for up to 90 days from original purchase for full refund, exchange or store credit.

Nordstrom's children's shoe department has an impressive selection of kids' shoes for newborns to teens. The store carries such brands as Stride Rite, Ecco, Puma, Primigi, and Jumping Jacks, just to name a few, along with their own private-label

shoes. Salespeople take their time, making thorough measurements.

★ OLLY SHOES

7702 B Richmond Highway

Alexandria, VA

703-717-0009

www.ollyshoes.com

Return Policy: Purchases with receipt may be returned for up to 30 days for full refund.

Olly Shoes is an international chain whose focus is on fit. It has a patented system that takes the unique measurement of each shoe and links it into software that allows salespeople to superimpose your child's foot inside the shoe. The store carries a very large selection of European and American brands, such as Primigi, Basically Barefoot, Umi, and Enzo.

★ RAMER'S SHOES

3810 Northampton Street, NW

Chevy Chase, MD

202-244-2288

Return Policy: Non-sale items that are unworn and with original receipt may be returned for full refund or exchange for up to 90 days.

You'll find brands such as Stride Rite, Keds, and Capezio through size four and a half here. Ramer's sets itself apart with its friendly and attentive service. Kids will love the toy box and the little piano.

★ SHOE TRAIN CHILDREN'S SHOES

11325 Seven Locks Road

Potomac, MD

301-299-9662

Return Policy: Purchases may be returned for up to 30 days for full refund. Anytime thereafter returns may be made for store credit.

If a company makes children's shoes, Shoe Train carries them. With literally hundreds of children's shoes to choose from, Potomac's Shoe Train is the place to go for the best overall selection in the area. From sizes for infants to teens, the store has it all.

★ **STRIDE RITE**

1100 South Hayes Street
Arlington, VA
703-418-0910

8075 Tysons Corner Center
McLean, VA
703-761-1121

118001 Fair Oaks Mall
Fairfax, VA
703-273-4170

7101 Democracy Boulevard
Bethesda, MD
301-469-7880
www.striderite.com

Return Policy: Shoes in original packaging may be returned within 30 days for full refund.

Stride Rite has been the leader in children's shoes for over eighty-five years. The company's focus has always been on engineering shoes to help support growing feet. Unfortunately, for many years its first walkers also looked like a cross between heinous orthopedics and Frankenstein shoes. However, recently the company has learned to marry superior function with great style. Children's shoes are carried in sizes zero through twelve.

your intrepid explorer: baby-proofing basics

Your home, once viewed as a safe haven from the perils and pitfalls of the outside world, can quickly emerge as a complete hazard zone once you have a baby living with you. In no time at all, every staircase, bookshelf, and electrical outlet is exactly where your little one will be heading. At this point you can either decide to redecorate with Gymboree flair, and replace every piece of furniture with padding in a primary-color palette, or you can take a few necessary precautions to protect your little inquiring mind from complete disaster.

In this chapter I provide some basic tips should you decide to baby-proof yourself, as well as the stores that carry the supplies you will need; I have also included companies that will come to your house, assess the situation, and baby-proof for you. Whichever route you take, your first step should be to visit the International Association for Child Safety website (www.iafcs.com). This website has the latest information on safety awareness and baby-proofing, and can also help you find IAFCS consultants in your area.

baby-proofing consultants

★ **BABY'S HOME SAFE HOME, INC.**
P.O. Box 396
Lutherville, MD 21094
410-308-BABY
www.babyproofinghelp.com

★ **CHILDREN'S SAFETY CARE, LLC**
243 Grangehall Drive
Gaithersburg, MD 20877
301-977-8334
www.childrenssafetycare.com

★ **SAFE START BABY**
35753 Roundleaf Court
Round Hill, VA 20141
888-240-7233
www.safestartbaby.com

diy tips

Many people baby proof their own homes, and there are good online resources that will guide you through the process. Babyguard (www.babyguard.com) is one that I'd recommend. Based out of McLean, Virginia, the site sells baby-proofing products with recommendations on how to keep every aspect of your baby's environment safe.

Another option is buying a book or video, such as *Mr. Baby Proofer*. This thirty-minute video shows parents how to create a safe environment for newborns. You can also ask for advice at any of the baby superstores, such as buy buy BABY. A salesperson will talk you through what you need in order to create a safe home.

Even if you don't officially "baby proof" your home—after all, we turned out okay and most of our parents didn't wrap rubber pads around every table—here are some basic safety tips to keep in mind:

★ Poisons or toxic materials (i.e., all cleaners) should not be stored under the sink; place them high up, out of baby's reach.

★ Attach all busy boxes, mirrors, and crib toys on the wall side of the crib, so that your baby cannot use the objects to climb out of the crib. Do not mount a wall hanging above the crib, where your child can pull it down and perhaps dislodge nails.

★ Toilet lids should be locked closed.

★ Keep all trash containers locked up and out of baby's way.

★ Remove tall lamps or coat racks, or block them with furniture, so that your baby can't pull them over.

★ When cooking, all pot handles should be turned inward so your baby cannot reach them. Use back burners when possible.

★ Separate plants and babies. Some plants are poisonous, and a young child may eat the leaves or pull the whole plant on top of himself.

★ Keep hanging cords from answering machines, phones, lamps, and appliances out of baby's reach.

★ Take pills or medication out of sight of children; they mimic what they see.

★ Remove all soaps, razors, and shampoos from the edge of the bathtub.

★ Use tape to secure electrical cords to walls, not tacks or staples, which can fall out or be pulled out and swallowed.

★ Discard plastic dry cleaner bags before entering the house. Babies can suffocate in them or pull off pieces and choke on them.

★ Keep emergency phone numbers, including the poison control center, near all telephones.

★ Use a foam grid padding beneath carpeting to prevent it from sliding.

* Place some glue inside the tips of doorstops, since babies like to pull them off. Then stick the cap back on the doorstop.

* Remove magnets from your refrigerator door. If they fall to the floor and break, a child may pick up the pieces and swallow them. Invest in baby magnets or plastic non-breakable ones.

* Place a piece of carpet or foam on the whole base of a fireplace, so your child won't bang into the brick.

* Get a bathtub spout cover to prevent your child from hitting his head against it.

* Keep the door of a home gym closed when you are not in it. Babies can get their fingers stuck in the spokes of exercise bikes, put their fingers in the gears, or pull weights onto themselves.

* Glass panels in coffee tables can break under the weight of a child. Replace with acrylic.

* Mobiles should be removed when a child is five to seven months old. A baby of that age can pull the mobile down or get injured if the little strings from the mobile become wrapped around his fingers.

* Cords for window blinds should be lifted high and out of reach. Babies can accidentally wrap cords around themselves.

* Wash out cleaning-fluid bottles before putting them in the recycling bin. Just a drop of cleaning fluid can cause serious injury to a baby.

* Never leave infants alone in the bathtub. Ignore telephone calls and doorbells; babies can drown in just an inch of water. Never leave a tub or any buckets or pails with water standing in them.

* Check the underside of upholstered furniture for loose staples or sharp points.

Chapter Ten

toys, toys, and more toys

These days I can't tell you what I did last Saturday night or who I talked to this morning, but my precious childhood memories are completely intact. My sister and I spent Saturday mornings with *The Smurfs*, *He-Man*, and *Thundercats* over a bowl of Pops. We played carpool, driving up and down our driveway on Big Wheels with our Cabbage Patch Dolls on the back. And to this day, I owe an incredibly steady hand to the ingenious game of Operation. Life was good. These playthings of our childhood are the tangibles of those early beginnings. So let's not underestimate the importance of toys for both you and your child. One of the best things about becoming a parent is getting to be that kid again.

You may or may not be surprised at how much toys have changed since you were a kid, and some of the old favorites are actually making a comeback right now. I mean, how could anyone actually improve on the Snoopy Sno-Cone Machine or the Slinky? Check out www.playthingspast.com for a trip down memory lane.

These days everybody weighs in on the educational value of toys. Magazines like *Parenting* and *Child* are good resources for finding out about the latest toys; if you want to be completely neurotic, check out consumer guides such as the Oppenheim Toy Portfolio as well. Each year it rates the best toys for every age group. The Consumer Products Safety Commission also recommends and rates toys on its website (www.cpsc.gov), as do Amazon.com and other toy websites.

Safety is also something to keep in mind. The Consumer Products Safety Commission requires manufacturers to recall any toy that it deems unsafe, and the manufacturer then notifies the retailers to pull any such toys from the shelves. You should always make sure that your toys have not been recalled. You can do so by calling the CPSC hotline at 800-638-2772 or checking its website (www.cpsc.gov). Most stores will post any recall information at the checkout counter. Some pediatricians do the same.

Toy stores fall into the same categories as other stores: There are chain stores and independent stores. The chains generally have better prices and more lenient return policies, but the independent stores often carry more unique toys and provide you with more personalized service. Many neighborhood toy stores are good for gifts and provide gift wrapping. Don't forget to check the Internet, especially Amazon.com, which includes Toysrus.com and Imaginarium.com. It's a great place to shop for toys, especially when you know exactly what you are looking for. But beware of buying bulky items online, because the shipping charges can be hefty.

the stores

★ ANGLO DUTCH POOLS AND TOYS

5460 Westbard Avenue

Bethesda, MD

301-951-0636

www.anglodutchpoolsandtoys.com

Return Policy: Unopened items with receipt may be returned for full refund for up to 15 days from original purchase date.

This store was established in 1985 as a pool-supply company. Soon after, it began carrying water toys; land toys followed shortly after this. Twenty years later, it still has a reputation of aiming to please, offering wonderful personalized service and stocking pretty much every toy imaginable.

★ BARSTON'S CHILD'S PLAY

5536 Connecticut Avenue, NW

Chevy Chase, DC

202-244-3602

www.barstonschildsplay.com

Return Policy: Items with receipt may be returned for full refund for up to 2 weeks. Items with no receipt may be returned for store credit.

Barston's Child's Play is not your average toy store. Children of all ages will enjoy the wide range of books, music, arts and crafts, and costumes that pack the shelves. The store also carries a huge selection of trains, puzzles, and games. The store has plenty of informed staffpeople, who are actually willing to help you.

★ BRUCE VARIETY

6922 Arlington Road

Bethesda, MD

301-656-7543

Return Policy: Items with receipt may be returned for up to 7 days from purchase date.

This five-and-dime-type store seems old-fashioned, but you can find all those trinkets and household items that no one else has. The offerings at this fun and quirky store change frequently, but it always has an aisle or two of toys for a good cross-section of ages. The prices are reasonable and the staff is quick to help you find what you need.

★ BUY BUY BABY

1683 Rockville Pike

Rockville, MD

301-984-1123

6398 Springfield Plaza

Springfield, VA

703-932-9797

www.buybuybaby.com

Return Policy: Returns for full refund may be made for up to 30 days from original purchase date.

Buy buy BABY is a baby superstore. It has the same look and feel as a Babies "R" Us or Great Beginnings, but I find the service is far superior and the salespeople are very knowledgeable. Toy selection is small compared to those at other large chains, but it is well-edited, and you are guaranteed to leave with something for everyone on your list.

CRADLE & CRAYON

Reston Town Center
11913 Freedom Drive
Reston, VA
703-437-0900
www.cradleandcrayon.com

Return Policy: Full refund on items returned within 14 days of purchase. Anytime thereafter, items can be exchanged or returned for store credit only.

Cradle & Crayon carries a small but worthwhile selection of toys and gifts. The infant and toddler lines of toys are Haba, Alex, Bunnies by the Bay, Cloud B, and Little Giraffe, among others. The boutique's friendly staff is eager to assist, and oftentimes it's the store's owners themselves who offer helpful suggestions.

CURIOSITY ZONE

43135 Broadlands Center Plaza
Ashburn, VA
703-723-9949
www.curiosityzone.com

Return Policy: Purchases in original packaging and with receipt may be returned at any time.

In addition to being the incredible hands-on science center for kids, The Curiosity Zone also has a fabulous toy store featuring high-quality, hard-to-find educational toys that kids love, at surprisingly reasonable prices. You can purchase gift certificates over the phone, which are then mailed to you, and there is free gift wrapping with in-store purchases.

DANCING BEAR TOYS & GIFTS

12 North Market Street
Frederick, MD
301-631-9300
www.dbeartoys.com

Return Policy: Unopened items may be returned for full refund or store credit for up to a year.

This specialty store stands out from other toy stores by stocking unique toys from all over the world. The shelves are lined with wonderful handmade toys, classic toys, and games. They also carry music and instruments for children, as well as puppets, books and puzzles.

DOODLEHOPPER 4 KIDS

228 West Broad Street
Falls Church, VA
703-241-2262

7521 Huntsman Boulevard
Springfield, VA
703-912-7200
www.huntsmandoodlehopper.com

Return Policy: Items with receipt may be returned for store credit up to 2 weeks after original purchase.

Doodlehopper 4 Kids has an impressive roster of toys, in addition to its vast selection of children's clothing and books. The store caters to children from ages newborn to ten, offering everything from baby's first set of blocks to puzzles and crafts for older children. Staffpeople are very helpful and knowledgeable.

★ **FAIR DAY'S PLAY**

7050 Carroll Avenue

Takoma Park, MD

301-270-4999

Return Policy: Unopened and undamaged items with receipt may be returned for full refund at any time. Unopened and undamaged items without receipt may be returned for store credit at any time.

Fair Day's Play provides fun, unusual, and top-quality games, toys, puzzles, and books. It carries one of the largest selections of wooden toys in the area, and a large number of its products are fair trade and union or domestically made.

★ **FAIRY GODMOTHER**

318 Seventh Street, SE

Capitol Hill, DC

202-547-5474

Return Policy: Undamaged items may be exchanged or returned for store credit.

Located in a historic house, this small store is filled with classic toys and books. Collectibles include Steiff and Madame Alexander dolls and accessories. It has a wonderful selection of English, French, and Spanish literature, plus educational CDs, DVDs, audiotapes, arts-and-crafts kits, puppets, and more.

★ **IMAGINATION STAGE GIFT SHOP**

4908 Auburn Avenue

Bethesda, MD

301-280-1660

301-961-6060 (Box Office)

www.imaginationstage.com

Return Policy: Items with tags intact and with receipt may be returned for full refund for up to 14 days from original purchase date.

Imagination Stage is known for its theater productions, from modern pieces to classics and commissioned originals, performed year-round in the four-hundred-seat Lerner Family Theatre. It also offers a wide range of classes and camps for children and teens interested in drama, music, and dance. However, an often-overlooked treasure of this place is the Just Imagine Gift Shop, packed with imaginative gifts both large and small, including dress-up costumes, toys, books, and much more.

★ **KB TOYS**

21800 Dulles Town Center Drive

Dulles, VA

703-406-7847

Fair Oaks Mall

11750 Fair Oaks

Fairfax, VA

703-591-6007

8661 Colesville Raod

Silver Spring, MD

301-563-6862

www.kbtoys.com

Return Policy: Any toy in its original condition may be returned for full refund up to 30 days from original purchase.

These superstores are filled with just about every brand-name toy imaginable. They also carry furniture lines and party supplies from all of the Disney shows. Staffpeople can be helpful but at times can also be a challenge to locate.

★ **KINDER HAUS TOYS**

1220 North Fillmore Street

Arlington, VA

703-527-5929

www.kinderhaus.com

Return Policy: Unopened toys with receipt may be returned for refund up to 14 days from original purchase.

This independently owned toy store—the sister store to the Imagination Station bookstore—offers kids a virtual sensory overload with its floor-to-ceiling shelves packed with toys. From name brands such as Mattel and Lego to handcrafted wooden toys and puppets, Kinder Haus offers it all. The new store has an additional play area to keep little ones occupied while parents shop. They also offer free gift-wrapping.

★ **NATIONAL GEOGRAPHIC STORE AT EXPLORERS HALL**

1145 Seventeenth Street, NW

Downtown, DC

202-857-7591

www.shop.nationalgeographic.com

Return Policy: Any purchase may be returned for full refund or store credit.

The National Geographic store carries very cool educational toys. It carries its own line under the National Geographic name, as well as other lesser-known brands. This is a great place to find that special gift for the kid who has it all.

★ **NOODLES & NOGGINS**

7145 Main Street

Clifton, VA

703-815-8600

www.noodlesandnoggins.com

Return Policy: Items with tags intact and with receipt may be returned for full credit up to 45 days from original purchase date.

Somewhat off the beaten track but worth the trip, Noodles & Noggins carries interesting, fun toys, as well as games and books for kids of all ages. The store also hosts in-store concerts for children by local musicians such as Rocknoceros and The Banjo Man. Gift wrapping is free.

★ **SULLIVAN'S TOYS**

3412 Wisconsin Avenue, NW

Cleveland Park, DC

202-362-1343

Return Policy: Unopened items may be returned for store credit.

Considering Sullivan's relatively small space on Wisconsin Avenue, it packs a punch. Bins brim with knickknacks, dress-up clothes, and accessories, books, movies, party supplies, craft projects, and toys for every child on your list. An entire room is dedicated to the serious artist. Gift wrapping is free.

★ **TOYS "R" US**

6001 Kingstowne Village

Alexandria, VA

703-922-4968

11810 Rockville Pike

Rockville, MD

301-770-3376

13035 Fairlakes Parkway
Fairfax, VA
703-803-1050

46300 Potomac Run Plaza
Sterling, VA
703-404-8697
www.toysrus.com

Return Policy: Purchases may be returned up to 30 days from original purchase date. Refunds are issued in the form of original payment.

A national chain for over sixty years, Toys "R" Us has an impressive assortment of toys, games, sporting goods, electronics, software, baby products, children's apparel, and juvenile furniture. However, the great selection doesn't necessarily guarantee the same quality of service.

★ **TREE TOP KIDS**
7505 Leesburg Pike
Falls Church, VA
703-356-0088

11895 Grand Commons Avenue
Fairfax, VA
703-815-2121

10219 Old Georgetown Road
Bethesda, MD
301-897-4940

11325 Seven Locks Road
Potomac, MD
301-299-8300

3301 New Mexico Avenue, NW
Wesley Heights, DC
202-244-3500

1382 Chain Bridge Road
McLean, VA
703-356-1400
www.treetopkids.com

Return Policy: Returns with receipt may be made within 2 weeks for full refund. Returns without receipt may receive store credit.

Tree Top Kids has an impressive array of quality toys from all of the high-end brands. From books to collectible trains and trucks, costumes, tricycles, and outdoor play yards, Tree Top Kids truly has something to suit every interest in the family. Staff-people are incredibly friendly and offer helpful recommendations based on age and interests. The stores also host free events, from story times to musicians and entertainers for children.

★ **TUGOOH TOYS**
1419 B Wisconsin Avenue, NW
Georgetown, DC
202-333-0032

Tugooh Toys is a long overdue addition to the many stores popping up in Georgetown geared towards the neighborhood's youngest shoppers. Tugooh is the sister store to Yiro, the organic children's clothing store across the street, and store owner Grace hits another home run offering products that are fun, educational, and environment friendly. Toys for children ages newborn through eight are offered, from mobiles and playmats to kitchen sets, building blocks, and bikes. This small Georgetown gem packs a big punch.

★ **WHY NOT?**

200 King Street

Alexandria, VA

703-548-4420

Return Policy: Returns may be made within 7 days of purchase for full refund.

At Why Not? moms and dads can find top-of-the-line toys for infants and toddlers. Brands include North American Bear Co., Fisher-Price, Doudou et Compagnie, and Corolle. The store stocks a wide selection of books, board games, and model trucks and trains. Staffpeople are helpful and attentive, and there is a large playpen area downstairs with a train set and play kitchen to keep kids safely occupied while parents shop.

bookstores

DC babies and their parents love city bookstores! Together they can listen to stories, pick out videos and CDs, and, best of all, discover the joys of reading. This multimedia universe is one of the most exciting aspects of baby culture today. In every case, talented writers, artists, and musicians are creating lasting treasures for your children. And these days it seems like every celebrity has lent her or his name to a children's book. Madonna? I certainly didn't see that one coming.

This section lists the best children's bookstores in DC, including places where you and your toddler can listen to a reading of his or her favorite book. I have listed all of the major chain stores, as well as the best independent bookstores in town. Also, don't forget your local public library. The DC metro area's expansive public library systems are a great way to introduce your child to the wonder of children's books. The branches offer many services for children, including book readings, puppet shows, and short films. Check out dclibrary.org or publiclibraries.com for Maryland and Virginia.

the stores

❋ Indicates stores with story time for toddlers. Call for updated schedules.

★ **ALADDIN'S LAMP CHILDREN'S BOOKS** ❋
2499 North Harrison Street, Suite 10
Arlington, VA
703-241-8281
Story Time: Wednesday, Friday, Saturday
Aladdin's Lamp Children's Books has been locally owned and operated for more than seventeen years and has a loyal customer following of both children and parents alike. The store's shelves are stocked with the best children's books, and it hosts story time, workshops, and visiting authors. Regularly scheduled story-time hours are Fridays at 11 A.M. with the very popular Miss Jenny, for children ages eighteen months to three years, and Wednesdays and Saturdays at 11 A.M., with a special guest or a staffperson, for ages two and a half to six.

★ **BARNES & NOBLE** ❋
3040 M Street, NW
Georgetown, DC
202-965-9880
Story Time: Wednesday, Friday

3651 Jefferson Davis Highway
Alexandria, VA
703-299-9124
Story Time: Tuesday, Saturday

4801 Bethesda Avenue
Bethesda, MD
301-986-1761
Story Time: Monday, Tuesday

12193 Fair Lakes Promenade Drive
Fairfax, VA
703-278-0300
Story Time: Monday, Friday

555 Twelfth Street, NW
Downtown, DC
202-347-0176
Story Time: Tuesday

2800 Clarendon Boulevard
Arlington, VA
703-248-8244
Story Time: Wednesday, Saturday

6260 Seven Corners Center
Falls Church, VA
703-536-0774
Story Time: Tuesday, Thursday

12089 Rockville Pike
Rockville, MD
301-881-0237
Story Time: Wednesday, Saturday

7851-L Tysons Corner Center
McLean, VA
703-506-2937
Story Time: Wednesday, Saturday

1851 Fountain Drive
Reston, VA
703-437-9490
Story Time: Wednesday, Saturday
www.bn.com

You will never find children's books and videos in short supply at Barnes & Noble. Items are often deeply discounted, and don't forget to check the clearance tables for incredible savings. Most Barnes & Noble stores have regular story times for children. I have listed the days for regular story times for each store, but you should call ahead to confirm the schedule.

★ **BARSTON'S CHILD'S PLAY**
5536 Connecticut Avenue, NW
Chevy Chase, DC
202-244-3602

1661 Rockville Pike
Rockville, MD
301-230-9040
www.barstonschildsplay.com

Beyond the fantastic toy store it is known to be, Barston's Child's Play carries a large selection of books for children aged six months to fifteen years. Whether you are in search of the literary classics or the newest adventure from J. K. Rowling, Barston's stores stock shelves for readers of all stages and interests. The stores have plenty of informed staffpeople on hand who can provide advice.

★ **BORDERS** ❋

600 Fourteenth Street, NW
Downtown, DC
202-737-1385

Eighteenth and L streets, NW
Downtown, DC
202-466-4999

5333 Wisconsin Avenue, NW
Friendship Heights, DC
202-686-8270

1201 Hayes Street
Arlington, VA
703-418-0166

8518 Fenton Street
Silver Spring, MD
301-585-0550
Story Time and Sing-along: Wednesday

11301 Rockville Pike
Kensington, MD
301-816-1067
Story Time: Tuesday

534 North Frederick Avenue
Gaithersburg, MD
301-921-0990
Story Time: Wednesday

8027 Leesburg Pike
Vienna, VA
703-556-7766
Mr. Knick Knack Story Time: Saturday

11054 Lee Highway
Fairfax, VA
703-359-8420
Story Time: Tuesday, Saturday

5871 Crossroads Center Way
Falls Church, VA
703-998-0404
Tiny Tots Story Time: Tuesday

Thomas Avenue and Abingdon Road
Arlington, VA
703-416-1590
www.borders.com

Borders stores have great children's departments with almost any book your little one might want, as well as small tables and areas where they can sit and read. Like Barnes & Noble, Borders has everything: a cafe, the latest magazines, and books for the entire family.

★ **CANDIDA'S WORLD OF BOOKS**

1541 Fourteenth Street, NW
Downtown, DC
202-667-4811
866-667-4811
www.candidasworldofbooks.com

Candida's World of Books is an independent bookstore located in Logan Circle that specializes in foreign-language material. In addition to books in more than fifteen languages, they also offer Rough Guide world-music CDs, journals, and language learning. The children's book department carries original, bilingual, and major-language translations.

★ DANCING BEAR TOYS & GIFTS

12 North Market Street
Frederick, MD
301-631-9300
www.dbeartoys.com

In addition to featuring unique playthings from around the world, this specialty store carries a wonderful selection of children's books. With an emphasis on customer service and plenty of hands-on opportunities for young toy testers, Dancing Bear is a welcome destination for all ages.

★ DOODLEHOPPER 4 KIDS

228 West Broad Street
Falls Church, VA
703-241-2262

7521 Huntsman Boulevard
Springfield, VA
703-912-7200
www.huntsmandoodlehopper.com

In addition to toys, Doodlehopper 4 Kids also offers a wide array of books. Everything from Mother Goose classics to the newest works on the kid-lit scene line the well-stocked shelves, calling to bookworms of all ages. The staffpeople are knowledgeable and helpful, and gift wrapping is free.

★ FAIRY GODMOTHER

318 Seventh Street, SE
Capitol Hill, DC
202-547-5474

Located in a historic house, this small store is filled with classic toys and books. There is a wonderful selection of English, French, and Spanish literature, plus educational CDs, DVDs, audiotapes, arts-and-crafts kits, puppets, and more.

★ IMAGINATION STAGE GIFT SHOP

4908 Auburn Avenue
Bethesda, MD
301-961-6060
301-280-1660 (Box Office)
www.imaginationstage.org

Imagination Stage is known for its theater productions, from modern pieces to classics and commissioned originals, performed year-round in the four-hundred-seat Lerner Family Theatre. The often-overlooked treasure trove is the Just Imagine Gift Shop, packed with great gifts. In addition to fun costumes and toys, it has a wonderful selection of books, including children's classics and Imagination Stage originals.

★ IMAGINATION STATION ❋

4524 Lee Highway
Arlington, VA
703-522-2047
Story Time: Tuesday, Friday
www.kinderhaus.com/imagine.html

Imagination Station, sister store of Kinder Haus Toys in the Lee Heights Shops, is a small, independently owned bookstore specializing in children's selections. Authors and book characters often visit the store.

★ KARIBU BOOKS ❋

15624 Emerald Way
Bowie, MD
301-352-4110

3500 East-West Highway
Hyattsville, MD
301-559-1140

3283 Donell Drive
Forestville, MD
301-736-8853

3817 Branch Avenue
Hilcrest Heights, MD
301-899-3730

Pentagon City Mall
South Hayes and South Fifteenth streets
Arlington, VA
703-415-1118
www.karibubooks.com

Locally owned and operated since 1993, Karibu Books is a specialty bookstore chain dedicated to providing books by and about people of African descent. Karibu carries more than eight thousand titles including a large selection of children's books. KaribuKIDS is a story time featuring games, performances, and special guests; it takes place every third Saturday of the month at the Bowie Town Center location.

★ KRAMERBOOKS & AFTERWORDS

1517 Connecticut Avenue, NW
Dupont Circle, DC
202-387-1400
www.kramers.com

Serving up good food and books since 1976, Kramerbooks is a local institution. I wouldn't classify this as a children's bookstore, but it has a decent selection of books for the little ones, and with plenty of places to sit, eat, read, and hang out, the atmosphere is definitely kid-friendly. It's got generous hours, from 7:30 A.M.–1:30 A.M.

★ LAKESHORE LEARNING STORE

7009-A Manchester Boulevard
Alexandria, VA
703-719-0202
www.lakeshorelearning.com

This education-focused supply store is a favorite among teachers and parents, as well as kids. The store is full of arts-and-crafts supplies, educational toys and games, and music for kids. In addition, it has a large selection of educational books for children of all ages.

★ A LIKELY STORY ❉

1555 King Street
Alexandria, VA
703-836-2498
www.alikelystorybooks.com

Story Time: Monday, Wednesday and Friday mornings

Named one of the best children's bookstores in the country by *Child* magazine, and a recipient of the 2006 Women's National Book Association's Pannell Award, A Likely Story strives to provide parents and children with a large selection of quality children's literature. Throughout the year, the store hosts book signings, costumed characters, story times, and other events for children. Regular story times are held in the morning, and there is a large selection of summer camps for children ages three and up.

★ NOODLES & NOGGINS

7145 Main Street
Clifton, VA
703-815-8600
www.noodlesandnoggins.com

Somewhat off the beaten track and known more for its impressive selection of educationally challenging games and activities, Noodles & Noggins also has a small selection of books for children ages one to eight.

★ **OLSSON'S BOOKS & RECORDS**

1307 Nineteenth Street, NW
Downtown, DC
202-285-1133
202-785-2662

418 Seventh Street, NW
Downtown, DC
202-638-7610

106 South Union Street
Alexandria, VA
703-684-0077
703-684-0030

2111 Wilson Boulevard
Arlington, VA
703-525-4227
703-525-3507

Reagan Washington National Airport,
  Terminal C
Arlington, VA
703-525-4227
703-525-3507

2200-G Crystal Drive
Arlington, VA
703-413-8121
www.olssons.com

Olsson's Books & Records is DC's oldest independent book and music store. Each of the six DC metro stores features a well-edited selection of books and music from a wide range of genres. There are wonderful selections of children's literature, both new and classic, and the cafes are nice places to peruse your findings over some tasty treats.

★ **POLITICS & PROSE** ❋

5015 Connecticut Avenue, NW
Chevy Chase, DC
202-364-1919
Story Time: Monday
www.politics-prose.com

On any given Monday morning one will find a virtual parking lot of strollers outside of this favorite local book haven. Politics & Prose has an incredible children's section, and its Monday morning story time is a hot ticket for the four-and-under set. There is always something of interest happening, from book signings to special appearances by kids' entertainers. Don't forget to check out the cafe in the back.

★ **RIVERBY BOOKS**

417 East Capitol Street, SE
Capitol Hill, DC
202-543-4342
www.riverbybooks.com

This store specializes in used books, with a selection of over twenty-five thousand volumes; there's always a large selection for children. The store is very kid-friendly; free tea and cookies are served every day at 4:30 P.M.

★ SECOND STORY BOOKS

12160 Parklawn Drive
Rockville, MD
301-770-0477

4914 Fairmont Avenue
Bethesda, MD
301-656-0170

2000 P Street, NW
Downtown, DC
202-659-8884
www.secondstorybooks.com

Second Story Books, which has more than a million books at its three DC locations, is a great source for used and rare books. These stores have a good selection of children's books, both classic and recently published.

★ SULLIVAN'S TOYS

3412 Wisconsin Avenue, NW
Cleveland Park, DC
202-362-1343

Considering the relatively small space this store occupies on Wisconsin Avenue, Sullivan's packs a punch with a bounty of great toys and activities for children. A small selection of books in the back of the store warrants mention as well. Gift wrapping is free.

★ TREE TOP KIDS

7505 Leesburg Pike
Falls Church, VA
703-356-0088

11895 Grand Commons Avenue
Fairfax, VA
703-815-2121

10219 Old Georgetown Road
Bethesda, MD
301-897-4940

11325 Seven Locks Road
Potomac, MD
301-299-8300

3301 New Mexico Avenue, NW
Wesley Heights, DC
202-244-3500

1382 Chain Bridge Road
McLean, VA
703-356-1400
www.treetopkids.com

Tree Top Kids has an impressive array of children's books, with a focus on the classics. Staffpeople are friendly and offer helpful recommendations based on your child's age and interests. There are always lineups of free events, including story times, and children's musicians and entertainers.

★ WHY NOT?

200 King Street
Alexandria, VA
703-548-4420

At Why Not? moms and dads can find a wide selection of books for children. Staffpeople are helpful and attentive, and there is a large playpen area downstairs with a train set and play kitchen to keep kids safely occupied while parents shop.

part three

ENJOYING YOUR DC BABY:
everywhere you need to go

classes, play spaces, and other indoor activities

As your child grows, she is going to learn to run, jump, tumble, sing songs, and scribble pictures all on her own. But classes can help her develop social skills, learn how to function in groups, and be disciplined, among other skills. Above all, children have fun in these programs, and you will, too. Plus, it's nice to have some places to go during the winter.

All the places and programs listed here offer classes for children ages three and under, and in some cases, babies as young as three months are invited. However, you and your child will probably find an organized class more enjoyable if she is able to sit up on her own and actually be awake, so it's a good idea to wait until your baby is at least six to nine months old before signing up. I'll also say this: No matter how often they sterilize these places, kids are like walking petri dishes of germs, and when they get together in a large group the germs are passed around. Be ready for your little one to pick up what's going around. This is one more reason to wait until he or she is at least six months old before starting a class.

Here are a few things to think about as you decide on programs:

★ Take a trial class or attend an open house before you sign up. You may have to pay for it, but you'll have a better sense of what you are getting into.

★ Choose classes with children the same age as your own.

★ Look for big, open, clean rooms with plenty of space and light, accessible by elevator or ramp. You do not want to walk up five flights of stairs carrying your baby, diaper bag, and stroller.

★ Check equipment provided: It should be scaled down to small-child size, and any gymnastic-type facilities should include lots of mats and other safety features.

★ Ask about class sizes: Small to medium-size groups are best. But do not be too concerned if the class is very big on the first day; all participants don't show up every week. Illnesses, naps, and vacations normally account for a quarter of a class being absent in any given week.

★ The teacher makes all the difference and some are definitely better than others. The other children and their mothers and nannies also can affect the atmosphere of a class. If you are the only mom in attendance, for example, you may feel awkward spending time with ten nannies every Thursday afternoon at 2 P.M. (You can always ask to switch to a class with more moms.)

★ Location is important. Enroll in a class near your home, and remember that you will be pushing a stroller. If it's less than ten blocks away, you will be more likely to actually go and to make it there on time.

Prices and schedules change almost every semester, so call ahead for the latest information. Classes often run in sessions of ten or twenty weeks; prices vary widely, from free story times to $1,000 for a semester of language classes.

Here are recommended classes and programs in the DC metro area:

classes and play spaces

★ **ABRAKADOODLE**

Corporate Headquarters:
1800 Robert Fulton Drive
Reston, VA
703-860-6574
www.abrakadoodle.com

Jan Holland-Chatman
DC/Montgomery County
202-636-4020
http://www.abrakadoodle.com/dc01.html
Jholland-chapman@abrakadoodle.com

Susan Walia
Fairfax County
703-760-0767
http://www.abrakadoodle.com/va01.html
SWalia@abrakadoodle.com

David and Georgia Edwards
Loudon County
703-443-0527
http://www.abrakadoodle.com/franchise_04018.html
DEdwards@abrakadoodle.com

Ages: 20 months to 12 years

Abrakadoodle is an organization that was founded by a group of educators and focuses on art education for children. Offered are a range of classes for children twenty months to twelve years old. The Twoosy Doodlers class is for children twenty to thirty-six months old. Children and their caregivers experiment with paints, papers, glues, and a variety of materials and ideas in art exploration. Mini Doodlers is for children three through six years old. Children develop their creative sides through carefully designed lessons that spark the imagination, inspire creativity, and teach skills. Classes are usually four to six weeks, and cost $35–$48 per session, on average.

★ ART IN HAND
Julie Liddle
703-264-0407
www.artinhand.org
JALiddle@cox.net
Ages: 18 months to 5 years

Founded by a registered art therapist, Art in Hand offers fun ways to introduce creativity through art. Classes are designed for toddlers (eighteen months through three years old) and preschoolers (three-and-a-half to five years old). Classes are designed to be fun but with an emphasis on enhancing children's emotional growth; stimulating brain development and skill acquisition (language and emergent literacy, problem-solving, fine motor and social skills); promoting sensory integration; and including parents in the creative process.

★ ARTWORKS FINE ART STUDIO
7847 Old Georgetown Road
Bethesda, MD
301-656-0044

416 Main Street
Gaithersburg, MD
301-330-2055
www.artworksclasses.com
Ages: 3 to 12 years

Artworks Fine Art Studio teaches children the fundamentals of drawing and painting, step by step. Preschoolers begin by learning basic drawing and pastel techniques, then can move on to watercolors and oils.

★ BABY BALLERINA
22360 South Sterling Boulevard
Sterling, VA
703-430-3033
www.babyballerina.net
Ages: 1 to 6 years

Baby Ballerina nurtures children's imaginations and fosters self-confidence and creativity through dance. The studio offers tumbling, tap, ballet, and jazz, and recitals are held throughout the year, including a Baby Nutcracker at Christmas. There is a weeklong Summer Princess Camp Program for two- to six-year-olds, with dance, crafts, and a performance at the end of the week.

★ BABY SIGNS BY MAUREEN
17511 Redland Road
Derwood, MD
240-447-3152
www.funfit.us

1234 Ingleside Avenue
McLean, VA
240-447-3152
www.mcleancenter.org

2450 Lyttonsville Road
Silver Spring, MD
240-447-3152

4301 Willow Lane
Chevy Chase, MD
240-447-3152
www.montgomerycountymd.gov/rec

11931 Seven Locks Road
Potomac, MD
240-447-3152
www.babysignsbymaureen.com
Ages: 6 months to 2 years
In Baby Signs classes, babies can learn to communicate even before they can talk. Over the course of six fun-filled sessions, parent and child (six months through two years old) learn forty of the most common signs in the context of playful songs, games, and activities.

★ **BALLET PETITE**
4701 Sangamore Road
Bethesda, MD

367 Main Street
Gaithersburg, MD

11325 Seven Locks Road
Potomac, MD

837-D Rockville Pike
Rockville, MD

301-229-6882 (all locations)
www.balletpetite.com
Ages: 18 months to 6 years
Ballet Petite offers an extensive list of dance and movement classes at studios around the DC Metro area that integrate costumes, props, and books. And don't let the word "ballet" dissuade you from enrolling a testosterone-filled boy. I can vouch that Connor thoroughly enjoyed dressing up as a knight and growling at the girls dressed as princesses. (Though the fairly structured environment did have him bouncing off the walls by the end of the forty-five-minute class.) For the littlest ones (eighteen to twenty-four months), there is Baby Dance, in which parents use motion and touch to stimulate their babies' sense of movement and music. Six-week sessions cost from $240–$350. Advanced registration is a must.

★ **BLACK ROCK CENTER FOR THE ARTS**
12901 Town Commons Drive
Germantown, MD
301-528-2260
www.blackrockcenter.org
Ages: 3 and up
Black Rock Center for the Arts has several theaters, and features different music, dance, and theater performances each season. The extensive education program includes classes and summer camps for children ages three and up. Piano lessons, hip-hop, ballet, and drama are just a few of its offerings. Of note are their classes for children with developmental disabilities.

★ **CAPITOL HILL ARTS WORKSHOP**
545 Seventh Street, SE
Capitol Hill, DC
202-547-6839
www.chaw.org
Ages: 6 months and up
Capitol Hill Arts Workshop (CHAW) offers classes in visual arts, dance, music, and drama, as well as tumbling and tae kwon do. There is a very popular Mommy and Me music class for toddlers based on the Kindermusik curriculum (see page 136).

★ THE CENTER FOR BALLET ARTS

11215 H, J, K Lee Highway
Fairfax, VA
703-273-5344
www.thecenterforballetarts.com
Ages: 3 and up

The Center for Ballet Arts offers dance classes for the entire family, starting with Kinderballet for three-year-olds up to advanced levels in ballet, modern, tap, jazz, and flamenco. Classes are designed to promote flexibilty and strength as well as technique; Pilates and yoga are offered too. Annual performances include a fall concert and *The Nutcracker* in December.

★ THE CENTER FOR MUSIC, MOVEMENT, AND ART

St. John's Episcopal Church
6701 Wisconsin Avenue
Bethesda, MD
301-251-1524
301-251-1148
www.centerformusic.org
Ages: infant and up

The Center for Music, Movement, and Art offers classes in—you guessed it—music, movement, and art. Classes incorporating the philosophies, curricula, and materials of established programs such as Music Together, Kindermusik, Musikgarten, and Suzuki, are offered in a warm, nurturing environment. Classes are offered for infants and up accompanied by a caregiver, and include Musical Baby, Family Music Time/Musical Beginnings, Imagine That!, Instrumental Exploration, and Keyboard.

★ CENTRE DE DANSE

3254 Prospect Street, NW
Georgetown, DC
202-337-0268
202-365-8576
www.centrededanse.info
Ages: 3 and up

Centre de Danse is a ballet studio located in the heart of Georgetown. Theresa Kramer, the director, danced professionally for thirteen years before opening the school in 1983. Her studio offers classes for boys and girls ages three and up. Most children's classes are offered in the afternoon, and prices start at $17 for a single class. Classes run from September through June.

★ THE CHEVY CHASE COMMUNITY CENTER

5601 Connecticut Avenue, NW
Chevy Chase, DC
202-282-2204
Ages: 6 months and up

The Chevy Chase Community Center offers a seemingly endless list of different classes for the entire family from sports like basketball and fencing to crafts such as sewing, pottery, and animation. Among its offerings for toddlers and preschoolers are karate, tumbling, Music Together, Toddler Spanish, ballet, and art. There is also a popular summer camp.

★ THE CITYDANCE CENTER AT STRATHMORE

5301 Tuckerman Lane
North Bethesda, MD
301-581-5204
www.citydance.net
Ages: 2 and up

The CityDance Center at Strathmore offers a large selection of dance classes that give children—and adults—plenty of opportunities to get moving. From classic ballet to modern and African dance, there is truly something for everyone here.

★ **CLASSIC TALES 'N TUNES**

3210 King Street
Alexandria, VA

1415 South Queen Street
Arlington, VA

5722 Lee Highway
Arlington, VA

300 North Park Drive
Arlington, VA

223 Little Falls Street
Falls Church, VA

703-848-9808 (all locations)
info@classictnt.com
www.classictnt.com
Ages: 18 months and up

Classic Tales 'n Tunes is a fun program that fosters language, cognitive, social, and motor skills through activities such as shared reading, making music, creative movement, and play. Each lesson has a theme, and all of the music and literature of the day relates back to it. Classes are small and instruction is differentiated to challenge each child at his or her own level. Some Spanish and American Sign Language are blended into the curriculum. Classes are designed primarily for children eighteen months to under five years old. Each session runs quarterly and includes a set number of weekly forty-five-minute classes.

★ **COMMUNIKIDS LANGUAGE SCHOOL FOR CHILDREN**

Wisconsin Avenue Baptist Church
3920 Alton Place, NW
Tenley, DC
202-363-0133
www.communikids.com
Ages: 1 to 8

CommuniKids offers total language immersion classes for children in many languages, including Spanish, French, Chinese, and Arabic. Through fun, age-appropriate activities, children learn the language of choice. Weekly camps for children ages three to five in Spanish, French, and Chinese are offered in the summer. The camps run for nine weeks, but parents can sign their children up for as many or few weeks as they wish. A one-week camp in Hindi is also available.

★ **EMERY RECREATION CENTER**

5701 Georgia Avenue, NW
Cleveland Park, DC
202-576-3211

Among the amenities at Emery Recreation Center are a playground, gymnasium, and several classrooms. Of note is the preschool cooperative play program, a half-day program for children ages two and a half through five.

★ **THE FAMILY ROOM**

411 Eighth Street, SE
Capitol Hill, DC
202-640-1865
www.thefamilyroomdc.com
Ages: infant to 8 years

The Family Room is an indoor play area for families. Children love the climbing structure, as well as the mountains of toys, art supplies, and books. The daily admission fee allows access to certain classes in crafts and music, as well as story times. Other classes are offered for an additional fee. For adults, there are books and magazines as well as a few exercise classes, such as Pilates. Adults and infants under one are free; daily fees are $10 for the first child and $5 for siblings. It also offers memberships of $60 a month for one child; discounted rates are available for siblings.

★ FUNFIT FAMILY FITNESS CENTER

17511 Redland Road
Rockville, MD
301-975-0099
888-8-FUNFIT
www.funfit.us
celia@funfit.us

Ages: 6 months to 13 years

Funfit Family Fitness Center was opened by two local sisters to show parents and their children how much fun exercising can be. The classes encourage lots of movement and play using music and stories to spark kids' imaginations, which is a great class format for kids who do well with limited structure. There are also classes for children with special needs. Summer camps, for three- to twelve-year-olds, offer more of a set curriculum combining fitness activities with arts and crafts projects and even a bit of magic. During Open Gym, held a couple of days a week for infants through thirteen-year-olds, children can try a bunch of activities, from quiet (reading and playing with puzzles) to energetic (playing in the Moonbounce or riding the kiddie coaster!).

★ GLEN ECHO PARK

7300 MacArthur Boulevard
Glen Echo, MD
301-634-2222
www.glenechopark.org

Ages: infant and up

This complex is a one-stop entertainment center for the entire family. There is a carousel, multiple theaters, a children's museum, several different places offering arts-and-crafts activities, bumper cars, and the beautiful Spanish Ballroom, where dance classes are held and live music performed. Groups like Music Together, VisArt, Create Arts, and the Writer's Center, as well as the Corcoran College of Art and Design, offer classes in the park's art spaces for children, teens, and adults. These include ceramics, photography, drawing, calligraphy, glass blowing and kilnformed glass, painting, sculpture, contemporary and social dance, writing, music, and more. During the spring and summer months there are more than forty camps for children and teens.

★ GYMBOREE PLAY AND MUSIC CENTER

921B Ellsworth Drive
Silver Spring, MD
301-589-0064

6831 Wisconsin Avenue
Chevy Chase, DC
301-654-8988

318 South Pickett Street
Alexandria, VA
703-836-2277

8032 Leesburg Pike

Vienna, VA

703-506-6707

www.gymboree.com

Ages: infant to 4 years

With locations all over the Metro area, Gymboree has been one of the most popular places for kids' gym classes for over twenty years. Their classes engage kids in fun activities in an encouraging setting. Classes are divided by age group, and involve music, parachutes, slides, and other play equipment meant to foster a child's physical and social development. Music and art classes are also offered. Prices vary depending on the location, but generally there is a $25 one-time family membership fee. A session of twelve weekly classes costs approximately $175; there is a $30 materials fee for music classes. Discounts are available for siblings and taking multiple classes. Free trial classes are available.

★ **IMAGINATION STAGE**

4908 Auburn Avenue

Bethesda, MD

301-961-6060

301-280-1660 (Box Office)

www.imaginationstage.com

Ages: 12 months to 5 years

A wide range of classes for children and their parents or caregivers are offered at Imagination Stage. Children can start taking classes at twelve months old. "Just Imagine" is a forty-five-minute art class that requires active participation from the caregiver and provides a unique bonding experience with the child. Because classes are structured for one-on-one interaction, siblings are not allowed to attend; families who wish to attend a class with more than one

child should consider the Family Dance class. There is a long list of offerings for three- to five-year-olds who are ready to attend class without a parent or caregiver. Classes run on a weekly basis for eight weeks and cost about $145.

★ **JABERÜ**

4926 Del Ray Avenue

Bethesda, MD

301-951-1101

www.jabberu.com

Ages: 1 to 10 years

Jabberü offers small-group foreign-language classes. Spanish, Chinese, and French are taught by native or near-native speakers. All classes build proficiency in the chosen language through a mix of role-play, games, music, and storytelling.

★ **JEEPERS**

6042 Greenbelt Road

Greenbelt, MD

301-982-2444

700 Hungerford Drive

Rockville, MD

301-309-2525

www.jeepers.com

Ages: 2 to 12 years

These indoor amusement parks have all sorts of rides—at least five for each age group—so you don't have to worry about height limitations. There are also games, a soft play area, and food (mainly pizza). Jeepers are purely for entertainment; there's no pretense about any educational value, but they are great places to let off some steam during the long winter and summer months.

★ **JEWISH COMMUNITY CENTER**

Eight locations in the DC metro area

www.jcca.org

Ages: Infant and up

These centers are an unbelievable resource. Their early-childhood-development curriculum includes swimming, dancing, music, tumbling, and more. Connor and I took a nice swimming class at the Dupont Circle location when he was around five months old.

★ **JONAH'S TREEHOUSE**

2121 Wisconsin Avenue, NW

Upper Georgetown, DC

202-298-6805

www.jonahstreehouse.com

Ages: 6 months to 5 years

Jonah's Treehouse has a spacious play studio for babies and young children up to age five. During scheduled free play times, kids can romp around on specially designed mat shapes; negotiate obstacle courses, tunnels, and wooden bridges and slides; and play with huge colorful balls, puppets, and more. Children are grouped by age starting with six-month-olds, and classes combine free play, structured movement, music, poetry, and drama. Classes run in sessions of twelve and fourteen weeks and meet on a weekly basis. Costs start at $245.

★ **JOY OF MOTION**

7315 Wisconsin Avenue, Suite 180E

Bethesda, MD

301-986-0016

1643 Connecticut Avenue, NW

Downtown, DC

202-387-0911

5207 Wisconsin Avenue, NW

Friendship Heights, DC

202-362-3042

www.joyofmotion.com

Ages: 3 and up

These locations offer a wide range of dance and exercise classes for six-month-olds and up. The Kid-motion series is designed for six-month- to three-year-olds and their caregivers to participate in together. During the sixty-minute classes, teachers lead toddlers in activities that help them develop locomotor and cognitive skills in a fun way. Six-week sessions meet weekly for $84.

★ **JW TUMBLES**

2499 North Harrison Street

Arlington, VA

703-531-1470

43150 Broadlands Center Drive

Ashburn, VA

703-729-3880

3223-B Duke Street

Alexandria, VA

703-212-9430

www.jwtumbles.com

Ages: infant to 9 years

JW Tumbles offers classes for children up to nine years of age. For the younger set, classes are divided into four age groups: four to ten months, eleven to eighteen months, nineteen months to two and a half years and two and a half to three years old. While they incorporate music and games, the focus of these classes is really on the physical development of children at each developmental stage. Caregiver participation gradually decreases with each class level, from full class participation in the four-month-old group to the three-year-old group, which teaches kids to follow directions from a teacher. JW Tumbles is great for active kids.

★ KIDS MOVING COMPANY

7475 Wisconsin Avenue
Bethesda, MD
301-656-1543
Ages: infant to 9 years
www.kidsmovingco.com

In the creative and challenging classes at Kids Moving Company, children move and play using balls, scooters, and gymnastics equipment, including a full-sized trampoline. Every class is taught by a team of well-qualified teachers, with a maximum of ten students per class. Weeklong camps during spring and summer breaks are also available for children age three to five.

★ KINDERMUSIK

Gail Trafelet
Bethesda, MD
301-657-0763
gtrafelet@verizon.net
www.ismw.org

Tracey Kretzer
Arlington, VA
571-643-1002
MissTracey@ParentChildU.com
www.parentchildu.com

Capitol Hill Arts Workshop
Capitol Hill, DC
202-547-6839
megan@chaw.org
www.chaw.com

Tracey Kretzer
Arlington, VA
571-643-1002
MissTracey@ParentChildU.com
www.parentchildu.com

Rebecca Linafelt
Takoma Park, MD
240-353-9637
beckytod@aol.com
www.kmwithbecky.kindermusik.net

Cynthia Stoop
Bethesda, MD
301-251-1148
cstoop@pressroom.com
www.centerformusic.org

Parent Child University
Alexandria, VA
571-643-1002
MissTracey@ParentChildU.com
www.parentchildu.com
Ages: infant to 5 years

For twenty-five years Kindermusik has been creating music- and movement-based curricula for children. In class, a certified Kindermusik educator leads a group of parents and their children through activities, using music and movement based on the award-winning curriculum. Above is a list of certified teachers in the area who implement the Kindermusik curricula into their class offerings. Also offered are books, CDs, games, and instruments that help children develop cognitive, physical, social, emotional, and language skills.

★ THE LITTLE GYM

1071 Seven Locks Road
Potomac, MD
301-294-4840

6911 Telegraph Road
Alexandria, VA
703-971-4FUN

43330 Junction Plaza
Ashburn, VA
703-723-0011

20980 Southbank Street
Sterling, VA
703-444-9122

4211 Fairfax Corner East Avenue
Fairfax, VA
703-818-9600
www.thelittlegym.com
Ages: infant to 12 years

Classes in gymnastics, dance (ages three through twelve), sports skill development (ages three through six), and karate (ages four through twelve) are offered at The Little Gym. Their core program is Developmental Gymnastics, a fun, noncompetitive, motor-skills-enhancing class for children ages four months through twelve years. Classes are held on weekday mornings and evenings, and on Saturday mornings, but as always make sure to check the current schedule. Single-session three-hour "camps" are held during the summer and school holidays.

★ LITTLE SPROUTS

12243 Darnestown Road
Gaithersburg, MD
301-947-4356
www.littlesproutsplay.com
Ages: infant to 6 years

This is an indoor playground for infants to children age six. A variety of classes and activities, such as Music & Movement, Art, and Kids Cooking, are available. Also scheduled is Open Play during which parents can take their little ones to the indoor play area for some unstructured fun. Families purchase a six- or eight-session card for $80 or $100 respectively, and can drop in on any class or Open Play-time based on the schedule.

★ MONTGOMERY COUNTY RECREATION DEPARTMENT

4010 Randolph Road
Silver Spring, MD
240-777-6900
www.montgomerycountymd.gov/rectmpl.asp?url=/content/rec/index.asp
Ages: infant and up

An impressive list of classes for kids and parents are offered at the eighteen recreation centers of Montgomery County; you can view their complete program guide online. The Tiny Tots program is designed for children six months to four years of age to participate in with a parent or caregiver. Included is baby sign language, interactive story times, art, music, and dance classes. Classes meet weekly for eight weeks for forty-five to sixty minutes. Costs range between $65 and $120, and classes fill quickly, so be sure to register early.

★ MUSIC TOGETHER

Headquarters
66 Witherspoon Street
Princeton, NJ 08542
800-728-2692
www.musictogether.com

Little Steps
5631 Williamsburg Boulevard
Arlington, VA
703-536-4706
www.littlestepsmusic.com

Miss Amy's Music Makers
1880 Columbia Road, NW
Kalorama, DC
202-290-2467
www.missamysmusicmakers.com
amyashley44@aol.com

Music With Maddy
8124 Birnam Wood Drive
McLean, VA
Maddy505@aol.com
www.musicwithmaddy.com

Ages: infant and up

Music Together pioneered the concept of a research-based, developmentally appropriate early childhood music curriculum. Classes are open to infants, toddlers, and preschool-age children. The program strongly emphasizes and facilitates adult involvement, so parents and caregivers are encouraged to attend. The classes are conducted by various groups and instructors throughout the DC metro area (listed above). Eight-week sessions meet weekly for forty-five minutes. The cost is $160.

★ MUSIKIDS

Chevy Chase Baptist Church
5671 Western Avenue, NW
Chevy Chase, MD
301-215-7946

4900 Auburn Avenue
Bethesda, MD
301-215-7946

1701 Rockville Pike
Rockville, MD
301-215-7946
www.musikids.com

Ages: infant to 5 years

MusiKids offers two programs for children ages six months to five years. The Music and Movement class is based on a more traditional music class format, with circle time, use of rhythmic instruments followed by movement, and finally quiet time. The Movers & Shakers class, for more active children starting at eight months, is recommended for kids who don't enjoy sitting in a structured circle and need to be up and moving more. Classes are kept small, and are taught by experienced early childhood music and movement teachers.

★ MY GYM

11325 Seven Locks Road
Potomac, MD
301-983-5300

5810 Kingstowne Center
Alexandria, VA
703-971-5437

1045 Edwards Ferry Road
Leesburg, VA
703-777-4496
www.my-gym.com
Ages: 3 months to 9 years

My Gym's programs foster cognitive, physical, and emotional growth in age-appropriate classes for children three months to nine years of age. Weekly classes incorporate music, dance, games, gymnastics, and other activities, which help children develop strength, balance, and coordination, as well as social skills. The play equipment is rearranged each week so children can find new and exciting ways to use it.

★ SILVER STAR GYMNASTICS

2707 Pittman Drive
Silver Spring, MD
301-589-0938
www.gosilverstars.com
Ages: 1 year and up

Gymnastics and tumbling classes are available for children eighteen months and older in this eighteen-thousand-foot gym. In addition, Silver Star also offers camps for children ages three and older during summer and winter break. Specially designed equipment for preschool-age children is used, as well as spotting and safety mats when introducing new skills. The gym also offers great birthday party packages.

★ SING ALONG WITH KAREN

10621 South Glen Road
Potomac, MD

8215 Old Georgetown Road
Bethesda, MD

14330 Travilah Road
Rockville, MD

301-537-SING (all locations)
www.singalongwithkaren.com
Ages: infant to 4 years

Karen, a professional guitar player and singer, really (and refreshingly) brings things back to the basics with songs that will take you back to your own childhood. *The Wheels on the Bus* and *Row, Row, Row Your Boat* are just a couple from her repertoire. She has been the early childhood music teacher in five area preschools and is a children's recording artist. Each forty-five-minute Mommy, Me & Music class incorporates singing, finger- and hand-plays (think *Itsy Bitsy Spider*), interactive games, and circle time. Classes are small and organized by age. The youngest classes are for children ages three to seven months, and the oldest classes are for three- and four-year-olds. There are also sibling classes.

★ SPIRAL FLIGHT

1826 Wisconsin Avenue, NW
Georgetown, DC
202-965-1645
www.spiralflightyoga.com
Ages: infant and up

This yoga studio offers plenty of classes for kids and parents, including Itsy Bitsy Yoga, Tummy Time, Postpartum Pilates (for two!), Kids Yoga, and Teen Yoga. Private one-on-one lessons for adults and children are also available in the class of your choice.

★ **SWAN BALLET DANCE SCHOOLS**

9416 Main Street

Fairfax, VA

703-425-9400

13655 Lee Jackson Memorial Highway

Chantilly, VA

703-803-8877

www.swanballetdance.com

Ages: 2 years and up

These dance schools offer classes in ballet, jazz, and tap. Classes are held Monday through Saturday year-round, and are structured by age and skill level. Annual performances include *The Nutcracker* and a spring recital.

★ **TINY DANCERS**

10875 Main Street

Fairfax, VA

703-385-5580

7474 Limestone Drive

Gainesville, VA

703-754-2210

info@tinydancers.com

www.tinydancers.com

Ages: 18 months to 12 years

Tiny Dancers offers performance-based ballet, tap, and jazz classes for young children ages eighteen months to twelve years. The curriculum begins with Wiggletoes for kids eighteen to thirty months and a parent and then moves on to Mom & Me classes for two- and three-year-olds. Tiny Dancers uses elaborate costumes and props, coupled with classical music and favorite tales, to build a solid technical foundation in a fun environment filled with creative self-expression.

★ **TRANQUIL SPACE YOGA**

2024 P Street, NW

Dupont, DC

202-223-9642

7475 Wisconsin Avenue

Bethesda, MD

301-654-9642

www.tranquilspace.com

Ages: infant and up

A vast range of classes in the Vinyasa Hatha yoga style are offered at Tranquil Yoga Space. Baby and Me classes are open to post-pregnancy moms with their not-yet-crawling babies. Parent and child classes are for children ages three through five and emphasize partner poses, and interaction between parent and child. Poses are introduced through songs, stories, and creative play. The kids' class is for children ages six through nine and introduces yoga in a fun, relaxed atmosphere, while teaching children about yogic concepts and philosophies, such as belly breathing, mindfulness, cooperation, and relaxation.

★ **UNITY WOODS YOGA CENTER**

4853 Cordell Avenue

Bethesda, MD

301-656-8992

2639 Connecticut Avenue, NW

Woodley Park, DC

301-656-8992

4001 North Ninth Street

Arlington, VA

301-656-8992

4201 Albemarle Street, NW
Tenley, DC
301-656-8992

4321 Wisconsin Avenue, NW
Chevy Chase, DC
301-656-8992
www.unitywoods.com
Ages: infant and up

Unity Woods Yoga offers classes in the Hatha yoga style for students of all levels. The center offers pre- and postnatal classes, plus a parent and baby class for babies six weeks through crawling.

★ **WEE PLAY**
441 Carlisle Drive
Herndon, VA
703-870-7400
www.weeplayinfo.com
Ages: 12 months to 5 years

Located in a three-thousand-square-foot, bright, colorful studio, Wee Play offers innovative classes designed for children ages twelve months to five years and their parents or caregivers. Classes are organized by age group and consist of structured play with a weekly theme. Each session is broken down to five segments: table time (choice of play dough, puzzles and other fine-motor activities), circle time, an art project, active free play time, and snack time. Six- to eight-week sessions meet weekly for forty-five to sixty minutes and cost between $70 and $90.

★ **YMCA**
Twenty locations in the DC metro area
www.ymcadc.org
Ages: 6 months and up

Swimming, gymnastics, basketball, volleyball, softball, soccer, computers, arts and crafts, summer camps, pre-school, day care, before- and after-school—the YMCA has something for everyone. Once you've established membership, you can check class offerings and schedules and sign up online.

★ **YOGATALES**
8020 Norfolk Avenue
Bethesda, MD
301-951-9642
www.yogatales.com
Ages: 2 years and up

This studio offers postnatal yoga focused on abs, glutes, and arms, and Baby 'n' Me for little ones four weeks to crawling. Adult classes are $18 each or $150 for ten; Baby 'n' Me classes are $22 each or $200 for ten. Reservations are required for all classes.

museums and theaters

★ **DISCOVERY CREEK CHILDREN'S MUSEUM**

Stable at Glen Echo Park
7300 MacArthur Boulevard
Glen Echo, MD

Historic Schoolhouse
4954 MacArthur Boulevard NW
Palisades, DC

Meadowlark Botanical Gardens
9750 Meadowlark Gardens
Vienna, VA

Kenilworth Aquatic Gardens
1550 Anacostia Avenue, NE
Capitol Hill, DC
202-337-5111
www.discoverycreek.org
Ages: 6 months to 9 years

Discovery Creek Children's Museum is composed of four environmental-education centers, one mobile site, and a central office. The museum is open to the public on Saturdays and Sundays, 10 A.M.–3 P.M., at the Stable at Glen Echo Park. Programs take place during the weekdays at the other locations by reservation only. All classes and programs at Discovery Creek are focused on teaching children an appreciation for the natural environment. Weekend Family Programs for children ages two through eleven emphasize hands-on interaction with nature through hikes, crafts, and games—drop-ins are welcome. There are other programs designed for one child and one caregiver, including Polliwog Pals (ages six to twenty-four months),

Toddler Treehouse (ages two and three), Outdoor Enthusiasts (ages four to six), and C&O Safari (ages seven to nine). Children and their caregivers learn about nature first-hand through art projects, story times, games, and instructor-led hikes. These programs are popular, and require pre-registration.

★ **NATIONAL BUILDING MUSEUM**

401 F Street, NW
Downtown, DC
202-272-2448
www.nbm.org
Ages: 2 years and up

The National Building Museum covers all aspects of architecture, design, engineering, construction, and urban planning. It is filled with exhibits that incorporate hands-on experiences, video, and signage geared to kids inviting them to examine what they're seeing through counting games and other explorations. Regular weekend family programs are offered, as well as short summer camps and the exhibits designed especially for children. Kids will enjoy exploring the Great Hall (hailed by architect Philip Johnson as "the most astonishing interior space in America") and viewing the tops of the eight Corinthian columns—among the world's tallest. They can also build an arch up to seven feet tall using soft blocks available in the Great Hall.

★ **NATIONAL TROLLEY MUSEUM**

1313 Bonifant Road
Silver Spring, MD
301-384-6088
www.dctrolley.org
Ages: 18 months and up

Kids will love the seventeen vintage streetcars that they will be able to get up close and personal with at this museum. Looking at the trolleys that were vital to the transportation of Washingtonians until 1959, kids will get a glimpse into their city's history. But let's be honest, they'll really love being able to ride actual streetcars on the one-mile demonstration railway, and so will you. There's also a model representing a Washington streetscape from the 1930s with model trolleys, plus photographic and artifact exhibits.

★ **THE SMITHSONIAN INSTITUTION**
202-633-1000
www.si.edu
www.si.edu/visit/kids_and_families.htm
Ages: 12 months and up

With all that the Smithsonian has to offer, no one can claim a lack of activities in this town. As Washingtonians, we are incredibly lucky to have the world's largest museum complex right here in our backyard. Composed of sixteen museums and the National Zoo, the Smithsonian has over one hundred thirty six million objects, artworks, and specimens and more than one hundred different activities a month to explore and enjoy. There is literally something for everybody spanning every interest and every age, and the possibilities could fill up a separate book. The sites I list here are more geared toward the interests of DC babies (infants to age four) than others, but I have found most to be very family friendly and would encourage you to check them out, if only for the wide open spaces to run around in on a cold or hot day. The museums are all free, and most events are as well. You can search for all types of activities for family and kids on the Smithsonian website.

The following are Smithsonian museums and theaters not to be missed with your DC baby.

★ **DISCOVERY THEATER**
The South Dillon Ripley Center, 3rd sublevel
1100 Jefferson Drive, SW
The Smithsonian
Capitol Hill, DC
202-633-8700
www.discoverytheater.org
Ages: 2 to 14 years

For over twenty-five years the Smithsonian's Discovery Theater has been offering the best in live performing arts for young people. Each season, more than three-hundred performances of thirty productions feature puppets, storytellers, dancers, actors, musicians, and mimes. Shows focus on classic stories, folk tales from around the world, and events in American history; some are written specially for Discovery Theater. The performance schedule is Tuesday through Friday at 10:15 A.M. and 11:30 A.M. There are occasional Saturday performances at 12:00 P.M.

★ **NATIONAL AIR AND SPACE MUSEUM**
Seventh Street and Independence Avenue, SW
Downtown, DC
202-633-1000
202-633-4629 IMAX theater showtimes
www.nasm.si.edu
Ages: infant and up

The National Air and Space Museum is a must for the entire family. Parents can appreciate the historical accomplishments while babies and toddlers enjoy the brightly colored aircraft suspended in air at every turn. There are many exhibits, so there's no need to worry about your child's short attention span (and there's no pressure to see everything in one visit, because it's free). The museum is always packed and quite noisy, so running around (and screaming) can go unnoticed. The Lockheed Martin IMAX Theater and the Albert Einstein Planetarium are not to be missed. The theater shows amazing IMAX films throughout the day on a giant screen. The two-hundred-thirty-seat planetarium simulates the night sky with stars, planets, and other cosmic objects, and teaches children about the wonders of the universe.

★ **NATIONAL MUSEUM OF NATURAL HISTORY**
Tenth Street and Constitution Avenue, NW
Downtown, DC
202-633-1000
www.mnh.si.edu
Ages: infants and up

This museum is made for kids. They'll be captivated immediately when they encounter the Hall of Mammals. Here you'll find two hundred seventy-four mammal specimens, nearly a dozen fossils, and plenty of hands-on exhibits. Continue on to the Insect Zoo, where kids can touch and hold all sorts of tiny insects and even watch the tarantula feeding. The newly opened *Butterflies and Plants: Partners in Evolution* showcases live butterflies and plants in an enclosed pavilion. *Soils*, opening in late 2008, will focus on the exciting world of the living soil right under our feet. Visitors will be able to dig in and explore a hidden world teeming with fascinating life-forms of all kinds.

★ **STEVEN F. UDVAR-HAZY CENTER**
14390 Air and Space Museum Parkway
Chantilly, VA
202-633-1000
www.nasm.si.edu/museum/udvarhazy
Ages: infant and up

The Steven F. Udvar-Hazy Center displays the National Air and Space Museum's collection of historic airplanes and spacecraft. Located near Washington Dulles International Airport, the center is housed in several adjoining airplane hangars, which provide the necessary space for displaying this unbelievable collection. There's also an observation tower, from which visitors can watch air traffic at Dulles Airport; an IMAX theater; gift shops; and more. The James S. McDonnell Space Hangar displays hundreds of famous spacecraft, rockets, satellites, and small space-related artifacts, the centerpiece of which is the Space Shuttle Enterprise.

Chapter Thirteen

outdoor activities

If you love the outdoors, the nation's capital is a great place to live. We live in the city of monuments and memorials, and just about every one of them has an accompanying park. When I first moved here, I could not get over how incredibly green DC becomes in the spring. The rest of the world only sees the images on the news of the White House, the Capitol Building, and occasionally a quick glimpse of a monument here or there. I'm convinced it's a conspiracy. Otherwise, everyone would want to live here! We are also home to some of the country's most remarkable attractions, like the pandas at the National Zoo. Furthermore, just a ten-minute drive takes you into Maryland and Virginia, with the Potomac meandering through some of the most beautiful countryside in the nation. There's no other city in the world like DC. Obviously I love living here and think it's a great place to raise children. I'm sure you will, too.

This chapter explores some of the best parks and playgrounds to visit with your city baby, as well as other fun outdoor attractions. There are more parks in the DC metro area than I can list here, so I have limited myself to only those that I think are the best for kids—with playgrounds, sandboxes, and at least one climbing structure. In addition, many parks have recreation centers that offer fabulous classes, including Mommy and Me and a variety of activities for older children. In addition to the magnificent public parks around the city, there are some really great playgrounds in schools, many of which are open to the public after school hours. All of the playgrounds I've listed are great for the littlest ones and preschoolers. In some cases, I have used the term "tot lot," which most often means that the play area has a rubber "soft-top" surface and is completely fenced in.

The following is a list of the DC, Loudoun, Fairfax, and Montgomery county websites dedicated to their respective parks and recreation services and locations. You would not believe the number of classes, activities, and summer programs that these local organizations have. The offerings and schedules are constantly expanding, so make sure you check them out and sign up for email updates where they're available. Most of the programs are deeply discounted for area residents and often even free.

DISTRICT OF COLUMBIA
www.dpr.dc.gov

ARLINGTON COUNTY
www.arlingtonva.us/prcr

LOUDOUN COUNTY
www.co.loudon.va.us/prcs

FAIRFAX COUNTY
www.fairfaxcounty.gov/living/parks

MONTGOMERY COUNTY
www.mcparkandplanning.org/parks

parks/playgrounds

DC

★ **CHEVY CHASE PLAYGROUND**
4101 Livingston Street, NW
Chevy Chase
202-282-2200

This park has a great playground suitable for older kids as well as toddlers. The play area is completely contained and there's ample space to take along the big wheels, trikes, and scooters. The sandbox is always full of toys that are sure to keep children occupied for hours. In addition, the park has a baseball diamond, basketball court, two tennis courts, and plenty of places to sit and enjoy an afternoon.

★ **EAST POTOMAC PARK**
1100 Ohio Drive, SW
202-485-9880
www.nps.gov/nacc

This three-hundred-plus-acre peninsula between the Washington Channel and the Potomac River is dotted with nearly seventeen hundred cherry trees, making it one of the best places to see the blossoms in season. Hains Point lies at the southern end and houses a mini-golf course, a playground, a public outdoor pool, golf course, tennis courts, picnic facilities, and a recreation center. The golf course snack bar is a great place to grab a bite.

★ **FOREST HILLS PARK**
3200 Chesapeake Street, NW
Forest Hills/Chevy Chase
202-673-7647
www.dpr.dc.gov

This playground is a hidden gem for the littlest set of Washingtonians. Kids love the fire truck for climbing, as well as the seesaw, the swings, and the sandbox, which keeps tiny ones busy for long stretches of time. The tennis courts are great for zipping around on tricycles.

★ **GARFIELD PARK**
200 F Street, SE
Capitol Hill
202-673-7665

Located in the heart of historic Capitol Hill, Garfield Park has fairly new playground equipment in the gated tot lot, including swings for both babies and toddlers. There is a separate playground for older children, as well as tennis courts, basketball courts, and picnic tables. The park is rarely crowded.

★ **GUY MASON RECREATION CENTER**
3600 Calvert Street, NW
Glover Park/Upper Georgetown
202-282-2180
www.guymasonstudioarts.com

This recreation center, located next door to Whole Foods on Wisconsin, has a baseball field, a multipurpose court, a large playground for infants and preschoolers, and picnic areas, among other features. Within the playground area are two separate jungle gyms with several slides, a big sandbox, swings and a small "sprayground." The Center offers a variety of classes, including Little League and Music Together. There are tons of restaurants located across the street on Wisconsin Avenue, so it's easy to grab a quick bite before or after your visit.

★ HARDY PARK AND RECREATION CENTER

Q and Forty-fifth streets, west of Foxhall Road

Foxhall

This park is located just behind Rock Creek International School (formerly called the Hardy School). In addition to a huge open playing field and tennis and basketball courts, it has a fantastic playground for tots and toddlers. The playground is completely fenced in, and it has a wood train and attached cars that kids love. There are swings for babies and toddlers, slides, and a separate playground for older children.

★ HORACE MANN ELEMENTARY SCHOOL PLAYGROUND

4430 Newark Street, NW

Spring Valley/Wesley Heights

Particularly great for athletic kids, Horace Mann's playground serves the elementary school's kindergarten through six graders but is open for locals after school and on weekends. A notable feature is the huge tube slide that goes down a sloping hill. There is a separate large area with two playgrounds, one featuring a child-size wooden structure for younger kids and the other a modern metal structure for older kids.

★ KALORAMA PARK AND RECREATION CENTER

1875 Kalorama Road, NW

Kalorama

202-673-7606

www.kaloramapark.com

Located in the center of the residential neighborhood of Kalorama is this three-acre park and recreation center. The park has two fenced-in playgrounds (one for tots and the other for bigger kids) that are very well maintained thanks to neighborhood donations. Basketball courts, a community garden, and plenty of space to run around take up the remaining area. Summer camps and neighborhood events are held in the small recreation center.

★ KENNEDY RECREATION CENTER

1401 Seventh Street, NW

Capitol Hill

202-727-1000

In addition to the two lit basketball courts, a baseball field, a tennis court, weight room, and gymnasium, the Kennedy Recreation Center has two great playgrounds—one for preschoolers and the other for somewhat older kids. There is also plenty of space for families to enjoy a picnic.

★ LAFAYETTE PLAYGROUND

5701 Broad Branch Road, NW

Chevy Chase

The expansive Lafayette Playground is located on the grounds of Lafayette Elementary School. There are a number of separate play areas, including a small, fully fenced-in and gated area for toddlers. The tot lot has a great sandbox, swings, and two slides for climbing and sliding. Beyond the tot lot, there is tons of equipment for climbing, in addition to monkey bars, an area where kids can spray water, and more swings. Many picnic tables are available. The baseball field located below the playground has a great track for tricycles.

★ MACOMB PLAYGROUND

Macomb Street between Thirty-fourth
   and Thirty-fifth streets, NW
Cleveland Park

This pristine neighborhood playground in Cleveland Park was completely renovated a few years ago by area residents. Features include basketball courts, and an awesome tot lot. There are approved plans to install a spray park in the lower playground area.

★ MONTROSE AND DUMBARTON PARKS

R Street between Twenty-eighth and
   Thirty-second streets, NW
Georgetown

Open rolling lawns and wooded wilderness on over twenty-seven acres compose Montrose and Dumbarton Parks in Georgetown. Within Montrose Park proper is a large, completely fenced-in playground with a cushiony surface. Plenty of slides, monkey bars, and a miniature merry-go-round that kids can spin themselves on keep the playground hopping. There is also a nice sandbox, as well as plenty of swings for babies and toddlers. On the west side of the park are two tennis courts and picnic tables.

★ PALISADES PARK AND RECREATION CENTER

5200 Sherrier Place, NW
Palisades

This park has something for children of every age. For older kids, the big wooden structures, tall tube slide, monkey bars, walls to climb, and poles to slide down offer hours of high-energy play. Tots love the small but fun sandbox.

★ ROCK CREEK PARK

5200 Glover Road, NW
Friendship Heights/Chevy Chase/
   Rock Creek Park
202-895-6070
202-895-6239
www.nps.gov/rocr

Rock Creek is a vast, mostly wooded park spanning many acres through the DC metro area (the National Zoo is within it). Endless paved trails make strolling easy and fun. Hiking trails take you through more densely wooded areas and will make you feel as though you have left the city altogether. Throughout there are playgrounds as well as many picnic spots. It is also home to the Rock Creek Park horse stables, which offer horse rentals as well as riding lessons for children as young as three.

★ ROSE PARK

Between P and M streets, NW
Georgetown
www.roseparkdc.org/index.html

Rose Park is located between P Street NW and M Street NW, bounded on the west side by Twenty-sixth and Twenty-seventh streets and on the east side by Rock Creek Parkway. Its facilities include three newly resurfaced tennis courts, a basketball court, a baseball diamond, two playground areas, and substantial open space. The tot lot located on the south side of the park is fenced in and well-shaded. The northern playground, located in between the basketball courts and baseball diamond, is better for preschoolers. Friends of Rose Park organizes fun events for the whole family including the summer Concerts in the Park series.

★ **TURTLE PARK**

Forty-fifth and Van Ness streets, NW

Tenleytown

202-282-2198

www.turtlepark.org

A go-to for several generations of Washingtonians, this large playground is completely fenced in and features play equipment suitable for all ages. Kids love to cool off during the summer months in the "sprayground." In addition, there are adjoining tennis courts, playing fields, and a recreation center that is home to the cooperative preschool, summer camp, and cold-weather story and craft times. Each spring the park holds its annual fundraiser featuring games, crafts, a Moonbounce, and pony rides. At Story Time and Turtle Time—winter traditions enjoyed by parents, caregivers, and preschoolers— parent volunteers read stories, lead a craft project, and provide a snack.

★ **US BOTANIC GARDEN**

100 Maryland Avenue, SW

The Mall

202-225-8333

www.usbg.gov

This beautiful and fascinating living plant museum includes the Conservatory, Bartholdi Park, and The National Garden. Taking a stroll through the USBG and enjoying a picnic in the park or garden is a wonderful outing for the entire family. Inside the conservatory more than four thousand plants are on display and inside the forty-foot-high Palm House, now called the Jungle, is a visitor walkway suspended twenty-four feet above the floor. Bartholdi Park is an outdoor garden demonstration landscape and includes the historic Bartholdi Fountain.

The National Garden, west of the conservatory, is located on three acres and is a showcase for unusual, useful, and ornamental plants that grow well in the mid-Atlantic region. The major features of the National Garden are the Rose Garden, the Butterfly Garden, the Lawn Terrace, the First Ladies' Water Garden, the Regional Garden, and an outdoor amphitheater. Family events are always scheduled. During the holidays a must-see is the miniature train set on display in the Atrium.

★ **VOLTA PARK/GEORGETOWN RECREATION CENTER**

1555 Q Street, NW

Georgetown

202-282-0380

202-282-0381

Amenities at Volta Park and Georgetown Recreation Center include a baseball field with a sixty-foot diamond, one basketball court, a playground, an outdoor swimming pool, two tennis courts, and multipurpose rooms where classes are held. The playground has two climbing structures with slides, a separate sandbox, and two swing sets; it's great for toddlers through age five. The center offers many free classes and programs, including Arts for All Ages for preschoolers, Kids Art Abrakadoodle, and the Star Watchers Movie Club.

★ **WALTER PIERCE PARK**

Adams Mill Road and Ontario Place, NW

Adams Morgan

www.walterpiercepark.org

Extremely toddler- and parent-friendly, this fenced-in playground features well-kept equipment for babies and children through age five or six, as well as plenty of shade—a good thing during those hot summer months. There are benches and picnic tables within the fenced-in area, and beyond it in the larger park. The park includes a multiuse playing field, basketball courts, and a fenced-in dog run. Its central location between Adams Morgan and Woodley Park provides plenty of places to grab a drink or something to eat.

Maryland

⋆ CABIN JOHN REGIONAL PARK
7400 Tuckerman Lane
Rockville
301-495-2525
301-469-7835
www.mc-mncppc.org
/parks/facilities/regional_parks/cabinjohn

Take the little ones to the five-hundred-twenty-eight-acre Cabin John Regional Park—it's a must-see. There is an awesome miniature train that kids and adults can ride. A replica of an 1863 C. P. Huntington engine with five passenger cars transports visitors on a ten-minute, two-mile ride through the park. Among the other features at the park are tennis courts, baseball and softball fields, and picnic areas. The Park is also home to the year-round Cabin John Ice Rink and the Locust Grove Nature Center, which also organizes family concerts.

⋆ HADLEY AND FRIENDS PLAYGROUND
451 Beall Drive
Rockville

Located at the Beall Elementary School, this playground uses as its theme Marc Brown's lovable character Arthur. The park was designed to be completely wheelchair accessible and is great for toddlers. It features a pirate ship, a corkscrew slide and smaller slides, and a tightrope bridge.

⋆ HADLEY'S PLAYGROUND
Falls Road Local Park
Potomac
301-770-2144

This award-winning playground is completely wheelchair accessible and spans an entire acre. The playground has a rubber surface and there is tons of room to ride around on bikes, trikes, and scooters.

⋆ MEADOWBROOK PARK
7901 Meadowbrook Lane
Chevy Chase
www.mc-mncppc.org

Meadowbrook Park comprises nearly seventeen acres in Chevy Chase, and includes a large playground that is not exactly a tot lot but is well designed for the littlest climbers to explore. The park also has five softball fields, a lighted baseball field, four lighted tennis courts, football/soccer fields, indoor bathroom facilities, and a picnic area that can be rented. The park is also wheelchair accessible. It is located near the Meadowbrook Riding Stables.

⋆ NORWOOD PARK
4700 Norwood Road
Chevy Chase
301-299-0024
www.mcparkandplanning.org/parks

This park has a playground and picnic area, plus a softball field, a lighted baseball field, and five tennis courts. The cooperative Bethesda–Chevy Chase Nursery School is also located here and offers three- and five-day programs.

Virginia

★ ALGONKIAN REGIONAL PARK

47001 Fairway Drive
Sterling
703-450-4655
www.nvrpa.org

With a baby pool and lots of fountains, the Algonkian Regional Park is a lovely place to be on hot summer days. The large playground has four separate areas for toddlers through five-year-olds and for school-age kids as well.

★ AMERICAN HORTICULTURAL SOCIETY CHILDREN'S GARDEN

7931 East Boulevard Drive
Alexandria
703-768-5700
www.ahs.org

River Farm is a historic twenty-five-acre site on the banks of the Potomac River in Alexandria. Once part of George Washington's original five farms, today River Farm features an early-twentieth-century Estate House and both naturalistic and formal garden areas. Within River Farm lies the popular Children's Garden, which is made up of thirteen themed gardens designed to stimulate children's interest in plants and nature. These gardens are the Fairy Tale Garden, Hummingbird Garden, Beau Beau's Garden, Alphabet Garden, Wobby the Worm, Scratch and Sniff Garden, Boat Garden,

Hide-n-Seek Garden, Little House on the Prairie, Rock-n-Roll Garden, the Maze Garden, Rest Stop, and the Bat Cave.

★ BOHRER PARK AT SUMMIT HALL FARM

506 South Frederick Avenue
Gaithersburg
301-258-6350
www.gaithersburgmd.gov

The fifty-seven-acre Bohrer Park at Summit Hall Farm includes several open fields, a playground area with a separate tot lot, and two ponds. Of note is the extensive water park with a children's splash pool, designed for kids five years and younger. The splash pool features a frog slide and crab spray, and has a zero-depth entry (a gradual slope into the water, much like at the beach). There are play structures outside the pool, plenty of shade for little ones, and an eating area for families. There is even a bathroom located within the fenced-in area equipped with a changing station.

★ BURKE LAKE PARK

7315 Ox Road
Fairfax
703-323-6601
www.co.fairfax.va.us/parks/lakefront.htm#3

This park is popular with residents of northern Virginia. Overlooking the lake, the park and playground have scenic views, and there are many lovely paths as well. It features a carousel, train ride, mini-golf, and an ice-cream stand.

★ CHESTNUT HILLS PARK/HARRISON PARK

2807 North Harrison Street

Arlington

703-228-6525

Known to locals as Harrison Park, this is a popular destination for families all over North Arlington. Kids of all ages will enjoy the playground, which is fenced in to prevent tiny wanderers from venturing too far. The playground features a challenging jungle gym, tons of swings, a huge sandbox, and several imaginative playhouses. Native Virginian Katie Couric used to take her kids to this park before they moved to New York.

★ CLEMIJONTRI PARK

6317 Georgetown Pike

McLean

703-324-8581

www.clemypark.com

This twenty-six-acre park was built as a place for all children—with or without disabilities—to play in. Both the park and playground are completely accessible to children with handicaps. The two-acre playground consists of four outdoor "rooms": the Rainbow Room, School House, Movin' and Groovin' Transportation, and Fitness and Fun. At the center of the rooms is a carousel. All playground equipment features ramps instead of steps.

★ DOUGLAS PARK

Sixteenth and Quincy streets

Arlington

A great little neighborhood park and playground, Douglas Park was designed and maintained with toddlers and preschoolers in mind. The park also has a volleyball court, a stream with a bridge, nature trails, and a gazebo.

★ GREAT FALLS GRANGE PARK

9818 Georgetown Pike

Great Falls

703-750-1598

This beautiful park in Great Falls is a good place to pack a picnic and spend a day. The gorgeous falls and picnic area are lovely places to relax while toddlers enjoy the fairly new playground area complete with merry-go-round, tire swing, slides, and tubes. There is even a rock wall that older kids or daring toddlers can climb.

★ HADLEY'S MAIN STREET USA PLAYGROUND

21100 Dulles Town Circle

Dulles Town Center

703-404-7120

Brightly colored, this five-thousand-square-foot playground at the Dulles Town Center is appropriately shopping themed. It's laid out as a "Main Street USA," with everything from a local bank to a post office. It especially caters to tots and toddlers, with a rubber surface, and age-appropriate equipment to explore.

★ HIDDEN POND NATURE CENTER

8511 Greeley Boulevard

Springfield

703-451-9588

www.fairfaxcounty.gov/parks/hiddenpond/
index.htm

Twenty-five acres of undisturbed woodland, trickling streams and a lovely pond, lighted tennis courts, and a children's play area make Hidden Pond Nature Center a welcome refuge from city life. The nature center features exhibits and live displays that introduce visitors to the park and its inhabitants. A new two-thousand-foot trail and bridge connects this park to the larger Pohick Stream Valley Park.

★ LAKE FAIRFAX PARK

1400 Lake Fairfax Drive

Reston

703-471-5415

www.fairfaxcounty.gov/parks/lakefairfax

Lake Fairfax Park is another amazing urban refuge. The park comprises four hundred seventy-six acres of campgrounds, hiking trails, picnic and party areas, a carousel ($1.50 per ride), ballfields, and a playground. At the park's eighteen-acre namesake lake, there is a marina where you can rent pedal boats and canoes, take guided boat rides, and go fishing. And don't miss the unbelievable Water Mine Family Swimmin' Hole, which boasts more than an acre of slides, sprays, showers, and other kinds of water play for the whole family. Here, kids will enjoy playing on the covered wagons, floating on rattlesnakes, and running under overflowing water-filled ore carts, while adults may prefer a relaxing tube ride along Rattlesnake River. Older kids may brave Pete's Peak, an old mining moun-

tain with enormous twin waterslides, Big Pete and Little Pete. While not all of the Water Mine's attractions are great for babies, the deepest point in the pool is only four feet and there's definitely something here for everyone. Tenderfoot Pond will more than satisfy the toddler set, with its pint-sized water slides and themed sprayground. Life jackets in three sizes are available for use at the first aid tent on a first-come, first-served basis.

★ LEE DISTRICT RECENTER

6601 Telegraph Road

Alexandria

703-922-9841

www.fairfaxcounty.gov/parks/rec/leerec.htm

This center is located within one-hundred-ninety-three acres of parkland. While the majority of the activities and facilities offered at the RECenter are for high-school-age kids and adults, they offer a half-day preschool program for children ages two-and-a-half through four years. The park has a playground, tot lot, and a carousel that kids love. Classes and summer camps are offered in swimming, dance, fine arts, martial arts, basketball, gymnastics, tennis, volleyball, and more.

★ LYON VILLAGE PARK

1800 North Highland Street

Arlington

This one-and-a-half acre park has a playground designed for small children with a big sandbox and an awesome water play area. The "sprayground" takes running through sprinklers to a whole new level, with five in-ground sprays gushing water into the air. It also features a thirteen-foot-high water wheel and dumping bucket that splashes kids with water.

⋆ **POTOMAC REGIONAL OVERLOOK PARK**

2845 Marcy Road

Arlington, VA

703-528-5406

www.nvrpa.org/parks/potomacoverlook/

Situated on a hilltop, this park overlooks and slopes down toward the Potomac River. Considered a hidden natural treasure by locals, the park offers visitors two miles of hiking trails and a nature center with programs for all age groups. In addition, there are picnic areas and educational gardens (a vegetable garden, a butterfly garden, a wildflower/fern garden, an herb garden, and a landscape garden). Regularly scheduled lectures and concerts are offered year-round.

ZOOS

⋆ **LEESBURG ANIMAL PARK**

19270 James Monroe Highway

Leesburg, VA

703-433-0002

This zoo features many animals to pet and feed. Giant tortoises, lemurs, and a serval cat are just a few of the animal attractions little kids will enjoy up close. There are "safari" rides where visitors can view some of the animals that live in the rolling parklands, as well as pony rides and a live animal show. A beautiful lake is perfect for a picnic, and the park often hosts family events such as puppet shows and concerts.

⋆ **NATIONAL ZOOLOGICAL PARK**

3001 Connecticut Avenue, NW

Woodley Park/Rock Creek Park, DC

202-633-4800

www.nationalzoo.si.edu

Home to two thousand animals of nearly four hundred different species—including the great pandas—National Zoological Park is a place of discovery that could span an entire childhood. No matter what your age, you'll be mesmerized at every turn as you wander through this one-hundred-sixty-three-acre area set amid Rock Creek Park. Children love the Kids' Farm, which has hands-on features and animal contact areas. And there's more to this zoo than just wild animals. At the Giant Pizza Playground, kids can climb all over a colorful, rubber-surfaced pizza, crawl through a giant olive, move huge mushroom slices, and hide behind a tomato.

⋆ **RESTON ZOO**

1228 Hunter Mill Road

Vienna, VA

703-757-6222

www.restonzoo.com

Reston Zoo is a surprising find in the heart of urban Fairfax County. It's a thirty-acre, family-friendly zoo great for little kids. Zoofari wagon rides take you out to see the zebras, antelopes, bison, ostriches, and lots more. Staffpeople lead regular animal demonstrations and encourage animal interaction. There are plenty of places to get "up close and personal" with the animals. Animal feed and lamb bottles are available, too! You won't want to miss the alligators, camels, reptile house, or waterfowl.

other fun outdoor destinations and activities

★ **COX FARMS**

15621 Braddock Road

Centreville, VA

703-830-4121

www.coxfarms.com

This is a one-hundred-sixteen-acre family-owned and -operated farm in Centreville. Family members also run two farmer's markets, one located in Vienna, and the other on the farm. During the fall there is a festival where kids and their parents can pick pumpkins, have fun on huge slides, go for hayrides, and pet some of the farm animals.

★ **HOMESTEAD FARM**

15600 Sugarland Road

Poolesville, MD

301-977-3761

www.homestead-farm.net

Homestead Farm is a two-hundred-thirty-acre working farm open almost year-round to the public (it is closed the month of November). Families can pick their own fresh berries, apples, pumpkins, and squash. During December, people can chop down their own Christmas tree. Produce-filled fields, a large pond, and cows, goats, chickens, and sheep are reached via tractor-pulled hayrides.

kid-friendly restaurants

When you think of a "kid-friendly restaurant," you may immediately conclude that dining out with your tiniest family member inevitably involves those nutritionally questionable kids' meals and pits of germ-covered balls. But I'm here to tell you that you don't have to dumb it down to enjoy a bite out with the family. While I love a good quarter-pounder now and then, there are a lot of great places around the city that have wised up to the fact that busy parents want a place to enjoy a glass of wine, good food (preferably served on nice linens) where kids are not only welcome but are catered to as well. After all, it's more than just a meal, it's an opportunity to spend time together.

This chapter features great places to eat out with the kids. All have boosters and high chairs, and most have children's menus. Some may be new to you, and others you may have been to but wouldn't have considered trying *avec les enfants*. The Hard Rock Café, for example, was hip about twenty years ago, but I'll bet you haven't had any compelling desire to try it recently. However, the food is pretty good, it has a full bar, and the decor could not be more fun for kids. If you think about it, kids are a little bit like visitors from a foreign country: everything is new and exciting to them, they're blissfully unaware of local customs, and the fact that something used to be cool about twenty years ago just doesn't matter. *Bon appétit!*

the restaurants

★ ADDIE'S

11120 Rockville Pike
Rockville, MD
301-881-0081
www.addiesrestaurant.com

Located in a converted bungalow, Jeff and Barbara Black's original restaurant (sister restaurant to Black Salt in the Palisades) offers amazing food in a laid-back setting. The delicious new American cuisine is well priced, and menu offerings include quesadillas and hamburgers that can either be tricked out with chipotle crème fraîche or prepared traditionally for less adventurous palates. They are well known for their hardwood-grilled selections such as the Black Pearl salmon and gulf shrimp as well as the oyster po' boy.

★ AMERICA

50 Massachusetts Avenue
Union Station, DC
202-682-9555
www.arkrestaurants.com

With its sweeping views of Capitol Hill, this enormous eatery sprawls over three levels in Union Station and spills tables out into the Main Hall as well as the sidewalk. With nearly a hundred entrées, ranging from wild mushroom stew to cilantro pasta and peanut-butter-and-jelly sandwiches, kids and parents alike will be pleased. Colorful art–deco murals covering the high ceilings and walls add to the boisterous and fun environment. Even the loudest tantrum would fade into the background here. In addition to a kids' menu, the restaurant has monthly "kids eat free" events.

★ AMERICAN CITY DINER

5532 Connecticut Avenue, NW
Chevy Chase, DC
202-244-1949
www.americancitydiner.com

American City Diner has been serving up classic 1950s diner fare since 1989. Offering breakfast, lunch, and dinner twenty-four hours a day for the past two decades, it has maintained a loyal following of Washingtonians who have come to rely on the good food and fast service. The nightly 8:30 P.M. showings of classic movies are a fun thing to do while enjoying one of the many delicious variations of burgers, pizza, or classic meatloaf and mashed potatoes.

★ ARTIE'S

3260 Old Lee Highway
Fairfax, VA
703-273-7600
www.greatamericanrestaurants.com

Here you will find very good traditional American fare such as salads, burgers, crab cakes, and filet mignon. The nautical decor, big booths, and loud bar area make it particularly kid-friendly, along with the children's menu, which includes chicken fingers, grilled cheese, and smoked salmon. Brunch is served on Saturday and Sunday, and a selection of favorites—scrambled eggs and French toast,

among many others—are offered. I hear adults can get a mean Bloody Mary. The restaurant doesn't take reservations, but you can call ahead and put your name on the list.

★ ARUCOLA OSTERIA ITALIANA

5534 Connecticut Avenue, NW
Chevy Chase, DC
202-244-1555
www.arucola.com

With a menu that changes daily and a die-hard neighborhood following, Arucola serves up exceptional Italian cuisine, highlighting the cuisine of Piedmont. Kids will love the hustle and bustle of the open kitchen and the wood-fired pizza oven, not to mention the tasty pies that it produces.

★ AUSTIN GRILL

919 Ellsworth Drive
Silver Spring, MD
240-247-8969

7278 Woodmont Avenue
Bethesda, MD
301-656-1366

801 King Street
Alexandria, VA
703-684-8969

750 E Street, NW
Downtown, DC
202-393-3776

This fun and lively local chain serves reliable and delicious Tex-Mex. A children's menu features soft tacos, enchiladas, quesadillas, hamburgers, and even peanut butter and jelly. The children's menu also doubles as a coloring page with fun activities. Crayons and kids' cups add to the family-friendly vibe.

★ BANGKOK BISTRO

3251 Prospect Street
Georgetown, DC
202-337-2424
www.bankokbistrodc.com

This is some of the best Thai food I have ever had, and I consider myself a bit of an authority, having been born in Bangkok (a story that merits its own book). Bangkok Bistro serves regional dishes made from only the freshest ingredients. Personal favorites are the green curry chicken and shrimp pad thai. Kids love the chicken satay (or "chicken on a stick," as Connor calls it), fried rice, and steamed vegetables. Waitstaff could not be more attentive to their littlest customers.

★ BEST BUNS BREAD COMPANY

4010 South Twenty-eighth Street
Arlington, VA
703-578-1500
www.greatamericanrestaurants.com

The Best Buns Bread Company bakes for all of the Great American restaurants, several of which are included in this chapter. Everything is baked on-site daily. It sells a variety of breads, pastries, and sweets, including its delicious buttercream cupcakes. It's also a good spot to grab sandwiches, soups, and salads. Wonderful muffins and scones, and coffee to wash it all down, are also served.

★ CACTUS CANTINA

3300 Wisconsin Avenue, NW
Cleveland Park/Cathedral Heights, DC
202-686-7222
www.cactuscantina.com

Always packed, this Mexican restaurant has long been a favorite of area families. The kid-friendly environment (read: loud) keeps loyal customers coming back; they happily overlook the merely decent Mexican-American fare. The children's menu, which comes with crayons, offers things like chicken fingers and quesadillas. Kids love to watch the restaurant's tortilla machine; if they want to try to make their own, servers will also give them some dough to play with on request.

★ CAFÉ ASIA

1720 I Street, NW
Downtown, DC
202-659-2696

1550 Wilson Boulevard
Arlington, VA
www.cafeasia.com

"Café" may mislead those who aren't expecting the huge cavernous interiors, and often over-forty-five-minute wait for the decent Pan-Asian cuisine here. But while the overbearingly loud atmosphere may be a turnoff for some, when dining out with kids in tow, it's just what the doctor ordered. Grownups will savor the long list of inventive sushi, while children love the chicken satay and tempura.

★ CAFÉ DELUXE

3228 Wisconsin Avenue
Cathedral Heights, DC
202-686-2233

4910 Elm Street
Bethesda, MD
301-656-3131

1800 International Drive
McLean, VA
703-761-0600
www.cafedeluxe.com

With three locations in the DC metro area, Café Deluxe has become a go-to, whether you're dining *avec* or *sans* bébé. The open floor plan, relatively high ceilings, and bare floors mean that it's loud to begin with—which is a good thing. White tablecloths are conveniently draped with long sheets of white construction paper, and a small bucket of crayons is provided. The yummy food includes pasta dishes, grilled salmon, and creative salads; the children's menu offers standard favorites such as pasta and chicken fingers. Little ones are served drinks in kids' cups.

★ CAFÉ LA RUCHE

1039 Thirty-first Street, NW
Georgetown, DC
202-965-2684
www.cafelaruche.com

This truly authentic Parisian bistro, steps off the C&O Canal, is always abuzz (*la ruche* is French for "the beehive"), and is a longtime Georgetown staple. Friendly waitstaff go above and beyond to keep their littlest customers happy. Kids love the croque-monsieur, sandwich au jambon, and broccoli

au gratin. You'll probably need to hold them back from the signature pastries.

★ CAPITOL CITY BREWING CO.

1100 New York Avenue, NW
Downtown, DC
202-628-2222

2 Massachusetts Avenue, NE
Capitol Hill, DC
202-842-2337

2700 South Quincy Street
Arlington, VA
703-578-3888
www.capcitybrew.com

Capitol City Brewing Co. is a sure bet when dining out with the kids. The atmosphere is loud and hopping, and the service is fast and friendly. What more could you ask for? A full bar and home-brewed beer, as well as good pub fare, answer that question. The children's menu includes Federal Fingers and a Gettysburger Address, which may not get a giggle from toddlers but shows that this restaurant really makes an effort to accommodate its youngest customers.

★ CARLYLE

4000 South Twenty-eighth Street
Arlington, VA
703-931-0777
www.greatamericanrestaurants.com

This high-energy bistro serves innovative, award-winning New American cuisine in a casual, fun atmosphere. Year after year, Carlyle has been voted one of the top restaurants in Washington by the *Washingtonian* Readers' Poll, and its chef recently received the Restaurant Association of Metro Washington's "Chef of the Year" Award. Very friendly service, a boisterous atmosphere, and a children's menu make this a family favorite.

★ THE CHEESECAKE FACTORY

5354 Wisconsin Avenue, NW
Chevy Chase Pavilion, DC
202-364-0500

11301 Rockville Pike
White Flint Mall
North Bethesda, MD
301-770-0999

2900 North Wilson Boulevard
Arlington, VA
703-294-9966

1796 International Drive
McLean, VA
703-506-9311
www.cheesecakefactory.com

I usually prefer restaurants without "factory" in the name and menus without pictures of the food, but this popular nationwide chain is fairly kid-friendly. Large booths and a noisy environment are very conducive to family dining, despite the lack of a separate children's menu. Some friends don't entirely agree with me on this one, saying granite tables and the lack of kids' cups are a recipe for disaster. However, trough-sized portions of standard kids' fare such as quesadillas, pizza, and burgers are sure to please and are easily shared.

★ CHEF GEOFF'S

3201 New Mexico Avenue, NW
Wesley Heights, DC
202-237-7800
www.chefgeoff.com

This quintessential neighborhood restaurant serves everything from yellowfin tuna to steaks, great burgers, pizzas, salads, and sandwiches. Finish the meal with homey desserts like "milk and cookies," or a piece of chocolate truffle cake. At the restaurant's jazz brunch, held on the patio on Sundays, you and your family can enjoy specialties like eggs Chesapeake or the Texas scramble while listening to a live jazz band. The children's menu is full of kid-pleasers, which makes Chef Geoff's perfect for families.

★ CLYDE'S

3236 M Street, NW
Georgetown, DC
202-333-9180

1700 North Beauregard Street
Alexandria, VA
703-820-8300

5441 Wisconsin Avenue
Chevy Chase, MD
301-951-9600

707 Seventh Street, NW
Downtown, DC
202-349-3700

11905 Market Street
Reston, VA
703-787-6601

8332 Leesburg Pike
Vienna, VA
703-734-1901
www.clydes.com

A DC institution, Clyde's offers popular American bistro fare in a booth-filled, tavernlike setting. A children's menu includes burgers, hot dogs, a fruit plate, and more for only $6. Clyde's is also a popular brunch spot on the weekends.

★ **COASTAL FLATS**
11901 Grand Commons Avenue
Fairfax, VA
571-522-6300

7860-L Tysons Corner Center
McLean, VA
703-356-1440
www.greatamericanrestaurants.com

Part of the Great American Restaurant Group, Coastal Flats offers a menu of American-style entrées similar to those at the group's other locations, but with a focus on seafood. The 1950s Florida-themed eatery has a children's menu and includes grouper fingers, steak, grilled cheese, a cheeseburger, and smoked salmon. As with all the restaurants in the Great American group, no reservations are taken, but you can phone ahead to be placed on the waiting list.

★ **DAILY GRILL**
1200 Eighteenth Street, NW
Dupont Circle, DC
202-822-5282

1310 Wisconsin Avenue, NW
Georgetown, DC
202-337-4900

One Bethesda Metro Center
Bethesda, MD
301-656-6100

2001 International Drive
McLean, VA
703-288-5100
www.dailygrill.com

Daily Grill serves big portions of traditional grill recipes at affordable prices. These restaurants are great for American classics such as BLTs, meatloaf, and mashed potatoes, as well as huge (and I mean huge!) salads and reliable brunch items. The children's menu features tot-sized versions of meatloaf, pasta, pizza, and more. Crayons are provided for doodling on the paper-covered tables.

★ **DC BOATHOUSE**
5441 MacArthur Boulevard
Palisades, DC
202-362-2628

Family-friendly and perfect for dining out, DC Boat House offers nothing fancy or unusual, just standard American fare, such as baby-back ribs, chicken, pasta, tuna steak, and a list of hot sandwiches and subs. Despite its name, DC Boathouse has no river view but does attempt to uphold its namesake motif with the crossed-oar logo, the crew gear, college T-shirts on the wall, and the huge skiff suspended from the ceiling.

★ ESPN ZONE

555 Twelfth Street, NW

Penn Quarter, DC

202-783-3776

www.espnzone.com

Though it's not exactly Zagat material, the ESPN Zone has all of the necessary ingredients to please a crowd of kids. Be forewarned: Unless you are a sports-bar aficionado, this is one that you will be going to for the kids. (But I guess at some point, we all have to take one for the team.) Downtown's ESPN Zone is forty-one thousand square feet of sensory overload. Big screens throughout the restaurant show every sporting event being broadcast on the planet, and the entire second floor is a wall-to-wall virtual-gaming extravaganza. From motocross to skiing, soccer, and wave-running, it's all there for the taking. (I'll admit the air-hockey is a personal guilty pleasure.) The food is typical bar fare, with burgers, steaks, ribs, and a few salads, but it's actually pretty good. The children's "Rookie Menu" is for kids twelve and under.

★ FIVE GUYS FAMOUS BURGERS AND FRIES

Over 30 locations in DC metro area

866-345-GUYS

www.fiveguys.com

If you're hankering for a good burger, look no further: Five Guys has the best burger in Washington, according to *Washingtonian* magazine's readers, who have given it this title in the annual readers' poll six years running. The menu is short and straightforward, offering grilled cheese, hot dogs, and made-to-order burgers with everything from jalapeños to sautéed mushrooms as toppings. Decor is nonexistent, but then again, you're not there for the ambiance.

★ FURIN'S OF GEORGETOWN

2805 M Street, NW

Georgetown, DC

202-965-1000

www.furins.com

Another one of our Georgetown staples for breakfast and lunch, Furin's is a family-owned and -operated mainstay. Inside it's very low-key, with first-come, first-served seating only; there's also an outdoor seating area. The menu features basic egg dishes, classic sandwiches, and fresh salads, and the friendly staff always remembers who you are. Thanks to its proximity to the Four Seasons, it's also a great place for celebrity sightings. After a recent Saturday morning breakfast, Connor is now on a first-name basis with a certain Mr. Spacey.

★ GARRETT'S RESTAURANT AND RAILROAD TAVERN

3003 M Street, NW

Georgetown, DC

202-333-1033

www.garrettsdc.com

A major stop on the Georgetown pub crawl for over twenty-seven years, you may (or may not) remember making a few stops here yourself back in the day. In fact, highly sought-after DC litigator Brian Schwalb was once a highly sought-after bartender here. But Garrett's Restaurant and Railroad Tavern has been a longtime local family favorite (a bit earlier in the evening), serving up pub favorites and various American dishes with a down-home Southern flair. Kids love the vintage train memorabilia and items on the separate children's menu. You will have come full circle when you walk back through those welcoming doors with Georgetown's next generation of crawlers.

★ GENEROUS GEORGE'S POSITIVE PIZZA AND PASTA

3006 Duke Street
Alexandria, VA
703-370-4303
www.generousgeorge.com

Decent food at unbelievably cheap prices coupled with tons to look at and lots of balloons make this a popular family restaurant. The native Virginian founder and operator is famous for turning out huge portions of pizza, subs, and "pasta pies," a carb-crazy concoction of pasta, lasagna, or eggplant parmigiana served in a pizza shell. Monday is "kids eat free" night.

★ HARD ROCK CAFE

999 E Street, NW
Penn Quarter, DC
202-737-7625
www.hardrock.com

This may seem like a painfully cheesy suggestion, a destination for the uncool tourist set. But remember the whole "visitor from a foreign country" thing? Kids will love the rock memorabilia throughout, including the oversized guitars jutting out from the bar in the center of the restaurant. The food is typical theme-restaurant fare, heavy on the burgers, and the ambiance is loud, with rock videos playing on screens throughout. The children's menu offers kid-sized favorites.

★ IOTA CLUB & CAFE

2832 Wilson Boulevard
Arlington, VA
703-522-8340
www.iotaclubandcafe.com

The cafe side of Iota serves upscale bistro-style cuisine, with soups, salads, burgers and sandwiches. Most performances are for adults, but they do have occasional afternoon shows for kids; see the club's website for the current schedule. Cafe seating is first-come, first-served.

★ JOHNNY ROCKETS

50 Massachusetts Avenue, NE
Union Station, DC
202-289-6969

3131 M Street, NW
Georgetown, DC
202-333-7994

1100 South Hayes Street
Arlington, VA
703-415-3510

1718 Connecticut Avenue, NW
Dupont Circle, DC
202-332-8883

5900 Kingstowne Center
Alexandria, VA
703-921-5030
www.johnnyrockets.com

Blast-from-the-past 1950s-themed diner decor complete with chrome counters and stools may be lost on the small person dining with you, but the balloons, mini-jukeboxes at every table, and dancing waiters on the half hour won't. Your child will also get a kick out of Johnny Rocket gimmicks like waiters who "twirl straws" and serve "ketchup with a smile" (ketchup poured on a plate in the shape of a smiley face). The diner fare includes burgers, hot dogs, chili, grilled chicken sandwiches, tuna salad, and great fries. I've been hooked on the restaurant's chili cheese fries since the first one opened in L.A. twenty years ago. The children's menu includes hamburgers, hot dogs, chicken fingers, peanut butter and jelly, and grilled cheese. Don't miss the great old-fashioned malts, milkshakes, and homemade apple pie. Also, for those of us with early risers, they serve a decent breakfast and good coffee. The Georgetown location opens at 8:30 A.M.

★ KRAMERBOOKS & AFTERWORDS

1517 Connecticut Avenue, NW
Dupont Circle, DC
202-387-1400
www.kramers.com

For more than thirty years, Kramerbooks has been serving up good food and books. With a nice selection of books for the little ones, combined with a place to sit, eat, read, and hang out, it is definitely kid-friendly. The cafe has a children's menu, plus high chairs and booster seats. It also has generous hours, open from 7:30 A.M.–1:30 A.M. every day.

★ LOVE CAFÉ

1501 U Street, NW
U Street Corridor, DC
202-265-9800
www.cakelove.com

Sister to the Cake Love bakery across the street, at Love Café one can indulge in the "cupcake bar," where you can pick from a variety of icings to top your choice of flavored cupcakes or slices of their well-known cakes. But wait until after you try one of the scrumptious sandwiches, from the perfect traditional chicken salad to the mouthwatering grilled proscuitto panini. There is plenty of seating indoors and out.

★ MEIWAH

1200 New Hampshire Avenue, NW
Downtown/Dupont Circle, DC
202-833-2888

4457 Willard Avenue
Chevy Chase, MD
301-652-9882
www.meiwahrestaurant.com

Meiwah is no stranger to accolades, having received rave reviews from critics since its inception. Now with two locations (Downtown and Chevy Chase), the restaurant continues to be a favorite, providing Chinese-American dishes made from only the freshest ingredients, served by warm and friendly waitstaff. The expansive two-story location on New Hampshire Avenue, with roomy booths, is a perfect place to feed the entire family—there's just enough background noise to drown out any small outcries. There isn't a separate children's menu; however, there are plenty of kid-pleasing dishes, such as chicken fried rice, the delicious Peking duck, and steamed vegetables, just to name a few.

★ PEACOCK CAFÉ

3251 Prospect Street, NW
Georgetown, DC
202-625-2740
www.peacockcafe.com

Peacock Café is one of our personal favorites, and this restaurant is proof that you don't have to dumb it down when dining with the tots. First, the wait-staff could not be friendlier—if you're spotted pushing a stroller to the door, they actually run out to help lift the stroller down the two tiny front steps into the restaurant. Upon entering, kids are immediately handed a little take-home toy, coloring book, and crayons. The cool, upscale interior, delicious modern-American fare, and excellent bartending keep adults very happy, while pastas, grilled chicken fingers, burgers, and grilled cheese please even the pickiest eaters. Weekend brunch (call ahead—it's popular) is an absolute must. We love the eggs Benedict with shoestring fries, and the Bloody Marys are the best I've ever had.

★ SEQUOIA

3000 K Street, NW
Georgetown, DC
202-944-4200
www.arkrestaurants.com

This is another one of those places that was cool back in the day but is still going strong, and for good reason. Actually two reasons: good food and an even better view. If you are looking for a nice place down on the water, the front-row view of the activity on the Potomac will engage kids for the entire meal. On nice days, the patio is a great place to enjoy a leisurely lunch. There is no children's menu, but the expansive menu of new-American fare has something for everyone.

★ SILVER DINER

3200 Wilson Boulevard
Arlington, VA
703-812-8600

8101 Fletcher Street
McLean, VA
703-821-5666

11951 Killingsworth Avenue
Reston, VA
703-742-0801

11806 Rockville Pike
Rockville, MD
301-770-2828
www.silverdiner.com

An authentic-looking, old-fashioned diner, complete with comfy booths, tableside jukeboxes, and classic diner fare—including homemade meatloaf, fresh turkey with mashed potatoes, soups, sandwiches, burgers, and blue-plate specials—the Silver Diner is a great place to take kids. It also offers contemporary selections such as Cajun chicken pasta and a veggie stir-fry with Portobello mushrooms for those seeking something less traditional. These restaurants were featured in The Washington *Post* for their "Heart Healthy" selections; they don't use any trans-fat oils. A children's menu features kid-sized versions of sandwiches, breakfasts, shakes, and desserts. The menus double as coloring pages and come with crayons. Most of the Silver Diner locations have "Kids' Appreciation Nights" on Tuesdays from 5–8 P.M., which feature discounts on meals for kids twelve and under, plus activities such as coloring contests, balloons, crafts, and music.

★ **SWEETWATER TAVERN**

14250 Sweetwater Lane
Centreville, VA
703-449-1100

45980 Waterview Plaza
Sterling, VA
571-434-6500

3066 Gatehouse Plaza
Falls Church, VA
703-645-8100

www.greatamericanrestaurants.com

Also owned by the Great American Restaurant Group, these restaurants have a menu that features a long list of salads, fresh seafood, poultry dishes, steaks and meats (including Black Angus prime rib), plus an on-site brewery. A children's menu is available, and includes chicken fingers, grilled cheese, a cheeseburger, and smoked salmon (all served with fries and soda or milk). As with all the restaurants in the Great American group, no reservations are taken, but you can phone ahead to be placed on a waiting list.

★ **2 AMYS PIZZA**

3715 Macomb Street, NW
Cathedral Heights/Cleveland Park, DC
202-885-5700
www.2amyspizza.com

Walk into 2 Amys at any time of day, and you'll find the gourmet pizzeria abuzz with Washingtonians of all ages. Hailed by many critics as having the best pizza in the country, 2 Amys boasts traditional Neapolitan pies with homemade toppings from classic to chi-chi. Cockles and anchovies

please the older set while a traditional Margherita is guaranteed to be wolfed down by tykes. Crayons and paper-topped tables keep kids doodling and distracted.

ice cream and treats

★ **BASKIN-ROBBINS**

Locations throughout the DC Metro area
www.baskinrobbins.com

With more than thirty locations in the DC metro area, Baskin-Robbins' good, reasonably priced ice cream is an obvious go-to when you need to satisfy that sweet tooth. Stores have large freezers with ready-to-go pints of the tasty cold treat of your choice, and a large selection of ice-cream cakes (see page 179).

★ **BEN & JERRY'S**

Locations throughout the DC Metro area
www.benjerry.com

The socially conscious and politically active company Ben & Jerry's also finds time to produce some of the best ice cream there is. In addition to the delectable standards like chocolate and vanilla, these ice cream veterans turn out some original flavor combinations, and you can enjoy classics like Cherry Garcia and Chunky Monkey along with newer concoctions like Half-Baked. Scoop shops have ready-to-go pints as well as ice cream cakes (see page 179).

★ COLD STONE CREAMERY

Locations throughout the DC Metro area

www.coldstonecreamery.com

Cold Stone Creamery offers a huge selection of ice creams, made fresh daily, with an endless list of mix-in choices. In addition to choosing from preset combinations, visitors can make their own creations, with choices like fresh strawberries and other fruit, brownies, sauces, and all sorts of candies. Children's cakes are also available (see page 180).

★ GIFFORD'S ICE CREAM & CANDY CO.

555 Eleventh Street, NW

Penn Quarter, DC

202-347-7755

7237 Woodmont Avenue

Bethesda, MD

301-907-3436

21 Wisconsin Circle

Chevy Chase, MD

301-652-8965

100 Gibbs Street

Rockville, MD

301-315-2002

www.giffords.com

Gifford's Ice Cream & Candy Co. is the real deal. Since 1938 it has been serving homemade ice cream and candy made from the best ingredients. Cakes are also available (see page 181).

★ MAGGIEMOO'S

Locations throughout the DC Metro area

www.maggiemoos.com

MaggieMoo's ice cream and treatery offers an extensive variety of ice cream, made fresh daily, with an endless list of mix-in choices. Children's birthday cakes are also available (see page 182).

★ MAX'S BEST HOMEMADE ICE CREAM

2416 Wisconsin Avenue, NW

Glover Park/Upper Georgetown, DC

202-333-3111

Owner Max makes the ice cream on-site and it is quite possibly the best I have ever had. The walls of this small, aptly named shop are covered with pictures of his youngest customers who just keep coming back for more—along with willing parents. With only a couple of tables inside, most take their ice cream to go. Small scoops are available.

part four

IT HAPPENS SO FAST:
keeping up with your dc baby

birthday parties

You're no stranger to hosting a party—remember those gourmet soirees and urbane cocktail parties of life before baby? But those experiences really don't prepare you for your baby's first birthday party. In many ways, it's like throwing a party for your cat. The guest of honor is blissfully unaware of the raison d'être for the event . . . he or she doesn't even know what a party is. This is an event that needs equal doses of devil-may-care attitude and obsessively thoughtful planning.

If you don't have space at home, where will you have the party? Will the cuisine be geared for grown-ups or the little ones? Will the cake come from the supermarket or will you bake it yourself? Will the theme become so central to the success of your day that your poor husband has to don an Elmo costume?

Getting overwhelmed yet? Breathe in, relax, and turn the page. City Baby DC will help you figure out every last detail, and remind you of one important thing you may have forgotten: The first birthday is as much for you and your husband as it is for your mostly oblivious baby. You've made it a year. Celebrate!

entertainment

If you are hosting baby's first birthday party at your house, you are probably thinking about hiring some outside entertainment, and options certainly abound. However, keep this in mind: Your birthday baby will be more than content playing with a bunch of new toys, and after about an hour or so he'll probably pass out from all of the excitement. At this young age, it's not necessary to hire somebody to come in and perform—in fact it may very well freak out the little guys. My friend Hayley had her six-foot-two Italian husband dress up as Elmo for her son Teo's first birthday. Not only did all of the kids start screaming and crying when the enormous red furry monster came out speaking in an Italian accent, but the parents were a little scared as well. Unless you are trying to provide entertainment for some older birthday party guests, I would wait until your child is three or four before you hire the circus.

When you are ready, below is a list of some of the best children's entertainment for hire in the DC metro area:

★ **ANDY'S PARTIES**
   422 Main Street
   Gaithersburg, MD
   301-309-2FUN (386)
   www.andysparties.com

Pick a theme and provide the guest list—Andy's Parties will do the rest. This full-service children's party- and event-planning company takes care of everything, from the invitations to the post-party cleanup. During the event, a young and energetic team of staffpeople will lead up to eighteen guests (ages one through twelve) in music, games, and craft activities. Also included in the one-and-a-half hour party package are food, drinks, cake, and party favors. Rates begin at $300.

★ BIGGO PRODUCTIONS

DC Metro area

703-862-9466

www.biggoproductions.com

biggo2@biggoproductions.com

Biggo Productions has provided entertainment for children in the DC Metro area since 1984. Founded by an educator, Biggo Productions features Biggo the Clown as well as magicians who perform age-appropriate slapstick comedy and magic routines. Biggo Productions performs at parties for children ages one and up and costs $150 to $175 an hour.

★ BLUE SKY PUPPET THEATRE

4301 Van Buren Street

University Park, MD

301-927-5599

www.blueskypuppets.com

blueskypuppets@blueskypuppets.com

For thirty-three years, Blue Sky Puppet Theatre has been performing family-friendly shows throughout the Metro area. The touring company can take the performance to you for birthday parties, providing forty-five minutes of nonstop fun and laughs that kids of all ages are sure to enjoy. Prices start at $200.

★ BOB BROWN PUPPETS

DC Metro area

703-319-9102

www.bobbrownpuppets.com

BobBrownpuppets@aol.com

Bob Brown Puppets has been performing shows throughout the eastern and midwestern United States for more than forty years. Its two birthday shows, "Clowning Around" and "Kaleidoscope," offer entertainment specifically designed for children between the ages of three and seven. Puppeteers manipulate the marionettes in the middle of a large half-circle of children, which enables the party guests to interact with the characters.

★ BROCCOLI THE CLOWN, JAKE THE MAGICIAN, AND COOKIE THE CLOWN

DC Metro area

703-768-7352

www.broccolithemagicclown.com

bestclowns@aol.com

A two-time finalist for *Washington Family* magazine Children's Entertainer of the Year award, Jake Stern is an expert children's performer. A twenty-five year veteran of the DC party scene, Jake will perform a forty-five minute, high-energy show that will entertain children of all ages. Jake can be hired as Broccoli the Clown or Jake the Magician; both acts combine nonstop comedy and magic with balloon sculpture and audience participation.

★ **CATRIONA'S CASTLE**
DC Metro area
301-972-7549
www.catrionascastle.com

Catriona's Castle creates and leads theater-themed birthday parties for children ages two to ten years old. Each sixty-minute interactive show is based on a fairy tale or nursery rhyme. Guests get to dress up in elaborate costumes and use props to act out the classic tales together. A standard party includes invitations and favors for thirty and a special favor bag for the birthday child. Rates start at $395.

★ **CHILDTIME MAGIC**
DC Metro area
703-765-1923
www.childtimemagic.com
louis@childtimemagic.com

Magician Louis Meyers has been performing at children's birthday parties throughout the DC Metro area for the past ten years. Each forty-five minute show, tailored to the age group of the audience, incorporates music and humor, as well as the crowd-pleasing Abbott the Rabbit and Jansen the Amazing Dove. For an additional charge Louis will make balloon animals, provide goody bags, and give a special magic set to the birthday boy or girl.

★ **CLOWNING AROUND**
DC Metro area
301-738-1338
www.mywebpages.comcast.net/buckshot1/
   Clown.htm

Donna Stivers is a clown with pedigree, having graduated from Ringling Bros. and Barnum & Bailey Clown College. A current clown with the Big Apple Circus Clown Care Unit, Donna performs for patients at Children's National Medical Center, as well as at birthday parties around the area. Each show lasts approximately one hour (the length of the show varies depending on the age of the audience members), during which she does twenty to thirty minutes of slapstick magic tricks and creates a balloon sculpture for each child. Stivers also offers face painting, hand painting, and temporary tattoos.

★ **ENCHANTED PLAY**
DC Metro area
301-322-7399
www.enchantedplay.us

Enchanted Play offers themed parties for children ages three to eleven. One of the company's specialists will coordinate an entire party, from the invitations to the activities, cake, and party favors. Party themes primarily cater to girls' interests and include "Prima Ballerina" and "Princess Tea Party."

★ **FRANK CASSEL THE BANJO MAN**
DC Metro area
www.banjomanfc.com

Frank Cassel's banjo strumming and harmonica blowing are guaranteed to get kids dancing and singing at any occasion. His sweet and laidback nature will draw even the shyest party guests out and get them moving to his fun versions of classic and familiar tunes. Cassel, a fifteen-year veteran on the tyke party circuit with many other regular gigs around town, needs to be booked well in advance.

★ **FUN FACE PAINTING BY WOONY & COMPANY**
301-758-0460
www.woony240.com
woony240@aol.com

Woony & Company specializes in face painting for birthday parties and large events. For an additional fee the company will also make balloon sculptures and draw caricatures, and even take photographs.

★ **THE GREAT ZUCCHINI**
DC Metro area
202-271-3108
www.thegreatzucchini.com
eric_kanus@yahoo.com

Kids can't get enough of this guy. With more than sixteen years of experience, the Great Zucchini has performed at the White House Easter Egg Roll, the National Zoo's Guppy Gala, and thousands of birthday parties and events around town. His birthday-party performance consists of an interactive slapstick magic show for children ages two through six, offered in two packages. The Basic Magic Package is a fifty-minute magic show featuring lots of audience participation with the birthday child as the star. Kids learn a magic trick at the end of the show. The Basic Magic & Games Package includes everything in the Basic Magic Package plus an additional thirty minutes of games. Call months in advance to book the Great Zucchini.

★ **JONATHAN AUSTIN'S JUGGLING AND MAGIC SERVICE**
DC Metro area
804-230-4010
www.jonathanaustin.com
jonathanaustin@mindspring.com

Jonathan Austin started juggling at the age of twelve and was a popular performer by the age of fifteen. Since then, he has incorporated magic and riding a unicycle into his thrill-a-minute juggling act—often performing all three simultaneously. Claiming "there is nothing I won't juggle," his repertoire includes flames, bowling balls, paddles, and a slew of rubber chickens. Thirty- to forty-minute performances are suggested for younger crowds, but Jonathan will tailor his act to accommodate most needs.

★ **KAYDEE PUPPETS**
DC Metro area
703-385-4543
www.kaydeepuppets.com
kdpuppets@aol.com

Kaydee Puppets has been performing at area birthday parties since 1972. A thirty-minute birthday show includes two of your child's favorite stories performed by two puppeteers manipulating oversize large-mouth puppets. This is a good option for parties with kids as young as two, as the large puppets and highly interactive shows keep even the littlest (and wiggliest) partygoers engaged.

★ LAWRENCE THE MAGICIAN

DC Metro area

703-973-4678

www.magicuc.com

lawrence@magicuc.com

Lawrence the Magician performs "parlor magic," which includes close-up and stage illusions. Children's birthday parties are usually one hour (a bit long for the under-five set), during which he enlists the help of the guest of honor, turning him or her into a master magician. Partygoers will learn a magic trick and each will take home an origami favor. For kids who like Harry Potter, Lawrence also performs as Lawr the Wizard, complete with robe, wand, and hat.

★ MAD SCIENCE OF WASHINGTON

11251 Lockwood Drive

Silver Spring, MD

301-593-4777

www.madscience.org/dc

For children ages four and older, Mad Science will bring a highly interactive, exciting, and educational science show to your home. A "mad scientist" will lead the group through experiments that test the laws of gravity, light, and sound, leaving children thrilled and amazed. Guests can make cotton candy, rockets, and putty for an additional fee. Mad Science will also provide goody bags for guests. This is forty-five minutes of fun.

★ MIKE PERRELLO MAGICAL ENTERTAINMENT

DC Metro area

301-294-8874

www.mikepmagic.com

Magician Mike Perrello specializes in performing magic for young children. His magic shows feature the guest of honor as the star of the show while including and encouraging the participation of all guests. Magician Mike's oversize props (such as jumbo cards, balloons, ropes, silk flowers, and rings) make the hour-long show highly engaging for little kids. His fun and goofy sense of humor endears aspiring magicians. All guests get a prize at the end of the show.

★ MR. KNICK KNACK

DC Metro area

703-795-1800

www.mrknickknack.com

Connor and I first saw Mr. Knick Knack perform at Tyson's Corner two years ago, during what was intended to be a quick Nordstrom's shoe run. Steve Rossi, aka Mr. Knick Knack, plays guitar and sings throughout DC and has a huge following among the diaper-clad set. They move like bees to his original songs with a rock 'n' roll edge. At 10:30 in the morning, Connor and I were grooving to the music —and we're a tough crowd! Would it be too much to hire him for my next birthday?

★ MR. SKIP

DC Metro area

302-377-4555

www.mrskip.com

This performer, who has a background in early childhood development, has been a singer and songwriter of children's music for more than twenty years. Mr. Skip's performances for the eight-and-under set consist of all the classics as well as silly originals that get the kids singing and dancing.

★ **NOAH'S ARK ANIMAL WORKSHOP**
Brigette Norman
DC Metro area
800-396-1359
www.PartyWithNoahsArk.com

Owner Brigette Norman will set up and run one of her two themed workshops at your home. In the Noah's Ark Animal Workshop, kids get to make and accessorize their own stuffed animals. In the Glamour Girl Workshop, guests adorn themselves on the outside with glitter, makeup, and clothes while Brigette reinforces positive values and the importance of beauty that comes from within. Both workshops provide fun-filled entertainment for children ages three and up. Prices start at $15 per person.

★ **NOW THIS!**
6950 Oregon Avenue, NW
Hawthorne, DC
202-364-8292
www.nowthisimprov.com
bookus@nowthisimprov.com

Picture *Whose Line Is It Anyway?*—but in your living room, geared totally toward kids, and with tons of props and costumes. This improv theater group manages to sing and act its way through any idea or theme provided—even ones from a group of three- and four-year-olds. It's impressive, and the kids think so too. A thirty-minute, four-performer show in your home starts at $400. The group also performs its children's show on Saturdays at 1:30 P.M. at the Blair Mansion in Silver Spring.

★ **OH SUSANNAH**
DC Metro area
301-933-2006
www.susannahmusic.com

Susan McNelis has become one of DC's favorite children's performers. With two CDs and a bunch of awards under her belt, McNelis is in high demand. She has performed at the Kennedy Center, the National Zoo, and the National Theater, among other venues. Children love her upbeat voice and acoustic guitar rhythms, while parents like the witty and often sarcastic lyrics, which are often based on her experiences as a mom. Her one-hour "Oh Susannah" birthday party is a nonstop routine filled with music, dancing, puppets, and parachutes. The price is $275 for eighteen or fewer children (a sixty-minute party visit) or $325 for more than eighteen children (a ninety-minute party visit). Call at least six weeks in advance to reserve the date of your choice.

★ **THE RAINBOW ENTERTAINMENT COMPANY**
DC Metro area
703-239-0037
www.reciact.com

The Rainbow Entertainment Company is an interactive theater group for kids. In addition to drama classes that are taught throughout DC, the group is also available for birthday parties. After selecting a production from its repertoire (which includes "Snow White" and "Jack and the Beanstalk"), the group will come to your child's event equipped with costumes, props, and sets, and will lead the partygoers in acting out the story.

★ RALPH THE GREAT

DC Metro area

703-404-2737

www.ralphthegreat.com

Ralph the Great is a multitalented children's entertainer. Performances include music, magic, comedy, and lots of audience participation. Birthday parties run from forty-five minutes to one hour, and focus on the birthday child while always including other partygoers. With his off-the-wall antics and many talents, children are guaranteed a great time.

★ ROCKNOCEROS

DC Metro area

703-795-1800

www.rocknoceros.com

daniel@goteammusic.com

If you've had enough of The Wiggles, Rocknoceros will be a welcome change to the often sickly-sweet children's music that can drive a parent crazy. The rock music trio geared toward kids encourages movement, dance, singing, and lots of fun! With several regular gigs around town, the band's popular act is easy to check out ahead of time. Rocknoceros will perform a forty-five-minute set in your home or the venue of your choice. Kids ages two years and older just can't get enough of these guys.

rentals

★ ASTRO JUMP OF WASHINGTON, DC

DC Metro area

800-244-JUMP

703-339-8000

www.astrojump.com

Astro Jump is the largest moon-bounce rental company in the nation, in operation since 1986. These stores carry moon bounces in every size and theme you could imagine. In addition, they also carry inflatable waterslides, spin-art machines, popcorn and cotton-candy makers, and drink dispensers.

★ BALLOON BOUQUETS OF WASHINGTON, DC

DC Metro area

800-424-2323

202-785-1290

www.balloonbouquets.com

Balloon Bouquets is a national balloon delivery and decorating service that has been in business since 1976. In addition to delivering as many balloons as your venue can hold in any color imaginable, it can also make huge balloon sculptures of just about anything. It provides same-day delivery on most orders but requires twenty-four hours to make and deliver printed balloons.

★ PONY TO GO

540-955-5636

www.ponytogo.com

Pony To Go goes to your home for birthday and pony-themed parties with lots of extras! It outfits the birthday child in a hat and a bandanna—which he can keep. It will also take an entire petting zoo—

ranging from ten to fourteen animals—to your backyard; animals include bunnies, ducks, pigs, llamas, alpacas, miniature ponies, and much more. Rates start at $175; reservations must be made at least eight weeks in advance.

★ SQUEALS ON WHEELS

DC Metro area

703-424-0494

www.squealsonwheels.us

Squeals on Wheels is a traveling petting zoo, available in two different sizes—the small has eight to ten animals; the large has at least twenty. They also offer a Mini-Bug Zoo featuring walking sticks and other small insects. Pony rides and old-fashioned games are also available, on their own or combined with the zoo.

★ TALK OF THE TOWN VARIETY ENTERTAINMENT

14650 Southlawn Lane

Rockville, MD

301-738-9500

877-738-9500

www.tottevents.com

Talk of the Town is a family-owned and -operated company based in Rockville. This one-stop shop for party entertainment offers inflatables; trains; caterpillar tunnels; mazes; balloon typhoons; cotton-candy, snow-cone, and popcorn machines; carnival games; and entertainers, including clowns, magicians, fortune tellers, and more. For an additional fee, staffpeople will even coordinate the entire event for you, including food and party favors.

Birthday Cakes

★ THE ALEXANDRIA PASTRY SHOP AND CATERING COMPANY

3690 H King Street

Bradley Shopping Center

Alexandria, VA

703-578-4144

www.alexandriapastry.com

All of Alexandria Pastry Shop's cakes, pastries, and confections are made from scratch. The shop uses only sweet butter and fresh cream from Shenandoah Valley creameries, farm fresh eggs, chocolate from Belgium and France, and fresh fruit. Absolutely no preservatives are used. The bakery has binders full of pictures of cake designs, but bakers encourage new ideas. They also are able to scan photographs that can then be replicated with icing on top of the cake.

★ AMELIA'S CAKES

4465 Macarthur Boulevard

Palisades, DC

202-631-5463

800-637-0197

orders@ameliascakes.com

www.ameliascakes.com

Amelia's Cakes is a boutique bakery business started by a "mom with a sweet tooth" and some of her friends. They make a selection of popular treats for all seasons and occasions. Cake flavors include white butter, chocolate layer, carrot, German chocolate, and red velvet. Cupcakes and cookies are offered as well. Orders can be made by phone or online, and must be placed at least three days in advance. Appointments may be scheduled for a tasting.

★ BASKIN-ROBBINS

Locations throughout the DC Metro area

www.baskinrobbins.com

Baskin-Robbins is an old pro when it comes to ice-cream cakes. This business has been around for quite some time and for good reason—products are tasty, inexpensive, and always available (good for last-minute party planners, as I have been on occasion). With a little notice, cakes can be specially decorated.

★ BEN & JERRY'S

Locations throughout the DC Metro area

www.benjerry.com

In addition to the delectable ice cream in creative flavor combos like Phish Food and Neapolitan Dynamite, these socially conscious Vermont ice-cream magnates also turn out a mean cake as well. You need to order cakes ahead of time and a "Happy Birthday" is about the extent of the decorative touches offered, but the cakes are guaranteed to please little partygoers.

★ CAKE DELIVERY EXPRESS

202-785-1290

800-424-2323

www.balloonbouquets.com/webdoc6.htm

Cake Delivery Express delivers cakes (in flavors like truffle, mocha, and German chocolate), plus cookies, pies, and pastries baked to order by the Watergate Pastry Shop. For an additional charge, you can have writing, flower decorations, and edible photos printed on the cakes. Deliveries are made throughout the DC Metro area; same-day delivery is available, although the cake selection might be limited. All cakes are delivered with your choice of six 12-inch latex balloons, or three 18-inch long-lasting Mylar (foil) balloons.

★ CAKELOVE

1506 U Street, NW

U Street Corridor, DC

202-588-7100

935 Ellsworth Drive

Silver Spring, MD

301-565-CAKE (2253)

www.cakelove.com

For a simple, no-fuss (and no 3-D Spiderman) treat, CakeLove will "scratch bake" a delicious cake or cupcakes for your party. The all-natural delicacies are delicious, and you can choose virtually any type of cake and buttercream flavoring.

★ CARVEL

Locations throughout the DC Metro area

860-257-4448

www.carvel.com

When it comes to ice-cream cakes, this staple delivers, and is extremely affordable to boot. Carvel produces a wide range of cakes—all with the signature crunchy layers—including 3-D shapes and ones personalized with a photo. Drop by a store to see what can be custom ordered, or pick up an in-store cake to go.

★ CENAN'S BAKERY

122 Branch Road SE

Vienna, VA 22180

703-242-0070

www.cenansbakery.com

Cenan's Bakery prides itself on "bread and fine baked goods formed from all-natural ingredients without a trace of preservatives." Cenan's offers made-to-order cakes for birthdays and other special occasions. Choices include a mixed fruitcake, strawberry shortcake, carrot cake, and cheesecake, along with a large selection of mousse cakes.

★ CHARM CITY CAKES

Baltimore, MD
410-235-9229
www.charmcitycakes.com
ccdcakes@aol.com

Don't be dissuaded by the Baltimore address. If you're trying to wow everyone at the party, look no further and call now—Charm City Cakes requires at least ten weeks' notice on all cake orders. Owner and pastry chef Duff Goldman has pedigree to spare, with a degree from the Culinary Institute of America and a stint at French Laundry, not to mention his show on The Food Network, *Ace of Cakes*. These cakes are truly edible art with only one's imagination setting the limits. Staffpeople "welcome a challenge" in taking an idea (say a dragon) and turning it into a cake (result: a two-foot dragon eating a birthday cake). These cakes are delicious as well, with more than forty flavors available. Cakes start at $500.

★ COLD STONE CREAMERY

Locations throughout the DC Metro area
www.coldstonecreamery.com

Cold Stone Creamery offers an extensive variety of ice cream, made fresh daily, with an endless list of choices to mix in. Children's birthday cakes—with popular cartoon characters as cake toppers—are available in both rounds and rectangles, and can be customized with names and special-occasion messages.

★ CREATIVE CAKES

8814 Brookville Road
Silver Spring, MD
301-587-1599
www.creativecakes.com

Custom cakes can be made for any occasion. Cakes are topped with buttercream frosting in flavors such as chocolate deluxe, vanilla velvet, toasted almond, smuggler's rum, lemon lush, orange mist, and harvest spice. During December, Creative Cakes hosts two-hour gingerbread-house-decorating parties. Each child receives a constructed house and all the materials needed to decorate the house any way he or she chooses. Call well in advance to reserve a space for these!

★ CUSTOM CAKE DESIGN

8535 Ziggy Lane
Gaithersburg, MD
301-216-1100
www.customcakedesign.com/index.htm

Custom Cake Design will go above and beyond for any occasion. In addition to the sheet cakes for up to one hundred people, the bakers can also create cakes in cutout shapes, with sculptured 3-D artwork, or with airbrush color portraits. Some of the cake and icing flavors include chocolate, vanilla, lemon, orange, almond, butter rum, spice, and marble. You may mix flavors or add a filling for an additional charge.

★ ESPECIALLY FOR YOU

Alexandria, VA
703-660-9592
www.chefesp4u.com

Jo Ann Kottkamp creates amazing, imaginative 3-D cakes, which seem only to be limited by the imagination of her customers. Flavors include vanilla, chocolate, mocha, spice, and carrot, to name a few. Buttercream flavors include chocolate, hazelnut, fresh fruit, caramel, and toffee.

★ **FURIN'S OF GEORGETOWN**

2805 M Street, NW

202-965-1000

www.furins.com

In addition to being one of Georgetown's favorite local cafes, Furin's whips up fantastic cakes for every occasion. A delectable birthday treat in just about any flavor imaginable can be created; it can be decorated with anything you can think of, from a favorite Disney character to a beautifully wrapped edible present. The service is always friendly, and prices are extremely affordable.

★ **GIFFORD'S ICE CREAM & CANDY CO.**

555 Eleventh Street, NW

Penn Quarter, DC

202-347-7755

7237 Woodmont Avenue

Bethesda, MD

301-907-3436

21 Wisconsin Circle

Chevy Chase, MD

301-652-8965

100 Gibbs Street

Rockville, MD

301-315-2002

www.giffords.com

Gifford's Ice Cream & Candy Co. is the real deal. Since 1938 it has been serving homemade ice cream and candy made from the best ingredients.

Cakes are made from the stores' wonderful rich, creamy ice cream and are topped with a layer of marshmallow paste, which allows Gifford's to imprint almost any image on the cake. Stock cakes are available in the stores, but custom cakes must be ordered in advance.

★ **HARRIS TEETER**

Hyde Park Plaza

600 North Glebe Road

Arlington, VA

703-526-9100

Pentagon Row

900 Army Navy Drive

Arlington, VA

703-413-7112

Lee Harrison Shopping Center

2425 North Harrison Street

Arlington, VA

703-532-8663

Barcroft Plaza

6351 Columbia Pike

Falls Church, VA

703-256-6615

Shops at Foxchase

4641 Duke Street

Alexandria, VA

703-461-7082

Spectrum at Town Center

11806 Spectrum Court

Reston, VA

703-435-5800

www.harristeeter.com

These East Coast grocery stores offer ready-made cakes as well as cakes that can be picked out of a catalog in the store and made to order. Prices are very reasonable, and custom cakes can be made with twenty-four hours' notice. Worth mentioning is that special-occasion cakes and cupcakes can be ordered online. Convenience is a very good thing.

★ HEIDELBERG PASTRY SHOPPE

2150 North Culpeper Street
Arlington, VA
703-527-8394
www.heidelbergbakery.com

Heidelberg Pastry Shoppe stocks a selection of birthday cakes in its store for those situations when a last-minute cake is needed. Buttercream flavors available include vanilla, chocolate, lemon, mocha, or raspberry. You may also special-order a wide variety of cakes from the bakery with at least twenty-four hours' notice. Computerized color photos can be incorporated in the icing for an additional fee; you can check out the other cake-design options at the bakery or on the website.

★ HELLER'S BAKERY

3221 Mount Pleasant Street, NW
Mount Pleasant, DC
202-265-1169
www.hellersbakery.com

A Mount Pleasant fixture since 1922, Heller's produces delicious pastries, cakes, pies, and cookies. The shop makes specialty cakes for a range of occasions—not only for birthday parties but weddings and showers as well.

★ HOLLIN HALL PASTRY SHOP

7920 Fort Hunt Road
Alexandria, VA
703-768-9643
www.hollinhallpastry.com

Mel Meadows, pastry chef and owner of the Hollin Hall Pastry Shop, has been making sweet creations for three decades. More than fifty different cake designs are available with your choice of flavors. Meadows also welcomes your ideas for new cake designs. In addition, the shop can scan a photograph onto the icing of the cake. Free tastings are available by appointment. Cakes can be delivered to your home or party location the day of the event.

★ KENDALL'S CAKES

Falls Church, VA
703-536-2200
www.kendallscakes.com

Kendall's Cakes will decorate a cake in any theme imaginable. Designs are handpainted on single- or multi-tiered cakes. Available cake flavors are lemon, carrot, raspberry, chocolate truffle, chocolate raspberry, mocha, chocolate hazelnut, almond white chocolate, and rum. All orders must be made at least two weeks ahead of time and can be delivered for an extra fee.

★ MAGGIEMOO'S

Locations throughout the DC Metro area
www.maggiemoos.com

MaggieMoo's ice cream and treatery offers an extensive variety of ice cream, made fresh daily, with an endless list of mix-in choices. Children's birthday cakes—with popular cartoon characters as cake toppers—are available in both rounds and rectangles, and can be customized with names and special-occasion messages. In addition, MaggieMoo's will take an "ice cream social" to your home or birthday-party venue, dropping off the ingredients for, or serving, a make-your-own-sundae bar.

★ RAE BAKES [COOKIES]

202-333-4967

email@raebakes.com

www.raebakes.com

Rae bakes cookies, not cakes. Featured on the Food Network, and in the *Washington Post*, *Brides*, and the *Washingtonian*, the handmade, hand-decorated custom butter-sugar cookies are made to order using only the freshest ingredients. Most cookies are 3 inches by 4 inches, and all are individually wrapped in clear cellophane bags tied with coordinating tulle bows. Bakers can design a cookie to look like anything—including animals, planes, race cars, boats, miniature birthday cakes, and cupcakes, among other options. Prices begin at $5 each, but most cookies run between $6 and $10 each. A minimum order of $350 is required. Orders must be made one month in advance.

★ THE SWEET LIFE

Annandale, VA

703-750-3266

www.thesweetlife.com

These cakes can best be described as unbelievable. Pastry chef, award-winning chocolatier, and owner of The Sweet Life, Norman R. Davis has been featured in the *Washington Post* and on the cover of *American Cake Decorating* magazine. You have to see the multi-dimensional, life-size edible works of art to believe them. For a four-year-olds' birthday he created an entire underwater ocean scene complete with life-size sea creatures, coral formations, and "floating" seaweed. Every aspect of the cake was edible and, as I said, it was unbelievable.

party supply stores

★ BARSTON'S CHILD'S PLAY

5536 Connecticut Avenue, NW

202-244-3602

Chevy Chase, DC

1661 Rockville Pike

Rockville, MD

301-230-9040

www.barstonschildsplay.com

In addition to its noteworthy toy selection, Barston's Child's Play also sells party supplies. In the arts-and-crafts area of the store is a nice selection of solid-colored and themed paper cups and plates, as well as your standard selection of coordinating streamers and noisemakers. In addition, it's easy to pull together a respectable goody bag with the assortment of bubbles, stickers, and other knickknacks. The store also stocks cards and party costumes for children of all ages. Staffpeople are knowledgeable and happy to help.

★ MICHAELS

1509 Rockville Pike

Rockville, MD

301-881-8100

3089A Nutley Street

Fairfax, VA

703-698-9810

46301 Potomac Run Plaza
Sterling, VA
703-430-8645

11630 Plaza America Drive
Reston, VA
703-736-0530
www.michaels.com

Local headquarters for those crafty folks who set aside time for papier-mâché and intricate dried-flower arranging, Michaels is also an excellent resource for party supplies. Whether you are looking for a fun activity to occupy partygoers, like T-shirt decorating, or just looking for the glitter and glam with which to adorn tables, Michaels is a must. Staffpeople are very helpful, offering up ambitious suggestions (DIY piñatas, anyone?) and pointing you in the direction of themed cake pans, and marzipan- and piñata-making kits.

★ **THE PAPER STORE**

1803 Wisconsin Avenue, NW
Georgetown, DC
202-333-3200
301-657-2100

7712 Woodmont Avenue
Bethesda, MD
301-657-2100

The Paper Store has less to offer in straight paper and much to offer in party supplies. From high-quality coordinating paper tablecloths, cups, plates, and napkins in every color imaginable, to complete Disney-themed party decorations and supplies, the Paper Store is always one of my stops.

★ **SULLIVAN'S TOY STORE AND ART SUPPLIES**

3412 Wisconsin Avenue, NW
Cleveland Park, DC
202-362-1343

Considering the relatively small space of this store on Wisconsin Avenue, Sullivan's packs a punch. It's a one-stop shop for party supplies and craft projects, and a place to visit for last-minute goody-bag contents and final touches for the party decor.

haircuts

Baby's first haircut is a big deal. You may be planning on saving that first lock in the scrapbook, or even capturing the momentous occasion on film. But while you'll be excited over this monumental event, little ones can often feel overwhelmed and downright freaked out. Sitting still while a stranger comes at him or her with scissors? Can you blame your child for getting upset? Choosing the right place for this soon-to-be-regular routine can help set the stage for cuts to come. Basically, there are two choices here: a reliably good cut at a salon with no built-in distractions for kids (possibly the salon you already go to) or a decent, sometimes unreliable cut at a children's salon with many built-in distractions. Cuts at regular salons are usually a little bit more expensive (at the most, maybe $10 more), but you shouldn't have to pay over $25 plus tip for a child's cut. My friend Kelly, also mother to a boy, puts it succinctly, "Boys just need a good haircut and good clothes. That's it." And I agree—a good cut is worth the extra money. I dragged Connor around to most of the children's salons listed here, and although some did provide a chair-side TV and VCR, the poor guy endured some bad cuts. My personal preference is to go to a good salon, use bribery to encourage good behavior, and take a DVD player in case of emergency. Connor, you're a very good sport.

hair stylists & salons

★ **APONTE'S BARBER & STYLING SALON**
   2505 North Harrison Street
   Arlington, VA
   703-237-5698
A North Arlington institution, this old-school barbershop offers quick and friendly cuts for only $10. Little ones are rewarded with a lollipop.

★ **AQUA CUTS**
   11325 Seven Locks Road
   Potomac, MD
   301-765-1005
Video screens and a large fish tank are good distractions for toddlers at this Potomac hair salon.

★ **AVEDA**
   Locations throughout the DC Metro area
   800-644-4831
   www.aveda.com
Definitely on the expensive side, with a child's cut costing $45, but reliable in that you know you're getting a good cut.

★ BRADLEE BARBER SHOP

3638 King Street
Alexandria, VA
703-998-9830

This old-fashioned barbershop has some perks for kids. It has two cars and a horse to sit on; it provides a certificate to commemorate baby's first cut; and lollipops are given.

★ BRADLEY BARBER SHOP

6918 Arlington Boulevard
Bethesda, MD
301-907-7870

An inexpensive barbershop that offers classic no-frills cuts; barbers are friendly to children.

★ BUBBLES HAIR SALON

201 Pennsylvania Avenue, NE
Capitol Hill, DC
202-543-1245

2020 K Street, NW
Foggy Bottom, DC
202-659-5005
www.bubblessalons.com

Bubbles is an East Coast chain of sleek hair salons; the Capitol Hill location, which opened twenty-five years ago, was the first. These salons offer very good cuts at great prices and know enough to move quickly with squirming toddlers.

★ CARTOON CUTS

More than 30 locations throughout the
    DC Metro area
800-701-CUTS (2887)
www.cartooncuts.com

When you're looking for distractions that happen to come with a haircut, look no further than Cartoon Cuts. The East Coast kids' haircut chain boasts a waiting area filled with toys, puzzles, art supplies, and video games, and each stylist's area is equipped with a television showing—you guessed it—cartoons.

★ ECLIPS

1373 Beverly Road, NW
McLean, VA
703-356-0064
www.eclipshair.com

Eclips offers a kid-friendly environment with games in the waiting area and TVs and DVD players at each station, where kids can watch DVDs of their choice. The stylists are very friendly.

★ PAUL BOSSERMAN

3214 N Street, NW
Georgetown, DC
202-337-0020

This chic Georgetown salon, which coifs DC's most fabulous adults, is actually quite gracious to its youngest fashionistas. Try to make an appointment with Bok, who is a father with a young son and is extremely good with kids. He'll even cut a child's hair while he or she is sitting on the floor looking at books. When he's not being used as a research subject, this is where Connor gets his new 'dos.

★ SALON FAMILIA

3817 Livingston Street, NW

Chevy Chase, DC

202-966-6555

www.salonfamilia.com

This is a great salon for the whole family, with plenty of toys and a TV corner, as well as booster seats and little bows for girls.

★ 1620 LOFT HAIR STUDIO

1620 Wisconsin Avenue, NW

Georgetown, DC

202-333-3996

This husband-and-wife team gives great cuts for kids, and they are extremely patient with little ones who are less than happy to sit still.

★ WISCONSIN UNISEX BARBER

1518 Wisconsin Avenue, NW

Georgetown, DC

202-338-3116

As its name suggests, think basic. This traditional barbershop is surprisingly patient and good with kids, even those who are uninterested in getting a trim. The husband-and-wife barbers are quick, and produce a bowl of lollipops on your way out. They only accept cash.

pictures for posterity

Family portraits have come a long way since the Sears variety with the carpeted platforms, sky-blue backdrops, and forced poses. Don't get me wrong, they still exist and serve a good and inexpensive purpose. However, today, with as many photographers as there are moments that need capturing, there's a photographer and a style to fit anyone's taste.

The pictures seem to fall into two basic categories—traditional portraits or photojournalistic moments—but each photographer has his or her own style, so who you go with will ultimately be a matter of individual taste. Each photographer I have listed has a portfolio available on her or his website. First, take some time to look through the examples they have to get a sense of their approach. After you have narrowed it down to a few, call to discuss price, type (or types) of film used, the number of photos and/or proofs that are included, and how much extra they charge for prints. You should always plan on a meeting where you can view their work, and don't be afraid to ask for references.

All of the photographers listed specialize in child and family photography, and will go to homes and other sites all over the DC Metro area. Either I have used them myself or they come highly recommended from friends. I have divided them into two categories: photojournalistic photographers and traditional portrait photographers.

photojournalistic photographers

⋆ **ARTISTIC DESIGN PHOTOGRAPHY**
Jessica Garris-Scott
Bethesda, MD
301-951-0542
301-741-1575
www.artisticphotos.com
Jessica Scott prefers to shoot on location, either in your home or at a fun destination like The Mall. Prices start at $150 an hour with a two-hour minimum.

⋆ **BEVERLY REZNECK PHOTOGRAPHY**
202-244-1738
www.beverlyrezneckphotography.com
Beverly Rezneck is known for her black-and-white photojournalistic documentation of many Washingtonians' momentous occasions. She loves to photograph children and will do so at her in-home studio or at a location of your choice. Packages start at $450.

⋆ **EMILY DEISROTH PHOTOGRAPHY + DESIGN**
202-829-0412
www.emilydeisroth.com
Emily likes to photograph children and families in their natural environment or with the use of one of DC's many monuments as a backdrop. Fees start at

$225 for a two- to three-hour session. Prints are an additional charge.

★ **FOGARTY PHOTOGRAPHY**
301-585-3588
Erin@FogartyPhotography.com
Sessions with Erin Fogarty Owen start at $250 at a location of your choice. Prints are sold separately and range from $14 for a single 4x6 print to $165 for a single 20x30 print.

★ **JULIE FISCHER PHOTOGRAPHY**
202-246-5581
www.juliefischerphoto.com
info@juliefischerphoto.com
Sessions start at $275 at a location of your choice and often include one free 8x10 print. Additional prints are extra.

★ **LESLIE CASHEN PHOTOGRAPHY**
202-363-5682
She shoots at her home studio and primarily produces black-and-white prints. Rates start at $750.

★ **MARISSA RAUCH PHOTOGRAPHY**
202-337-1368
www.marissarauchphotography.com
Sessions start at $625 at a location of your choice. Prints are extra.

★ **MATT MENDELSOHN**
703-548-1669
www.mattmendelsohn.com
Matt likes to photograph kids and families at destinations in and around DC. Sessions start at $450 at a location of your choice. Prints are sold separately.

★ **PHOTOPIA**
Elizabeth Dranitzke
202-550-2520
www.photopiadc.com
Elizabeth loves to photograph families outdoors, often shooting around The Mall. She does home sessions as well and charges $400 a session for up to three people. Each additional person is $25; prints are available at an extra cost.

traditional portrait photographers

★ **FREED PHOTOGRAPHY**
4931 Cordell Avenue
Bethesda, MD
301-652-5452
www.freedphoto.com
The ten professionals who compose the Freed Photography team specialize in family and corporate portraiture. Packages start at $1,400.

★ **JIM JOHNSON PHOTOGRAPHY**
5185 MacArthur Boulevard, NW, Suite 106
Washington, DC
202-686-7300
800-557-3896
www.picturestorystudio.com
He specializes in portrait and wedding photography. Packages start at $1,200.

★ **KATHY KUPKA PHOTOGRAPHY**
Leesburg, VA
703-777-2054
www.kathykupkaphotography.com

Kathy likes to take portraits at her home studio in Leesburg, Virginia. Sessions usually last about two hours, and rates start at $150 for up to three people (dogs are welcome!). Sessions with four or more people begin at $400; prints are at an additional fee.

a note on playgroups and preschools

A playgroup is a small group of parents (or other caregivers) who get together with their children on a regular basis for play and interaction. Generally, parents and children meet at the same time each week for an hour or two at a member's home. Playgroups are a great alternative or addition to formal Mommy and Me classes, as playgroups are as much for the adults as they are for the children. Children develop important social skills, self-confidence, and independence. Parents and caregivers are able to connect with each other, providing an invaluable source of friendship and support. In addition, there is usually no fee associated with forming or joining a playgroup, as they are most often organized by neighbors or members of local listservs. There are hundreds of these playgroups in the DC Metro area, and they can easily be found or formed through the many support groups and listservs listed in chapter four.

In addition to these informal playgroups, there are also three, more organized ones in the area: Blue Igloo, Intown, and Little Graces. Each of these playgroups has an annual enrollment of around fifty children, who attend with a parent or caregiver each day. All of these groups meet five mornings a week, and like the informal groups, are places where children and their caregivers learn, play, and make friends. In these groups, however, teachers lead activities such as painting, singing, dancing, dramatic play, and story times. This set-up is similar to the structure of a preschool setting, so these groups are a good way to introduce children to it before they start preschool. Connor and I started Blue Igloo when he was a year old, and the friendships we both made are some of our closest to this day. Blue Igloo and Intown are not-for-profit and are run by the lead teacher and a board of parents with children who are enrolled. Little Graces is run by two local moms and is for-profit. The admissions process for all three requires an application submission and a child and caregiver to visit a session. Applications should be submitted by the March prior to the year of enrollment.

The following is the contact information for these three playgroups:

★ **BLUE IGLOO PLAYGROUP**
3220 N Street, NW
Georgetown, DC
www.blueiglooplaygroup.org
Email: admissions@blueiglooplaygroup.org
Ages: 6 months to 3 years

★ INTOWN PLAYGROUP

1334 29th Street, NW
Georgetown, DC
202-337-2720
www.intownplaygoup.org
Email: intowndirector@yahoo.com
Ages: 1 year to 3 years

★ LITTLE GRACES

5150 Macomb Street, NW
Kent, DC
www.stdavidsdc.org
Email: littlegraces@rcn.com
Ages: 3 months to 3 years

Before you know it, conversations in playgroup will switch from which solid foods your baby is currently consuming to which preschool is currently the feeder into Harvard. For better or worse, Washington, DC, has one of the most highly educated populations in the United States, and for this reason, it also has some of the oldest and most highly educated first-time mothers. Add the fact that we have the second most competitive school admissions in the country (after New York City), and you may feel like preschool admissions is a perfect storm—and you are headed straight into the eye of it. What you might think should be a thoughtful look into where your child will spend a few hours playing in the morning can quickly begin to feel like a cross between a strategy meeting at the UN and a sorority rush.

You will need to start thinking seriously about preschool when your child is between eighteen months and two years old (depending on his or her birthday), about a year before you will want to enroll. As you get started, keep things in perspective. Yes, we live in a highly competitive environment where parents are scrambling to provide the best education possible for their child, but this also means that there are many choices. When your options range from many highly regarded private schools to top public school systems in Virginia and Maryland, there really is no need to panic. My advice: Take your time and do your research.

★ First, think about what you know (or can guess) about the ever-changing likes and dislikes of your one-and-a-half-year-old, and consider what school environment might best suit him; for example, some schools provide a more structured setting, while others believe in a looser, free-play environment. Think about where your child may thrive most and what jibes with your own personal philosophy.

★ Second, think about logistics. Should the school be close to home, or is it easier to have your child somewhere close to your office? Will you need a school that allows for early drop-off or extended day, or both? The point is to come up with a list of your basic requirements; this will help you narrow the list of schools to consider.

★ Third, check out schools' websites and request catalogs. Take note of each school's admission and application deadlines, and any other requirements such as interviews or play dates. Again, it's best to start sometime in the fall the year before your child would be enrolling in a program.

★ Finally, schedule a visit at each of the schools on your short (or long) list. I can't stress the importance of this enough. The best way to get the true vibe of a school is to walk the halls, look into the classrooms of (hopefully happy) children, and speak with a teacher or two. No matter how fabulous the brochure looks or how much someone in playgroup likes a school, you won't know if it's right for your child until you check it out for yourself. Having the opportunity to compare several schools based on your firsthand experience is well worth your time.

There are two publications available that list all of the area schools: the *Independent School Guide for Washington, D.C. and Surrounding Area* and *The Metropolitan Washington Preschool and Daycare Guide*. Both offer information on the philosophy, admission process, and tuition for more than five hundred local schools. While they can't tell you which school is going to be the best fit for your child, they will help narrow down the choices.

If you still feel overwhelmed and think you may need some additional guidance, you are not alone and, fortunately, there is help out there. One option is to hire an educational consultant or counselor. This is someone who can objectively evaluate your child and, based on his or her knowledge of area schools, will be able to provide you with suitable options. Some consultants will also assist throughout the application process and provide a written recommendation. Consultants may be especially helpful with children who have special needs and would thrive in a certain environment. The two publications I've listed above provide a complete directory of counselors in the DC Metro area.

So now that you have an idea of what lies ahead, take a deep breath and remember that this is truly an exciting time in your child's life. It's not about what the "hot" school is—and you're not rushing Kappa Kappa Gamma. This is about finding the best place for your child to form meaningful friendships, to begin a love of learning, and, most of all, to be happy.

web directory

In addition to listing the websites for each entry in the book when available, I also wanted to include additional resources for DC parents that are only available on the web. Going online is a great way to save time shopping as well as getting plugged into parenting groups and happenings around the city.

There is an endless list of diverse parenting groups throughout the DC Metro area, many of which have message boards. Go to http://groups.yahoo.com and do a search for "DC parenting groups," for example, and you'll find a long list of local online communities. These message boards are a great way to instantly connect with other parents with similar interests on a local level.

local parent resources

www.citybabydc.com

www.washingtondc.craigslist.org

www.dc-baby.com

www.dcurbanmom.com

www.gocitykids.com

www.our-kids.com

www.washingtonian.com

www.lilaguide.com

parenting

www.babycenter.com

www.babiesnbellies.com

www.babyzone.com

www.dailycandy.com/kids/everywhere

www.parenthood.com

www.parenting.com

www.parenting.ivillage.com

www.urbanbaby.com

health

www.askdrsears.com

www.enfamil.com

www.kidshealth.org

www.webmd.com

maternity clothes

www.anntaylorloft.com

www.babystyle.com

www.bellybasics.com

www.bellydancematernity.com

www.duematernity.com

www.isabellaoliver.com

www.imaternity.com

www.japaneseweekend.com

www.lizlange.com

www.neimanmarcus.com

www.saksfifthavenue.com

furniture, gear and accessories

www.ducducnyc.com

www.leapsandbounds.com

www.onestepahead.com

www.poshtots.com

www.rosenberryrooms.com

www.thelandofnod.com

www.warmbiscuit.com

baby and toddler clothing

www.bestandcompany.com

www.blisscollection.com

www.bodenusa.com

www.hannaandersson.com

www.izzyandash.com

www.landsend.com

www.littlefollies.com

www.orientexpressed.com

www.papodanjo.com

www.retrobaby.com

books and toys

www.amazon.com

www.backtobasicstoys.com

www.educationaltoysplanet.com

www.etoys.com

www.fao.com

www.growingtreetoys.com

www.leapfrog.com

index

More Praise for *City Baby DC*:

"THE bible for every DC mom and mother-to-be. . . . Grab it to keep you and your baby feeling and looking great!"
—CLAIRE SHIPMAN,
Senior National Correspondent, *Good Morning America*
and mother of two

"Everything a mother needs to know about being a parent in the District of Columbia is in *City Baby DC*. The guide is a must-have for any new DC mother."
—MICHELLE CROSS FENTY,
attorney, first lady of DC, and mother of two

"This book is the ultimate guide for the ultimate mom—even when she's a local!"
—DEBORAH FINE,
president, NBC Universal's iVillage Properties,
and mother of two

About the Author

Holly Morse Caldwell is a DC resident and mom. She and her husband have lived in Georgetown for the past seven years, and are the proud parents of Connor and Charlie. She is on the board of the Blue Igloo Playgroup, and in her spare time she enjoys midnight feedings, constant diaper changes, and long carpool lines. This is her first book.